For Rowena,
with the
compliments
kindest regards.
Jeffrey,
8/1/97

WRITINGS BY JEFFREY BOSS

THE WOMAN MIRIAM
   (Harvest 37, 79-87, 1991)

MALE AND FEMALE CREATED HE THEM: AN EXPLORATION OF SEXUAL
DIFFERENCE IN THE BIBLICAL CREATION STORY
   (Harvest 351, 51-167, 1989)

WHAT IS FAITH - No. 11 of a series
   (Epworth Review 14, 70-76, 1987)

THE SEVENTEENTH-CENTURY TRANSFORMATION OF THE HYSTERIC
AFFECTION AND SYDENHAM'S BACONIAN MEDICINE
   (Psychological Medicine 9, 221-234, 1979)

THE ANTIQUITY OF CAESARIAN SECTION WITH MATERNAL SURVIVAL:
THE JEWISH TRADITION
   (Medical History 9, 17-131, 1961)

CONGENITAL MALFORMATIONS *(New Scientists 8, 335-337, 1960)*

THE CONTRIBUTION OF THE CHROMOSOMES TO THE TELOPHASE
NUCLEUS IN CULTURES OF FIBROBLASTS OF THE ADULT CRESTED NEWT
TRITURUS CRISTATUS CARNIFEX
   (Experimental Cell Research 18, 197-216, 1959)

and eighty-nine other published papers

BECOMING OURSELVES

Meanings in the biblical creation story

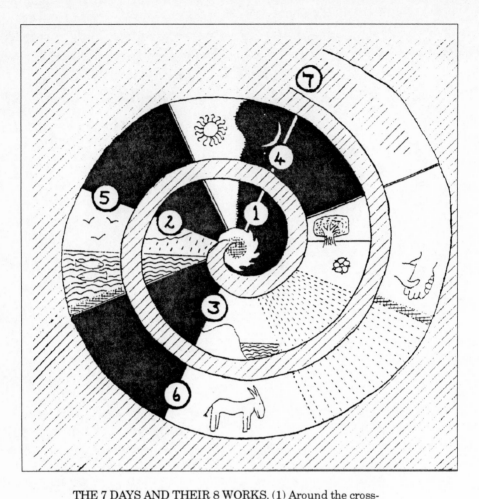

THE 7 DAYS AND THEIR 8 WORKS. (1) Around the cross-hatched circle, representing 'create', is a flared area representing the 'waters', with the darkness above them. Light is made and separated from darkness. (2) The waters divide into upper and lower. (3)Two works: dry land, plants. (4) Heavenly bodies, day and night, times and seasons. (5) Air life and water life; cross-hatching again for 'create'. (6) Two works: land animals, humankind; cross-hatching for third work in connection with which 'create' is said; clasped hands stand for humankind, as between lovers or dancers in a ring. (7) The Sabbath has no works, and its only product is itself; it is open to the infinitude beyond and at the centre of the spiral. The Seventh Day is shown without a black area, since of this day it is not said 'And there was evening and there was morning…' (Note how the spiral brings related works opposite one another.) Explanation of this figure in Chapter 2.

BECOMING OURSELVES
MEANINGS IN THE BIBLICAL CREATION STORY

With a new translation of Genesis 1-11
from the original Hebrew

JEFFREY BOSS

STROUD
MATTHEW LAMPSON
1993

Published 1993 by Matthew Lampson Publishing
Castle Coach House, Castle Pitch, Stroud, Gloucestershire, GL5 2HP

British Library Cataloguing in Publication Data

Boss, Jeffrey
 Becoming Ourselves:Meanings in the
 Biblical Creation Story
 I. Title
 222

ISBN 0-9520306-1-6

It is a policy of Matthew Lampson Publishing to publish books of original
research and scholarship in a style accessible to the general reader.

Typeset in New Century 10/12pt by Scriptmate and printed by Booksprint,
20 Shepherds Hill, London N6 5AH

For Bernice, Sarah, and Hannah,
with love and with thanks for
helping in their three different ways

and in memory of
Reginald Philip Boss (5.10.1896-19.7.1965), my father
with whom I would like to have shared this.

Acknowledgments

Several people have helped in the writing of this book. All have had an improving influence, and to none of them can be attributed remaining faults. I am grateful to Rabbi Dr. Jonathan Magonet who read an earlier version of the work, offering comments and encouragement of a sort which showed a care in reading which I appreciate especially in view of his being busy with so much else. Among the librarians who have helped, Dr. Hyam Maccoby, Librarian of Leo Baeck College, London, has never stinted with his inexhaustible scholarship. Bernice, my wife, has kept me going through the ups and downs of authorship, not least by her willingness to share the problems. Daughters have also rallied round; Sarah, having read the first version, made the suggestion which radically transformed it, while the existence of the last chapter is due to prompting from Hannah. Our friend Elizabeth Sheppard read the final version and gave encouragement at a time of doubt. Ann Kritzinger, the printer, has shown patience with a writer who had the printer's problems insufficiently in mind, and, by making me see the text from a printer's point of view, has enriched my understanding of authorship itself. My thanks to her are therefore more than formal. I am happy to acknowledge the courtesy of the following publishers who have permitted quotation from copyright works: Macmillan Press Ltd. for the quotation from John Hick *(Evil and the God of Love,* p.287) on p.61; Routledge & Kegan Paul for the quotation from C.C. Jung *(Collected Works,* vol. XII, para. 420) on p.111; Reform Synagogues of Great Brain for the quotation from Bunam (© *Forms of Prayer for Jewish Worship,* Vol. 1, Daily and Sabbath Prayerbook, R.S.G.B., 17) among the preliminary quotations; Yale University Press for the words of Edmond Jabès *(in* G.H. Hartman and S. Budick, ed., *Midrash and Literature)* among the preliminary quotations; *The Guardian* for the quotation of Nancy Banks-Smith on p.144; Penguin Books Ltd. for the passages from *The Koran* (transl. N.J. Dawood, Penguin Classics, fourth Revised edition, 1974, © N.J. Dawood, 1956, 1959, 1966, 1974) on p. 232 and among the preliminary quotations. Some passages in Chapters 12-14 have appeared in *Harvest,* the journal of the C.G. Jung Analytical Psychology Club of London, and I am grateful to the Club for permission to reproduce the construction in Figure 5.

Jeffrey Boss,
Stroud.
March 1993.

In the beginning of things
 Is the mother of things;
Knowing the mother, one knows also the children.

Tao Te Ching*

His is the creation and his the re-creation.

Al-Qurān*

The Lord created the world in a state of beginning. The universe...requires
continuous labour and unceasing renewal by creative forces. Were there a
second's pause by these forces, the universe would return to primaeval chaos.

Bunam of Pzhysha*

Now a book lives as long as it is unfathomed. Once it is fathomed it dies at
once...The Bible is a book that has been temporarily killed for us, or for
some of us, by having its meaning arbitrarily fixed.

D.H. Lawrence*

And if the beginning were only the book's desire for a beginning? Could this
beginning be God?

Edmond Jabès*

(* *The use of the asterisk is explained overleaf.*)

TO THE READER

The story of the creation of everything is not just a once-upon-a-time story. As it is told in Genesis, the first book of the Bible, it is about the human condition now and always, it is a here-and-now story about ourselves.

To understand this we need to look at the fine grain of the telling. Also, however, we need to look at its broad patterns. My attention to the fine grain is expressed in consideration of the words of the original Hebrew, although the book is written for the reader without knowledge of Hebrew, as well as those who have it.

To those who are biblical scholars I would make this remark: though the manner and style are for the general reader, this is an investigative work. If investigation leads to unconventional conclusions, so be it. Disagreements, I would hope, can be resolved by reference to the original text. That scholarship be made accessible is surely not a fault.

Beyond textual scholarship, I have speculated on the philosophical implications of the creation story. I make no apology. It is a story for our time.

NOTE

1. An asterisk* after the name of an author or work indicates that the full reference to the work cited is in the list on pages 249-255.

2. References to the Hebrew or Christian scriptures (Old and New Testaments) have the chapter and verse separated by a colon; e.g. Exodus, chapter 23, verse 4, would be referred to as Exodus 23:4. For the first 11 chapters of Genesis, however, the name of the book is omitted, so that, for example, Genesis, chapter 8, verse 22, would be referred to simply as 8:22.

3. Hebrew words (always in italics) have been spelled so as to give some approximation to the usual pronunciation. In them, *ch* and *kh* represent the sound of *ch* in the Scots *loch* and Welsh *bach*. The sign ' represents a guttural sound that need not be heard, but it has been put in to make comparison between related words possible. The same sign is used in some Arabic names.

Contents

FIGURES

LOCATIONS OF PASSAGES FROM GENESIS 1-11

CHAPTER 1: *INVITATION*

IN THIS BOOK I shall try to take you with me where I have explored. The exploration has been more gradual than slow, stretching across half my life, and I am now in my sixties. What I have discovered is an old philosophy, limitless in meaning, and still fresh for my life to-day. It may be so for yours. Come and see. For my part, I would like to share something of my experience.

The subject of this book is the Israelite story of the Creation, which forms the first eleven chapters of Genesis, at the beginning of the Bible. You may already be familiar with the story or, at least, have a nodding acquaintance with it. Whether or not most homes have a Bible, as they once did, the Bible is to be found in nearly all bookshops. It remains a best-seller. Everyday chat and popular writing suggests that it is common knowledge that the Bible says that the world was made in seven days, each twenty-four hours long, and that there was disaster when our ancestors, Adam and Eve, were misled by a serpent's offer of forbidden fruit. However, it often happens that what everybody knows and takes for granted somehow looks different when things are looked at more closely.

There is a variety of attitudes to the biblical Creation story. Some say that it is untrue because what it says is disproved by scientific discovery and reasoning. In my view, such critics are comparing two stories that have different ends, different methods, and which cannot be set against one another.

Then there are people, often called 'fundamentalists', who use the Bible as a source of instant right answers, as though it were the telephone directory or Nautical Almanac. This they justify by saying that the Bible is divinely inspired. For me, their use of the Bible attempts to limit what divine inspiration can do. After all, there may be true writing that cannot be used like the 'phone book. Consider also poetry, and metaphor, and proverbs, and the fiction that conveys truth as only fiction can; and there is much else besides. Also, I will not read something assuming before I begin that this writing is true and of a special sort, because it is inspired in a way that most other writing is not. It is dishonest to have a double standard of truth. On the other hand, I am open to persuasion by what I read. Therefore I may be persuaded by a work that it is divinely inspired. Only I would not use the expression 'divinely inspired'; it has been used in too many ways, and can lead to misunderstanding.

One of my students once asked me to take part in a debate between 'fundamentalists' and 'evolutionists' about the biblical Creation story. I declined because it would have been assumed that, whichever side I took, I

1

would be understanding the Genesis story of Creation in a particular way, holding it to be true or false according to that understanding. I could not agree with the 'evolutionists' that the story I know is false, although I agree with their rejection of the story as they understand it. I could not agree with the 'fundamentalists' that the story is true, since what they take to be true, like what the 'evolutionists' call false, is not the Creation story which I find when I read Genesis. I did not even attend the debate, since I did not want to witness violence to what is, for me, a great writing. It would have given me no comfort to hear the violent ones disagreeing among themselves.

A common approach to the Creation story in Genesis is to compare it with other Creation stories, either of the ancient Near East, or from all over the world. The comparison can tell us something about the human mind, and perhaps even something about the history of the Israelite narrative. Nevertheless, we can seldom, if ever, get the meaning of a writing simply from other writings that existed alongside it, or which may have influenced it. Here, perhaps, I differ in emphasis from some biblical scholars. The meaning of *Macbeth* is not in the Scottish history that Shakespeare might have read. When we know Macbeth that history may become relevant for us, but whether the play speaks truly or falsely of the human condition depends upon the play itself and not on some other writing. Whatever *The Merchant of Venice* may borrow from Marlowe's *The Famous Tragedy of the Rich Jew of Malta,* for example, the resemblances do not diminish Shakespeare's originality, any more than resemblances to Mesopotamian flood stories impair the uniqueness of the Israelite narrative. (We shall see that the biblical Flood story is part of the telling of the Creation.)

Some people, not fundamentalists, are concerned with the Creation story as if it were an imperfect record of history, meaning by 'history' the chronicles of humanity. Thus, if we follow Julian Ford*, the story of the Garden of Eden and the couple in it chronicles, through a shadowy memory, the history of humankind, as that history can be inferred from some current archaeology, ethnography, palaeontology, and study of folk-lore and language. Such speculation, which may be important for the study of the origins of the biblical Creation story, lies outside the field of this book.

Let me here repeat what I said at the outset. I am inviting you to join me on a path along which I have been exploring. This is not an academic discourse on the origins of the Creation story. Some would want the story to be first dissected into the 'documents' or 'sources' from which, they say, it was compiled. Why pull it apart, if we are not investigating history, and if what we have has unity of structure, even with diversity of style within the unity? In the story to be considered I have found no contradictions, no inconsistencies, which can be resolved only by taking the work to pieces and treating it as more than one writing.

Some say that we cannot understand the meaning of anything in the Bible unless we take into consideration its setting in life, the setting in which or for which it was written. The difficulty here is that what we know of the life situations of biblical writings comes very much not from independent evidence but from the Bible itself, and the rest is largely uncertain guesswork based on other peoples of the ancient Near East. There is no independent scholarly evidence that enables us to know, with even a low degree of certainty, what was the setting in life in which the Creation story arose, or what were its first uses or occasions of telling. Some guesses may be slightly less uncertain than others, and some are more fashionable than others. In fact it is not easy to say even approximately when the Creation story, as we have it, was written. Let us try to narrow down the range of possibilities.

Between three and four thousand years ago there were various peoples, which we can identify, living in Canaan. The ancient Canaan lay between the Mediterranean Sea and the Jordan, including the territory of the modern state of Lebanon in the north, and extending through the Negev to the south, but the name 'Canaan' does not correspond to exact boundaries. Among the Canaanites were those we call Phoenicians, who were to colonise around the Mediterranean Sea and trade into the Atlantic—eventually founding Carthage, near where Tunis now stands, and itself the metropolis of an empire. The Canaanites spoke related languages; some Canaanite nations differed from each other in language by no more than dialect variations. These languages were of the Semitic group, of which Arabic (not a Canaanite language) is to-day much the most widespread. One of the Canaanite languages, that spoken by the Israelites, is known to us as Hebrew. It has a recorded history of continuous use and change down to the present day. Of Israelite writings more than two thousand years old, by far the larger part of those that have come down to us are collected in the Hebrew scriptures, which Christians interpret as their Old Testament. The Hebrew scriptures themselves refer to Israelite books now lost to us.

As I have just written of Israelites, although to-day we speak more often of Jews, it may be helpful to relate the two terms. In 928 B.C.E. the kingdom of Israel split in two. In the south the tribes of Judah and Benjamin formed the kingdom of Judah, while the other ten Israelite tribes formed the northern kingdom, which kept the name 'Israel'. The word 'Jew' comes ultimately from a Hebrew word meaning someone of the tribe or kingdom of Judah. After the Assyrians destroyed the northern kingdom in 722 B.C.E., 'Jew' came to be a word for any Israelite, as to-day. Samaritans would, however, regard themselves to-day as non-Jewish Israelites, and their history is continuous with that of the northern kingdom. (The form 'Israeli' is, of course, reserved in English for a citizen of the modern state of Israel, whether Jewish or not.) As terms for the modern Jew, the French language has both 'israélite' and 'juif', where English almost invariably has 'Jew' or 'Jewish'.

To return to the dating of the Creation story, the first five books of the Bible are traditionally attributed to Moses, a character appearing in the last four of them, we would have to date him very roughly at about 1400 B.C.E.. Some modern scholars, however, put parts of these books, including most of the Creation story between six hundred and a thousand years later than that.

Nevertheless, there are features of the Creation story that point to a date not later than 1000 B.C.E.. For the purpose of this book the date is not important. The point that I am making is that we cannot use the date of the Creation story to get much help in interpreting it. My experience of the Creation story tells me that, whenever it was written, it is timeless. I have come to the belief that it conveys perennial truth, which each generation can hear in terms suitable to its own understanding and need. If what I write seems to you to be markedly of our own time, take that as a token of the Creation story's breadth rather than of my narrowness. The former is worthy of appreciation; the latter hardly matters. Only let me say this: the bearing which the Creation story has on life here and now is an aspect of that which I invite you to share.

The Hebrew text which I have used throughout this book is that called Massoretic. What appears as quoted passages is my own translation into English. The Massoretic text is that of the Hebrew scriptures in all to-day's standard printed editions. A thousand year-old manuscript, the oldest we have of all the Hebrew scriptures in a single book, shows the text we now have, down to the details. Manuscripts about two thousand years old, as among the Dead Sea Scrolls, have differences between copies of one and the same passage of scripture, but the smallness of the differences tends to confirm rather than cast doubt on the sense of the texts. It is worth bearing in mind that an older manuscript is not necessarily more like the earliest version than is a later manuscript. A copy considered authoritative is likely to have been made from another considered authoritative, and so on back. Thus there is a high probability that the received text (in this case the Massoretic) has come through a succession of copying of more than usual carefulness. The traditional procedures still in use among Jews for copying scripture by hand add weight to this supposition, especially as there is literary evidence for the antiquity and constancy of the procedures themselves.

It may also be that, in times past, a written text had to be accurately copied in order to conform to what people already knew by heart. For example, Gerhardsson* has shown that it was normal among Jews two thousand years ago to be word perfect in memorising much or all of scripture. A similar use of memory is indicated, to take quite a different example, when the detail needed to tell the Mediaeval Welsh *Dream of Rhonabwy* (in the Mabinogion*) is said to require that the teller exceptionally, as seems clear, use a book. Other examples of a requirement for word-perfect oral transmission can be found among Jews. So, while copyists, being only human, made mistakes, we should not ignore the precautions and circumstances which tended to keep a text constant before the invention of printing. Where the oldest biblical manuscripts differ among themselves, they may all have been accurately copied, of course, but be copied from different originals. Thus there can have been different lineages of copying, one of which has survived. Nevertheless, as already indicated, the differences are very rarely substantial in their effect on meaning.

It can happen, and does, that something in the Hebrew scriptures makes no sense, and that it seems pretty certain that there must have been a copyist's mistake somewhere in the line of transmission. Faced with such sentences, scholars try to think back to what the original might have been. However, this need not concern us. There are no such unintelligible sentences which I have met with in this work on the Creation story.

For convenience, scriptural passages are referred to in this book by the usual chapter and verse numbers. The division into chapters is fairly recent, having been made by Stephen Langton (1150-1228), Archbishop of Canterbury. It is sometimes awkward, although we have got used to it. For example, we shall see that Chapter 1 of Genesis finishes before the end of the seven days of the Creation, leaving the seventh day to begin Chapter 2. The verses were first numbered only in the Sixteenth Century. In dividing the Creation story into items to be considered, I shall not necessarily do so according to the divisions between chapters.

In this invitation I have indicated some of the approaches to the Creation story that I shall not be using. If you ask me just what my own approach is, I should reply: here is a piece of literature, a work of art, which I want to listen to, to hear what it has to say to me. Of course, it is rubbish for anyone to pretend that he examines anything without preconceptions. I started, years ago, with the assumption that what is written in the Creation story has something to say worth of an attentive ear, and I am biassed towards finding what I feel to be important. Nevertheless, I could have been disappointed. In the event, the riches which I have found, and am still finding, engage me beyond all expectation.

This work has been encouraged in the last six years by my reading of writers with a literary approach to the Hebrew scriptures. I have in mind especially books by Robert Alter*, Adèle Berlin*, Meir Sternberg*, and Phyllis Trible*. You will see that I find the Creation story constructed so as to show patterns within itself, patterns that give additional meaning. In this I have been greatly influenced by the method used by Rabbi Jonathan Magonet in a seminar on 6th November 1984 at Leo Baeck College, London. These names I mention by way of grateful acknowledgment; this is not a book of footnotes and cross-references. I have simply tried to exercise that scholarship which my task requires, and hope to share it with those who are not scholars in this field.

In taking you with me to share my pleasure, I am leading you along the path that I have found or made. It is not the only path. My aim is to show that a path is possible. I shall have succeeded if you go on to seek your own. For a way through the Creation story can be a way into one's own being.

CHAPTER 2

THE PATTERN OF SEVEN DAYS

———

THE STORY OF THE CREATION opens with an account divided between seven days. In our printed Bibles this runs from the first verse of the first chapter of Genesis to the third verse of the second chapter, that is, Genesis 1:1-2:3, in the manner of giving scriptural references that will be used throughout this book. In the translated passages, verse numbers are inserted for convenience.

***

[1] In the beginning God created the heavens and the earth. [2] And the earth was unformed and void, and darkness is upon the face of the deep, and the spirit of God is hovering over the face of the water.

[3] AND GOD SAID 'Let there be light', and there was light. [4] And God saw the light, that it was good. And God divided the light from the darkness. [5] And God called the light 'day', and the darkness he called 'night'.

AND THERE WAS EVENING AND THERE WAS MORNING, ONE DAY.

[6] AND GOD SAID 'Let there be an expanse within the water, and let it divide water from water'. [7] And God made the expanse, and divided the water which is below the expanse from the water which is above the expanse. And it was so. [8] And God called the expanse 'heavens'.

AND THERE WAS EVENING AND THERE WAS MORNING, A SECOND DAY.

[9] AND GOD SAID 'Let the water under the heavens be gathered to one place, and let the dry land appear'. And it was so. [10] And God called the dry land 'earth', and the gathering of the water he called 'seas'. And God saw that it was good.

[11] AND GOD SAID 'Let the earth shoot with shoots, herbage seeding seed and the fruiting tree making fruit after its kind, in which is its seed, upon the earth'. And it was so. [12] And the earth brought forth shoots, herbage seeding seed after its kind, and the tree making fruit in which is its seed after its kind. And God saw that it was good.

[13] AND THERE WAS EVENING AND THERE WAS MORNING, A THIRD DAY.

[14] AND GOD SAID 'Let there be lights in the expanse of the heavens to divide the day from the night, and the lights shall be for signs and seasons and days and years, [15] and they shall be for lights in the expanse of the heavens to give

light upon the earth'. And it was so. [16] And God made the two great lights, the greater light for rule by day and the lesser light for rule by night, and the stars. [17] And God put them into the expanse of the heavens, to give light upon the earth, [18] and to rule in the day and in the night, and to divide the light from the darkness. And God saw that it was good.

[19] AND THERE WAS EVENING AND THERE WAS MORNING, A FOURTH DAY.

[20] AND GOD SAID 'Let the water teem with teeming animal life and let flying things fly over the earth, over the face of the expanse of the heavens'. [21] And God created the great tanninim, and all creeping animal life which teemed in the water, after their kind, and every winged flying thing after its kind. And God saw that it was good. [22] And God blessed them, saying 'Be fruitful and increase and fill the water in the seas, and let flying things increase in the earth'.

[23] AND THERE WAS EVENING AND THERE WAS MORNING, A FIFTH DAY.

[24] AND GOD SAID 'Let the earth bring forth animal life after its kind, cattle and creeping things and the animal of the earth after its kind'. And it was so. [25] And God made the animal of the earth after its kind, and cattle after its kind, and everything that creeps upon the ground, after its kind. And God saw that it was good.

[26] AND GOD SAID 'Let us make humankind in our image, according to our likeness, and they shall have dominion over the fish of the sea, and over the flying things of the heavens, and over cattle, and over all the earth, and over every creeping thing that creeps upon the earth'. [27] And God created humankind in his image, in the image of God he created it, male and female he created them.

[28] And God blessed them, and God said to them 'Be fruitful and increase and fill the earth and subdue it, and have dominion over the fish of the sea, and over the flying things of the heavens, and over every animal that creeps upon the earth. [29] And God said 'See, I have given you all herbage seeding seed on the face of all the earth, and every tree in which is the fruit of the tree, seeding seed, shall be food for you. [30] And to every animal of the earth, and to every flying thing of the heavens, and to every creeping thing upon the earth in which is animal life, there is all green herbage for food'. And it was so. [31] And God saw all that he had made, and behold it was very good.

AND THERE WAS EVENING AND THERE WAS MORNING, THE SIXTH DAY.

[1] And the heavens and the earth were completed, and all their host.

[2] And God completed on the seventh day the work which he did, and he made a sabbath on the seventh day from all the work which he did.

[3] And God blessed the seventh day and made it holy, because in it he made a sabbath from all the work which God created to make.

***

In the telling of the seven days certain words and phrases recur. Two of the recurring sentences, shown with capital letters in the foregoing translation, mark off divisions of the telling. The first of these is *And there was evening* etc., which concludes each of the first six days, while the other is *And God said...* which introduces each of the eight works of the Creation. (Although the wording *And God said...* occurs in verses 28 and 29, it does not there lead into the calling forth of something new, and is therefore not introducing works of the Creation.) Westermann* discusses how a system of seven days may have come to be combined with another, of eight works. Such speculation about the history of the telling has its own interest. Nevertheless, the purpose here is to examine the text we have rather than texts, known or guessed at, which have some similarities to it or which may even have influenced it.

When the seven days and eight works are set out with the first four works alongside the others, both sets of four in order, a certain regularity appears, as in Figure 1.

		Spirit on the waters.			
Day 1	Work 1	Light is made and separated from darkness.	Heavenly bodies make a division between light and darkness	Work 5	Day 4
Day 2	Work 2	The water is divided to give an expanse between water and water.	Living things populate the lower water and the expanse.	Work 6	Day 5
Day 3	Work 3	Water gathers so that dry land appears.	Land animals are made.	Work 7	Day 6
	Work 4	Seeding plant life is called forth from the earth.	Humankind is created.		Work 8
		Sabbath.			Day 7

Fig. 1. *The Two Cycles of the Creation*

It can be seen that the accounts of the first and seventh days have material outside the eight works. If works are considered in pairs, side by side in the table, there is a relationship of topics between the first and fifth, second and sixth, and the third and seventh works. The relationship between the fourth and eighth works is indicated by verse 29, which makes plants human food. The two columns are similar also in that it is the third day of each which has two works.

Although this table shows how the sequence of the first four works has resemblances to the sequence of the other four, the arrangement tends to break up the continuity of the series as a whole. After all, the telling itself indicates no division after the third day, other than that used to end five of the other days. Now, if all the works are to be set in a continuous series, but showing the pairs evident in the table, it is necessary to set them out in a spiral, something like Figure 2.

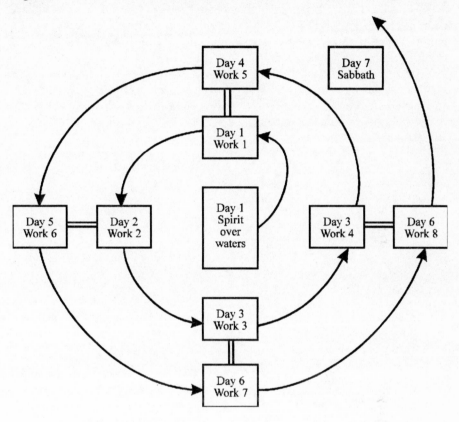

Fig.2. *The Two Cycles of the Creation: Spiral Representation*

The item referred to as 'Spirit over the waters' is the content of verses 1 and 2. As already noted, the text has these verses before the account of the first work, so that they are represented here separately from that work. The double lines join works which are pairs in the table already made, and which are related by their subject-matter. Since the account of the seventh day does not conclude with *And there was evening* etc., its openness is represented in the spiral by letting the arrow pass 'Day 7' instead of stopping at it. (This spiral is drawn with more detail on the frontispiece.)

It may be suggestive to consider the spiral as a whole. The entire configuration is open at both ends. Just as a spiral can continue indefinitely outwards, so also it does so inwards, around the point towards which it converges. Thus the way into the outer space and the way towards the central point are both infinite. Outer space and central point are single in that they are united by the coiled space between the turns of the spiral; this is clearer in the frontispiece than in Figure 2. Such consideration of the form of the spiral is not a mere game. It agrees, as I hope will become evident, with the accounts especially of the first, fourth, and seventh days in the Creation story.

To return to the text itself, the expressions *And God said...* and *And it was evening* etc. are not the only markers. Generally, we find with each work the sentences *And it was so* and *God saw that it was good.* These will be discussed in their places, with discussion why one or other is left out of the telling of certain works.

CHAPTER 3: *ONE DAY*

OUT OF THE GENERAL PATTERN of the seven days each may now be taken one by one. It is convenient therefore to repeat the opening of the story.

> [1] In the beginning God created the heavens and the earth. [2] And the earth was unformed and void, and darkness is upon the face of the deep, and the spirit of God is hovering over the face of the water. [4] And God said 'Let there be light', and there was light. And God saw the light that it was good. And God divided the light from the darkness. [5] And God called the light 'day', and the darkness he called 'night'. And there was evening and there was morning, one day.

What is meant by 'in the beginning'? The Hebrew word *(reshit)* translated 'beginning' may mean a start in time, but it has other shades of meaning. Sometimes it represents what is chief or principal. Here, for example, 'beginning' could mean what stands at the heart of the matter, or even what includes the rest. This openness of meaning can hardly be accidental. The Hebrew language, as used in scripture, is quite able to speak unambiguously of the outset of a matter, of the time when something starts.

Furthermore, the sentence *In the beginning God created the heavens and the earth* does not indicate the first step in a chain of events, since the story after the first day assumes that heaven and earth are not yet present. Rather, this opening sentence introduces, includes, and summarises what follows. The sentence *And the earth was unformed and void* clearly represents the basic state from which the reader or listener is led through the story. Some scholars, following the eleventh-century Rashi*, render the opening sentence as 'In the beginning of God's creating the heavens and the earth, the earth was unformed and void'. This gives a closer coupling of 'beginning' with the unformed state, so that we go from the basic principle to the basic state without, as it were, moving.

The question arises whether the intention of the writing is to show Creation producing what is 'unformed and void' or whether it is to start with Creation working on the 'unformed and void' already there. This question was being discussed at least as long ago as the Second or Third Century, according to the commentary Midrash Rabbah*. The question, however, makes an assumption. We can put the question only if we conceive of Creation with an onset at some point in time, and ask if the 'unformed and void' was already present at that time. Now we have already seen that the telling leaves it uncertain whether

11

the 'beginning' (or 'beginning of God's creating') does or does not refer to an onset at a point in time, and that the openness to different shades of interpretation must be deliberate. Here I will temporarily shelve this matter, Further comment will be possible when the fourth day's work is discussed.

Then we are told that *darkness is on the face of the deep*. The Hebrew word here for 'the deep' *(tehom)* is a biblical term for great seas, but it has especially the connotation of 'primaeval ocean'. In this sense it may perhaps be taken as a name of what is 'unformed and void'. The writing continues: *and the spirit of God is hovering over the face of the water.* The word translated 'spirit' can also be Englished as 'wind'. The wording thus presents two aspects. On the one hand it tells, beyond imagining, of the divine spirit moving on what is formlessness and emptiness. On the other hand we have something imaginable, a divine wind ruffling water. The unimaginable and its symbol inhere in the selfsame words.

***

Against this background the first work is told. *And God said 'Let there be light', and there was light.* This is the first example, in the story of the Creation, of the word of power. The coming into being is not a consequence of the saying: the saying itself is the bringing into being. The telling of the creation of light has four parts. First, there is the evocation of what is created; this is by the saying of the word of power. Then comes the value judgment, *And God saw the light that it was good.* Third is a supplement, amplifying what has been said of the evocation: *And God divided the light from the darkness.* Lastly, there is naming: *And God called the light 'day', and the darkness he called 'night'.* This naming I take as an example of adoption. By adoption I mean God's involvement with what otherwise might be thought of as an already completed work. These four elements of a Creation work, namely evocation, value judgment, supplement, and adoption, will be found in other works of Creation, although not every work is explicitly described with all four.

The act of adoption may merit comment. Here adoption is by naming. That is to say, it is through naming light and darkness that the Creator is shown to have a relation to them, beyond simply establishing their existence. Later it will be seen that naming can relate humankind to beasts, and can be a part of the relation between man and woman. The naming of light and darkness means therefore that they are not merely given their being and then, as it were, left like an abandonned manufacture or wound-up clock, or put aside to be picked up, like some plaything of higher powers. On the contrary, light and darkness exist always and everywhere only in relation to their Creator. As will be noted, the adoption within a Creation work is not necessarily by naming. Nevertheless, whatever the mode of adoption, it always implies that the Creator is involved with the created beyond the mere establishment of existence. Thus love is expressed in the very work of creation.

Although the telling of some works will be seen to lack a supplement, the latter is essential to the evocation of light. To put Creation into separable works means that created things are themselves by form, boundary, distinction. Without darkness, light is not itself; without light, darkness is not itself. This is true whether light and darkness are taken as distinct, or whether they are taken as the two opposite directions along a continuous scale of lightness and darkness.

And there was evening and there was morning, one day. Clearly, this means some degree of rounding off, of completion, even if not in all respects, since it refers to an entire cycle of day and night. Whether putting the evening first is to be taken as deliberately putting night before day, or whether it is the natural order in the language of a people who count days from sunset to sunset, is not obvious. More serious perhaps is how to understand the word 'day'. It may be more fruitful to consider this matter when more of the pattern of days has been reviewed. In particular, the word 'day' will come to notice in the examination of the 'days' which are in the telling of the fourth day.

CHAPTER 4: *A SECOND DAY*

WE NOW COME to the second work, which is the splitting of the waters, the deep, the primaeval ocean.

> [6] And God said 'Let there be an expanse within the water, and let it divide water from water'. [7] And God made the expanse, and divided the water which is below the expanse from the water which is above the expanse. And it was so. [8] And God called the expanse 'heavens'. And there was evening and there was morning, a second day.

The expression *And it was so* corresponds with *and there was light* in the account of the first day; in the Hebrew, 'and it was' is here the same word as 'and there was'. 'And it was so' is a recurring expression in the telling of the works, standing in each after the evocation. Here the evocation is the whole passage except verse 8. The first part of this verse is concerned with adoption which, as in the first work, is by naming. The evocation has no supplement.

This is the only Creation work recounted without the value judgment, and it has long been noted that we are not told that God saw that it was good. Rashi*, nine centuries ago, proposed that the expected sentence is omitted because the next work continues the distribution of the waters, so that the action is not complete with the work of the second day. Other explanations have been given. The mystical *Zohar* a little later than Rashi, gives the same explanation as he does, but also representing division as discord (and therefore not good), which the third day restored to amity.

Another explanation is that the sentence *And God saw that it was good* belongs here, but has somehow got lost in transmission. One argument for this, given in a note in the Stuttgart Bible*, a modern publication of the Hebrew text, is that in the Jews' old Greek translation, the Septuagint, the missing sentence is represented in verse 8. We must, however, be careful not to assume that the version which has an expected sentence is more faithful to the original than is the version which lacks it. A translator may tidy up irregularities of artistic importance, not only because he may be a bore, but also because the translation may be made for beginners, non-Jews or converts, for whom a difficulty is smoothed away, until they are perhaps ready for the Hebrew text itself.

In any case, it seems very unlikely that such a gross difference from all the other Creation works could have arisen, in this terse and compact telling of the seven days, from an error in copying, with the single copy thus produced then alone being accepted as authentic. Of course, the question of an error in copying does sometimes arise when the text of scripture presents something of which we can make no sense. However, what we have here is not some unintelligible detail but a major feature of the structure of the narrative.

The value judgment *and God saw that it was good* is also a way of putting a seal on a work. Leaving it out lessens the reader's sense of the completeness of the telling. As already noted, it is the next work which completes the distribution of the waters. In this sense, it cannot be said of the work of the second day, taken as a work in itself, that it is good. So, is the Creator doing something that is not good? It may help to bear in mind that another scriptural book has God saying 'I create evil' (Isaiah 45:7). The Revised Standard Version and the New English Bible, although not the 1611 translation, weaken 'evil' to 'woe' and 'trouble' respectively, but the context implies that 'peace' *(shalom),* with which 'evil' is here paired, has its widest and deepest meaning, so that 'evil' itself must be taken in its strongest and most universal sense. Also, the Hebrew scriptures have no devil. The *satan* (that is, 'adversary') is God's agent (Job 1:6-12, Zechariah 3:1-3). The fifteenth-century Christian, Nicolas of Cusa*, seems to be writing of the God who can do what is good and what is not good: 'God is absolute maximality and oneness, who precedes and unites absolute differences and distances, contradictions with no middle ground'.

The separation, in the story, of the upper from the lower waters leaves us with the question what is meant by these terms. The lower waters are not so much of a problem; their fate is made plain in the telling of the third day. The upper waters are more mysterious. They are not mentioned again in the Creation story, although the Psalms refer twice to water above the heavens (Psalms 104:3 and 148:4). Ginzberg*, summarising legends known from times after the scriptural books were written, tells how the lower waters were called female and the upper male. Some of these legends make the upper waters something normally held back, although from them the clouds are charged with rain.

THE THIRD WORK of the Creation takes up the further ordering of the lower waters.

> [9] And God said 'Let the water under the heavens be gathered to one place, and let the dry land appear'. And it was so. [10] And God called the dry land 'earth', and the gathering of the water he called 'seas'. And God saw that it was good.

Verse 9 gives the evocation, and verse 10 the adoption (again by naming) and value judgment. The evocation has no supplement.

The scriptural Hebrew word for 'sea' can be applied to a body of water whether salt or fresh, and is therefore wider in meaning than the English word. Also, the lower waters are said by the Hebrew scriptures to be not only beside the dry land, but also 'under the earth' (Exodus 20:4; Deuteronomy 5:8), whence springs come.

At this point, when 'earth' is being defined as a name for dry land, it may be useful to comment on the meanings of the words 'heavens' and 'earth'. In the telling of the second work we have *And God called the expanse 'heavens'*. If these heavens are potential in the 'earth' which is unformed and void, what is the meaning, in the introductory sentence, of *God created the heavens and the earth?* There is here a transition between two uses of the word 'earth'. When the hearer or reader meets, at the outset, *In the beginning God created the heavens and the earth,* the meaning of 'the heavens and the earth' is that which is commonest in the Hebrew scriptures when the two are coupled in this way: 'heaven and earth' means simply everything. There is then a description of one particular state of all this: *And the earth was unformed and void.* From this 'earth' come the expanse ('heavens'), dry land ('earth'), and water beneath the expanse ('seas'). Thus we have three uses of the word 'earth': coupled with 'heavens' to include everything, as the undifferentiated material ('without form and void') of created things, and as 'dry land'. (The division of created things into three—heavens, earth, seas—appears again in Exodus 20:11.)

In the telling, at verse 8, where God called the expanse 'heavens', the 'heavens' are not a special place for God's dwelling, but are that which we see spread above the earth, the sky and all that is in it. Conversely, God has a persistent concern with the earth, as is seen in the adoption of works on the fifth and sixth days. In the Hebrew scriptures all places have the divine presence (Jeremiah 23:24). The heavens are God's in the sense that they are unassigned to humanity (Psalm 115:16), so that an intervention of God into human affairs in a peculiarly full and awesome manner is described as God's coming down (Exodus 19:18). Thus the heavens are frequently said to be God's dwelling, and it is natural to look upwards in turning to God (Psalm 121:1). Nevertheless the Lord remains proprietor of the earth (Psalm 24:1), while even the farthest heavens cannot contain God (1 Kings 8:27). From these scriptural relations of God to the heavens and the earth there grew the realisation that the universe is not the dwelling-place of God, but that God is the dwelling-place of the universe. Therefore, in Jewish usage, 'the Place' became one of God's names. But that goes beyond the matter in hand.

***

The third day has two works. The second, which is the fourth work of the Creation, is recounted thus.

> [11] And God said 'Let the earth shoot with shoots, herbage seeding seed and the fruiting tree making fruit after its kind, in which is its seed, upon the earth'. And it was so. [12] And the earth brought forth shoots, herbage seeding seed after its kind, and the tree making fruit in which is its seed after its kind. And God saw that it was good. [13] And there was evening and there was morning, a third day.

Verse 11 has the evocation, the supplement of which is verse 12, which confirms the existence of what is evoked. The last sentence of verse 12 expresses the value judgment. In the spiral pattern, already considered on pages 9 and 10, this fourth work is paired with the eighth, and it is in the eighth work, in which God appoints a function for plants, that the fourth work finds its adoption.

The word pairs 'shoot with shoots' and 'seeding seed' may be clumsy in English. They reflect the Hebrew expressions *'ta-dshe deshe'* and *'ma-zria zera'* respectively, which are just such pairs.

THE TELLING of the fourth day recounts the fifth work of the Creation.

[14] And God said 'Let there be lights in the expanse of the heavens to divide the day from the night, and the lights shall be for signs and seasons and days and years, [15] and they shall be for lights in the expanse of the heavens to give light upon the earth'. And it was so. [16] And God made the two great lights, the greater light for rule by day and the lesser light for rule by night, and the stars. [17] And God put them into the expanse of the heavens, to give light upon the earth, [18] and to rule in the day and in the night, and to divide the light from the darkness. And God saw that it was good. [19] And there was evening and there was morning, a fourth day.

All four elements of the telling of a Creation work are present. The evocation is in verses 14 and 15, the supplement in verse 16, the adoption in verses 17 and 18, and the value judgment in the last sentence of verse 18. Each of the first three has a point of particular interest.

The evocation of the heavenly bodies gives 'signs'. Nothing is a sign unless it can be read or interpreted. Therefore the heavenly bodies are related to intelligent living beings, although the Creation story has not yet presented animal life.

The supplement expands on the 'lights' of the evocation. It speaks of a 'greater light' and a 'lesser light', avoiding the obvious mention of the sun and moon by name. This helps to put these wonderful and awe-inspiring bodies firmly in their place. Any power they have is from the Creator, whose lamps and time-markers they are, and who puts them for the use of those other created things that can read signs. The avoidance of naming the sun and the moon is characteristic of this account of the Creation. Elsewhere, as in Psalm 136:8 and 9, they are named, although referred to as being brought into being by God.

The adoption relates the created to the Creator by asserting the Creator's purpose. By continually effecting that purpose the lights are the Creator's continuing instruments. The wording of the adoption raises a question: why does it say *to divide the light from the darkness?* After all, we have read already, in the telling of the first work, *and God divided the light from the darkness.* Why does the telling attribute to a work of the fourth day a division which, it has already said, is made on the first day? In the table on p.8 and spiral on p.9, and on the frontispiece, the works of the first and fourth days are shown to be a pair within the Creation pattern. The two statements of the division between light and darkness differ only in that, in the work of the first day, the dividing is given as God's without mention of an instrument while, on the fourth day, God makes the division a purpose of his lights. I suggest that the fourth day's *divide the light from the darkness* is an intended echo of the first day, in spite of the difference in the form of the English and the Hebrew verb (because of the way the phrase is set in the sentence); the difference between *va-yavdel* ('and he divided') and *le-havdil* ('to divide') still leaves the echo heard. Either we have two dividings, or two references to one. If there are two dividings we would have to suppose that the writing is intended to say that God did the same thing twice. So when was it undone? This won't do. Undoing is clearly foreign to the telling of the seven days although, as will be seen, it has a place further on in the story. Rashi* makes two dividings by distinguishing two meanings to the word 'light', referring to the light of the first day as 'the first light'. He refers, in fact, to the legend, not in scripture, that there is a light, a work of the first day, unseen because of human wickedness, and reserved for the righteous at the last days; this legend is presented by Ginzberg*. (A legend associated with a difficulty in scripture may, of course, have arisen as an explanation of the difficulty, not independently of it. The legend may thus prevent recognition of an explanation inherent in the text itself.) The fact is that the telling itself makes no sense unless either some matter is drawn in from outside, as by Rashi, or the dividing of light from darkness is one matter mentioned twice, once with reference to light and darkness as such, and once to them as distinguished by the bodies ruling night and day. If we do not bring in material as Rashi did, may not one meaning of the pattern in the spiral be that the seven days are to be seen not as a succession but as a whole, partly or entirely without extension in time?

Here we obtain some help from the telling of the fourth day itself. The lights are to be for 'seasons and days and years'. Now, two meanings are possible for this marking out of time intervals by the movements and changes of heavenly bodies. The two meanings are implied by two different notions of time. One notion of time is that it flows of itself, without depending on the events which mark points or periods along its course. This notion is usually implied when we speak of time without 'the' or 'a'. Time is then something of itself. It can do things or have qualities. This is the notion of time which we have when we say 'Time flies', or which is there in the saying of Pindar* that 'time is the best saviour of the just'.

A second notion of time is that it depends on events. According to this notion of time, it is nonsense to think of it without there being a universe in which there are changes, happenings. According to this notion we can speak of 'a time' or 'the time' or 'times', but can say 'time' if at all, only because it is marked by days, seasons, clocks, human actions, events, or other such pacers and milestones. Which of these two notions is that present when the Hebrew scriptures speak of time? The answer may help with our interpretation of the 'seasons and days and years' in the Creation story.

The Hebrew scriptures refer to what English-speakers would call 'a time' in about three hundred instances. Several words are used, one of them (*ét*) about twice as often as all others put together. Whichever word is used, it always means the occasion or duration of one or more events. Time never has qualities or actions of its own. It is difficult to know how scriptural Hebrew could express accurately 'Time flies'. Modern Hebrew does it with a word *(zeman)* which, in scripture means a season or 'the time when...' As for saying that time is the best saviour of the just, not only would an ancient Israelite probably have found it philosophically meaningless or morally perverse, but he could have translated it into his own language only by paraphrase.

Because of the English translations, a reader might think that one scriptural book, Ecclesiastes, does indeed speak of time independent of events. The well-known Chapter 3 says that 'there is a time for...' everything. Does it not, then, present time as an independent framework on which an event has its place? Surely, this is not what it says when it tells us 'there is *a* time for'. Even if there is 'time' along which these 'times' are strung like beads, there is nothing to suggest that this continuous time is independent of events. On the contrary, Ecclesiastes (e.g. 8:9) has 'under the sun' as one of its recurring expressions, and the sun is a major time marker. This Chapter 3, in fact, speaks of 'times' but resembles the rest of the Hebrew scriptures in having no mention of 'time'. However, in Chapter 9 of Ecclesiastes, we have *time and chance happen to them all*. Is this not time as an independent entity, doing its own thing? Here there is an impression given by the translation; more literally, the sentence is *a time and an occasion will meet each of them.* (Some take the intended occasion to be death.)

I would therefore conclude that the consistent philosophy of time in the Hebrew scriptures is that there are times, but no 'time' independent of what marks them. It is the second of our notions of time that is relevant. This enables us to interpret 'seasons and days and years'. These are times, and arise from the bringing into being of the heavenly lights. This leads to the question whether the telling of the fourth day is about, among other things, the creation of time. The alternative is to see time being marked by works of the first, second, and third days. Against this alternative are two considerations. First, the reader's expectation, if any, of a series of events is disturbed at the start by the openness of meaning of 'in the beginning', as already discussed. Secondly, there is the division of light from darkness as an event of both the first and fourth days.

Rashi*, commenting on verse 1, pointed out that the items of the story of the seven days cannot be written in their order in time. I would like to go beyond this, and suggest that the earlier part of the story, at least, cannot be placed in time at all, and that it is the fifth work, the work of the fourth day, by which time, in any sense compatible with scriptural usage, is brought into being.

What then of the word 'day' which is used in marking off the episodes of the story? The expression *And there was evening and there was morning* indicates, as Radak* pointed out, that a day and night is meant, not simply light, which is the meaning of 'day' in verse 5. Now this cannot be meant literally, since 'days' in this cyclical sense, are first presented as the result of the work of the fourth day. Nevertheless, the word 'day' is still appropriate. The seven days of Creation are commemorated among Jews by the days of the week, the cycle marked by a Sabbath every seven days. To use anthropological language, we can say that the story of the seven days is the myth of which the week is the ritual. The seven days are ordinary days, borrowed by the telling of the myth from the practice of the ritual. The ritual gives words with which to refer to the unspeakable. The words *And there was evening...* point to something over and beyond time, something that words may grasp only to destroy, as a forceps can wreck a butterfly.

This argument about the creation of time may seem tedious, but it has a bearing on how we regard the whole Creation story, not just this opening narrative of the seven days. I do not see how any other view of the matter can take into consideration *all* that is told here of the first four days, and *also* the consistent philosophy of time of the Hebrew scriptures, while not bringing in material which the Creation story lacks. All this explaining is needed, not because the wording itself is obscure, but because we may need to work ourselves out of certain assumptions which cramp our understanding. Our assumptions are not necessarily those of the writer or earliest readers, nor need our 'natural' presuppositions be those which allow the text to offer its richest capability in our own time.

The Creation of the heavens and the earth includes the creation of time. Time is of the fourth day.

ON THE FIFTH DAY the work is the bringing into being of living things in the lower waters and the firmament, which are separated and made in the work of the second day.

> [20] And God said 'Let the water teem with teeming animal life and let flying things fly over the earth, over the face of the expanse of the heavens'. [21] And God created the great tanninim, and all creeping animal life which teemed in the water, after their kind, and every winged flying thing after its kind. And God saw that it was good. [22] And God blessed them, saying 'Be fruitful and increase and fill the water in the seas, and let flying things increase in the earth'. [23] And there was evening and there was morning, a fifth day.

The evocation is verse 20, with the first sentence of verse 21 as supplement. At the end of verse 21 is the usual value judgment. Verse 22 is the adoption, which is by blessing. Unexpectedly, the set expression *and it was so* does not appear at the end of the evocation. The possible reason for this can more conveniently be discussed later, when consideration is given to what is written of the creation of humankind.

In the account of the fifth day's work there are words that need some comment. In English, *teem with teeming animal life* repeats a word awkwardly. In biblical Hebrew, a doublet of this sort rings out with a kind of emphasis. I have tried to make the English reflect a pair of related words in the Hebrew *(yi-shretz-u, sheretz)*. In the work of the third day, you will recollect, there were the phrases *shoot with shoots* and *seeding seed*. In the passage now being considered, the English word 'teem' resembles the Hebrew word which it translates, in that both suggest fecundity as well as abundance.

The *great tanninim* present a problem. What is a tannin? The Authorised Version of 1611 has 'great whales', and this expression does catch something of the power and mystery of the tanninim. (For some of us, the power and mystery are brought out well when the 'great whales' are sung in Haydn's *Creation.*) Although tanninim are mentioned in the Hebrew scriptures on thirteen distinct occasions, none of the thirteen passages tells us just what a tannin is. The name is used for a dangerous natural animal, perhaps a poisonous snake (Psalm 91:13), but elsewhere the tannin seems to be some great creature, such as may be held to exist even if not observed. It is like Leviathan, a great beast which the Lord will eventually overcome (Psalm 74:13, Isaiah

27:1), or like Rahab (Isaiah 51:9), a beast or angel of which there are many legends, for details of which the curious reader may consult Ginzberg*. Job (7:12) couples a tannin with the sea, in that both are controlled by God's vigilance. Alongside this we may put the verse, 'Praise the Lord from the earth, O tanninim and all deeps'(Psalm 148:7). The word for 'deeps' is that used in this Creation story for the 'deep' on which the primal darkness lay. The plural ('deeps' for 'deep') is a fairly common device in scriptural poetry to give intensity of feeling. In fact, Psalm 148 relates to the Creation things praising the Lord: 'for he commanded and they were created' (verse 5).

The tanninim, then, are something very powerful, and are close to the deepest parts and processes of Creation. In this telling of the fifth day, the supplement in verse 21, giving the fulfilment of the evocation in verse 20, opens with the tanninim. They are the first-mentioned kind of animal life.

For this reason, it appears, they are 'created'. In the Creation story only three things are said to be created: heaven and earth, the great tanninim, and humankind. Now 'create' *(bara)* in scriptural Hebrew has not the same meaning as 'make' *(asah)*. Making can be divine or human: God makes the heavenly lights (Genesis 1:16) and a woman makes cloths and garments (Proverbs 31:22,24). It is not so with creating. In the Hebrew scriptures 'create' *(bara)* is found forty-eight times, and on every occasion the one who does the creating is God. As we shall see, in the telling of the seventh day of the Creation there is mention of *all the work God created for making* That is, creating, which only God can do, is needed for making, which can be divine or human. There is therefore a sense in which we can say that creation is prior to making in the story of the seven days.

God creates heaven and earth, all that there is. God creates the great tanninim, primal representations of animal life. God creates (in a passage still to be considered) humankind. With each of the three, therefore, something new is introduced, new in the sense that it differs from other things brought into existence, differs in a way that things 'made' need not differ from each other. The 'great tanninim' are the point at which animal life takes off from the line of the telling; here lies their power and their mystery. Those who love to read *Moby Dick* may not object to the old translation, 'great whales'.

It may be helpful to comment on *creeping animal life,* since the term, in English, does not include fish, although the context plainly implies them. The word 'creeping' *(romeset)* refers to land movement in which the belly is not lifted off the ground, or—and this is the point—to a gliding movement in water. Also, in some contexts, this verb 'creep' *(ramas)* seems to mean simply 'move', said of animals of various kinds.

The adoption of the work of the fifth day is by blessing, and God's blessing here is explicitly for increase and fecundity. On the bringing forth of plants, on the third day, in the fourth work, there is no such blessing, the making of seed being considered inherent in the plants themselves, rather than something requiring their Creator's distinct blessing. In this connection it is to be noted that

23

the biblical word for 'life' *(chay, chayim)* can be used of animals, including humankind, but not of plants. This adds to our impression of something new at *let the waters teem* and *created the tanninim.*

THE FIRST WORK of the sixth day is the seventh work of the Creation.

> [24] And God said 'Let the earth bring forth animal life after its kind, cattle and creeping things and the animal of the earth after its kind'. And it was so. [25] And God made the animal of the earth after its kind, and cattle after its kind, and everything that creeps upon the ground, after its kind. And God saw that it was good.

The evocation is in verse 24, and the supplement in verse 25. The closing sentence of verse 25 is the value judgment. There is no adoption, but an adoption of this work is implied in that of the eighth work, as will be noted in that connection.

Within the pattern of the seven days, this work, the seventh, has three relations, as in the spiral on p.9 and on the frontispiece. The work continues the bringing forth of animal life *(chayah)* explicitly mentioned in the telling of the previous work, and of this. The work is related to the next by their common adoption, as just noted. There is also (and here the spiral helps) the relation between the third work, making dry land, and this seventh work, populating it.

Land beasts are, in this telling, of three kinds: cattle, creeping things, and the animal of the earth. The creeping things are those with bellies on the ground. The animals with bellies off the ground are either domestic ('cattle') or wild ('the animal of the earth'). The order of the three differs between the evocation and the supplement. The creeping things, whose watery representatives have already turned up in the telling of the fifth day, are now mentioned last in both the evocation and the supplement. In the evocation, which shows the initiating will of the Creator, domestic beasts are mentioned first,–but only second to wild beasts in the supplement, which is about the natural fulfilment of what is willed. Wild beasts are prior to domestic in the natural order, but second to domestic beasts when the emphasis is more on end, direction, purpose. Thus the evocation points towards humankind, just as the heavenly bodies of the fourth day's work point towards the living things to which they serve as 'signs'.

***

The other work of the sixth day, the eighth work of the Creation, is the bringing forth of humankind. As the scriptural account of this work is fuller than the accounts of other works, it will be convenient to take the evocation, supplement, adoption, and value judgment separately, in turn, the evocation being first, corresponding to verse 26.

> [26] And God said 'Let us make humankind in our image, according to our likeness, and they shall have dominion over the fish of the sea, and over the flying things of the heavens, and over cattle, and over all the earth, and over every creeping thing that creeps upon the earth'.

What does it mean to be in God's image, according to God's likeness? The impact of this doctrine on the hearer or reader is, partly at least, due to what it says of the exaltedness of human nature. Three arguments have been used to diminish the impact, to avoid the challenge of the divinity which is here said to be inherent in humanity. One argument is that we are reading of the future, that humankind is not yet, according to this writing, in God's image and according to God's likeness. A second is that humankind, at the outset, in some way forfeited this godlikeness. Thirdly, it is argued that image and likeness are but feeble shadowings, far short of full godlikeness.

Later in the Creation story, after the Flood, we find a warning against shedding human blood because 'in the image of God he created humankind' (Genesis 9:6). The style of the warning shows that it is not only for some time in the indefinite future, but for now and always. Therefore the reason for the warning's validity, that 'in the image of God he created humankind', is intended to hold now and always. Thus the Creation story itself contradicts the argument that being in the image of God is meant to be only about some future time.

The second argument, that we are given to understand that humankind in some way forfeited this godlikeness, can, for the same reason, be valid only if the story has the forfeiture, if at all, after God's warning against bloodshed, which follows the Flood. It has not. Neither in the Creation story nor elsewhere in the Hebrew scriptures is there any indication that humanity is to be taken as less godlike than it is said to be just after the Flood.

The third argument, that image and likeness fall short of what is imaged and resembled, is more cogent. As Rudolf Otto* has said, and truly, the numinous divine is experienced as wholly other, overpoweringly majestic, and making the experiencer feel as nothing. Nevertheless Otto draws attention to the numinous power also of the human depths which can inspire the mystic's awe. The question, then, must be this: what are, in the Creation story, the respects in which humankind is in God's image and likeness?

The answer to the question is in the terms used in the account of this work of the making of humankind. When we read *in our image, according to our likeness,* coupled with it we read also of characteristics of divinity and humanity. It is surely implied that it is in these respects, at least, that the image and likeness correspond to what is imaged and resembled. In the evocation two characteristics are specified by the phrases *let us make* and *they shall have dominion.* That is to say, humankind is, with God, a maker and has, with God or delegated from God, dominion over other creatures. What is meant by *have dominion over* will be further filled out by what is written of humanity in the Garden of Eden. As for humankind's resemblance to God the maker, God is maker of humankind, which, is therefore, with God, maker of itself, as well as of much else. I am reminded of the late V. Gordon Childe*, who wrote on prehistoric archaeology a book called *Man makes himself,* which deals with one aspect of the matter.

The supplement adds to what has been said in the evocation.

> [27] And God created mankind in his image, in the image of God he created it,
> male and female he created them.

Like the heavens and the earth, like the great tanninim, humankind cannot be made entirely from something else. The making of humanity requires the creation of humanity. Since humankind is said to be created in God's image, we are thereby told that it is not only maker but also a creator, co-creator therefore with God.

So human activity is more than making, and goes behind it to the very act of creating. Nevertheless, as noted, the system of thought and expression within which this Creation story has its being gives God as the only creator. The clue to the paradox is in common ways in which we speak of our creativity. Consider the creative activity of the maker of music or stories or scientific experiments. It is exercised in many ways by many people. We see it in bringing forth something fresh in everyday human relations; we see it in a garden and in a child. We cannot create just anything, and everything we create needs more than ourselves alone. We are always co-creators. More than this, however, is in our common speech. An idea is 'inspired', a child is 'a gift'. It is not only that we work with what is other than ourselves. Even in the aspect of creativity that is all my own, I am aware of my being inspired, of receiving a gift.

Further, in all our creating, it is in ourselves also that we are liable to bring forth something new, some new function of our nature, some new component of our complexity, some new aspect of our singleness, with each new thing unique in humanity, and in the universe, although fellow to much else. Thus we are self-creators. Now an act of creation is an act of free will; in the telling, the phrase *let us make* says this. If we are creators with free will, and have a part in creating ourselves, it is not beyond us to influence how far and in what respects we fulfil God's image and likeness.

In this connection it is relevant that the Hebrew scriptures can speak of a human being as 'perfect' *(tam,* Job 1:1) that is, 'complete','finished', 'perfected'. One form of the word *(tamim)* is used not only for 'perfect' as applied to a human being (e.g. Genesis 17:1), but also to describe God's way (2 Samuel 22:31). The word 'perfect' (Greek *teleios)* is applied, in just this sense, to human beings, by the Christian Gospel also (Matthew 5:48), and with reference to being it in imitation of God. Since it would appear that the Creation story is meant to show the possibility of imitating God, it is not surprising that Israelite teaching, from the scriptures onwards, is concerned with this imitation, as Brocke* shows. (Brocke, however, denies that the Creation story's reference to humankind in the divine image is connected with this imitation. He may be right about the Creation story's historical influence, but still have missed something of the meaning of what is written.)

In God's creating humankind in his image, *male and female he created them.* This implies three things about being male and female. We see that the terms are first introduced at this point, although the previous work yielded beasts, whose sexual differentiation was certainly known to the writer, as it must have been to all readers since. Therefore we are true to the writing when we wonder why male and female are introduced only with humanity. The first point to be taken, obviously, is that this cannot be about biological sexuality in general, but only about some peculiarly human aspect of it.

Secondly, we are given to understand that we need to be male and female in order to be in the divine image. This can have a meaning wider than is at first obvious. In discussing the Garden of Eden I shall refer to the sexuality of each of the partners within a couple. In the consideration of Noah, reference will be made to the maleness and femaleness within the individual. Concerning the generations between Adam and Noah, the difference between male and female will be seen as a difference between social tendencies. With respect to those that issue from Noah and his sons, maleness and femaleness will be related to whole nations.

Thirdly, if to be in the image of God is to be male and female, then something is being said about God. The Hebrew scriptures are rich in metaphors and similes for God's powers and activities. Thus we read of God's hand, or that God hears. Human terms are used to give partial descriptions or inklings of what, in all lands and ages and irrespective of cultic words and ceremonies, is beyond speech. To achieve the range of description which scripture requires, the imagery has to be both male and female. Two instances of each may make the point. Male similes for God include a warrior (Psalm 24:8) and a husband (Hosea 2). One of the female images is that of the divine spirit hovering over the waters in the Creation, the word for 'hover' *(rachef)* being that for a bird fluttering over its young (Deuteronomy 32:11). Also female is the mercy of God, as in Psalm 145:9. The word there for 'mercy' *(rachamim)* is the plural, used as an intensive form, of the word for 'womb' *(rechem).* Beyond the use of metaphors and similes, the requirement that God's image and likeness be male and female represents a mystery that lies outside my ability to represent it in words. (To see the God of the Hebrew scriptures as male, as in some of to-day's textual criticism and sexual polemic, rests on misunderstanding Hebrew grammar and on incompetent literary criticism. Incidentally, the expression of such a view happens to be offensive to those whose worship and philosophy is in the line of these scriptures.)

Like the sixth work on the fifth day, this eighth work, on the sixth day, is adopted by a blessing of fruitfulness, but it is a blessing in other respects also.

[28] And God blessed them, and God said to them 'Be fruitful and increase and fill the earth and subdue it, and have dominion over the fish of the sea, and over the flying things of the heaven, and over every animal that creeps upon the earth'. [29] And God said 'See, I have given you all herbage seeding seed on the face of all the earth, and every tree in which is the fruit of the tree, seeding seed, shall be food for you. [30] And to every animal of the earth, and to every flying thing of the heavens, and to every creeping thing upon the earth in which is animal life, there is all green herbage for food'. And it was so.

This adoption refers to human increase, coupled with dominion over the earth and the provision of food for people and beasts. Neither the bringing into being of plants, on the third day, nor that of land animals, on the sixth, has an adoption in the telling. Now we find herb, fruit, and beast implicated in the adoption of this, the last-told work, the creation and making of humankind. The human standpoint of the telling is evident, and humankind, in the divine image and made according to the divine likeness, is God's agent, God's collaborator. It is in the joint adoption of three works that the creative assigning of dominion is affirmed. Here is starting material for any consideration of the meaning of 'dominion' in the Creation story.

Although the adoption of the work of bringing forth land beasts is suspended in this way, the fifth day's work of making the animals of sea and air has its own adoption, which also is a blessing. There, however, is the point at which animal reproduction is introduced into the Creation story; human involvement in animal fertility, if at all, cannot be at its initiation, its very existence.

The phrase *and it was so* needs some attention. As a rule, this follows the evocation. The expression was, however, missing from the account of the fifth day, in which animal life is brought forth to populate the firmament and lower waters. Here, in the telling of the sixth day, it is also absent at the end of the evocation, although turning up at the end of the adoption. The two evocations lacking the conclusion *and it was so* have also another feature in common. They are both evocations of things said, at some point, to be 'created' The phrase *created for making,* to be noted in the telling of the seventh day, shows that creation underlies making, is in some way logically antecedent to it.

Here, then, in the account of the sixth day, it is at the end of the adoption, not the evocation, that we are told that *it was so.* There are two possible meanings that come to the reader or hearer (Why should one not allow oneself to hear both meanings, and hold to both?) In the first place, it may be said that the adoption, coming later than the word *create* in the supplement, fulfils the word *make* in the evocation. Humankind is made (as in the evocation), but only insofar as it is in its divinely appointed relation to the other created things of the earth, through God's explicit blessing (as in the adoption). Secondly, it is possible to hear the sentence *And it was so* as closing all the making which depends upon the opening, *God created the heavens and the earth.*

The value judgment of this last of the eight works of Creation is certainly worded to refer to all the works, taken as a whole.

³¹ And God saw all that he had made, and behold it was very good.

The phrase *all that he had made* clearly refers not simply to one work, but to all the bringing into being that has been recounted. The expression *very good* need not mean better than just *good;* the word *very* (Hebrew *me'od)* has a sense of 'abundantly'. Therefore the expression could be rendered 'good in many respects' which answers to the inclusiveness of *all that he had made.*

The telling of this day closes with the rest of verse 31.

And there was evening and there was morning, the sixth day.

After *a* second day, *a* third day, and so on, we have here *the* sixth day. The change gives some feeling of conclusiveness. If the Creation is very good and well rounded off by the sixth day's works, how can humankind be in the Creator's image, for what is humanity's scope for creating and making? We have seen, however, that the sixth day's work is not necessarily fulfilled. Although being in God's image is not reserved, by the act of creation, for some future time, its manifestation, and thus humanity's self-creation, is variable and a matter influenced by the exercise of free will. Similarly, whatever meaning we give to *have dominion over,* the fulfilment of *subdue it* cannot be something achieved since time immemorial. What then has the Creation story to say about the fulfilment of the creation and making of humankind? To answer this question, it is necessary to consider the seventh day.

IN THE TELLING of the seventh day there is no evocation. What is brought into being is the day itself. Or one could say that what is made on the seventh day is the seventh day. There is no work; therefore there is no work for God to see to be good: no value judgment is possible. Also, there is no supplement. First, there is simply a completion, a perfection upon Creation.

> [1] And the heavens and the earth were completed, and all their host. [2] And God completed on the seventh day the work which he did, and he made a sabbath on the seventh day from all the work which he did.

The adoption of this follows immediately.

> [3] And God blessed the seventh day and made it holy, because in it he made a sabbath from all the work which God created to make [or created for making].

The expression *made a sabbath* translates one Hebrew word in each case *(wayishbot, shabbat,* both parts of the same verb). In scripture this verb can mean 'to rest' or 'to cease' from doing something, but it has these meanings because, in the first place, it means 'to make (*or* have) a sabbath'. There is no English word corresponding to the Hebrew word *shabbat,* translated 'sabbath'. Rest is a necessary feature of the sabbath, but rest does not define it. If one makes a sabbath, one of its effects is rest; however, merely taking a rest does not cause there to be a sabbath, whatever the day on which the rest is taken. The sabbath, as an institution among Israelites, is a celebration of Creation, including Creation's seventh day. Scripture does not define 'sabbath', any more than it explains what is meant by 'stone' or 'cow'. If the reader is to feel a way back to the meaning of sabbath, a consideration of Creation's seventh day may be one of the possible starting points.

The sabbath is blessed in this telling of the seventh day. Now, in every place where we find 'bless' in the book of Genesis, if there is some specified benefit, that benefit is or includes fertility, abundance. The blessing of the day may therefore be expected to be productive. Productive of what? The answer, which is in the telling, is holiness: *and made it holy.* The meaning of this may be clearer after notice has been taken of the two aspects of the sabbath.

The first aspect is given by the expressions *completed... the work* and *made a sabbath from all the work.* What does *work* mean? There are at least five distinct words for 'work' in scripture, as well as their derivatives, and each of the five differs from all the others in its exact meaning. The word used here is *mel'akhah*, which means 'labour' or 'occupation', but with a connotation of something going out from the doer. (It is the feminine form of *mal'akh*, which means 'messenger' or 'emissary', and hence 'angel'.) In the divine sabbath nothing goes out from God.

This aspect of the sabbath is explained further in the scriptural book of Exodus (31:17), where we read: *and on the seventh day* [God] *made a sabbath and became restored* (Hebrew *wa-yinnafash*). The verb *yinnafash* ('became restored') is from the noun *nefesh*, which is commonly translated 'soul'. Most often, however, in scriptural (not modern) Hebrew, *nefesh* means one's entire self. For example, later in the Creation story (Genesis 2:7), God breathes into the newly formed human being, who thereby becomes (not receives) a living *nefesh*. So, in the divine sabbath the Creator, otherwise seen in the diversity and change of creation, is presented as the Unity restored to being itself without the sending forth of 'work'.

The second aspect of the sabbath is put to us when we see that only this day lacks the conclusion *and there was evening…* etc. It is an open-ended day. From the point of view of human beings, who live in time, the sabbath opens into history and can be said to point, insofar as it is unrealised, to a time which is wholly sabbath.

Using the spiral on p.9 and on the frontispiece, the two aspects of the sabbath may be expressed thus. It opens into the surrounding space, but also into the space between the turns of the spiral, towards the infinitesimally small point of convergence. The infinitesimal point and the indefinitely extended exterior are both infinite and both parts of the same space.

Here we approach more of the answer to the question at the end of the previous chapter, on p.30: what has the Creation story to say about the fulfilment of Creation and the making of humankind? We, being in the divine image, can be co-creators of the seventh day in taking history towards the time that is all sabbath, while each of us can return to the inner centre where God is. To reach to the Creator in and beyond all things in nature and in history, and to reach to the Creator at the centre of ourselves, is all one, as the Creator is one. In our being created is our doing and our being, and in it they become one, our action and our stillness.

Now the meaning of the adoption of the seventh day can be considered again. The seventh day is only partly realised, or not at all, whether in history or in the individual. Nevertheless, it is presented to the reader of the Creation story as an essential of Creation. Therefore it stands as if to be ready for us, to bring us to itself. With its distinctness is its holiness. As we approach it we partake of the holiness. The story says that God blessed the seventh day and made it holy. This, in turn, means that we can be made holy through it. This is the fertility with which it is blessed: *and God blessed the seventh day and made it holy.*

***

The double meaning of the seventh day, its outwardness and its inwardness, is a polarity. It may be helpful towards an understanding of matters which will arise later in this book, if a pause is taken here to examine this notion of polarity. A polarity is not a pair of incompatibles antagonistic to each other. It is a pair of characteristics of one thing, neither of the pair able to subsist without the other.

A well-known example may make the matter plain. A magnetised iron bar has two poles, north and south. If it is floated or pivoted, this bar magnet will turn, if undisturbed, with its south pole towards the earth's north magnetic pole. Now let us try to separate the bar magnet's poles by cutting it in two. At the newly cut end of the half with the original north pole there is now a south pole; at the newly cut end of the part with the original south pole there is a north pole. The magnet was north-and-south right through, as is each of the magnets cut from it. It may also be to the point to note that north and south poles are complementary rather than antagonistic in their behaviour. Two freely floating magnets will tend to move so that the north pole of one comes towards the south pole of the other, and conversely; the behaviour of the compass needle, itself a magnet, in relation to the earth, also a magnet, exemplifies this.

The inwardness and outwardness of the seventh day are its two poles. If we try to accept the one without the other, we do not accept the seventh day.

In the other six days there are polarities arising from the bringing forth of new things by making distinctions. Thus we read of the division of the primal waters into upper and lower, of light from darkness and day from night. Male and female are necessarily created together, and this polarity will have further attention when later parts of the Creation story are considered. There can be a complementarity even in the meaning. Were there no darkness, no night, no male, what would we mean by day, light, or female? It is similar with holy and profane. The seventh day, being made holy, implies that there is also the profane, but the profane is needed for holiness to be perceived in the first place. When it is perceived it is seen not to be necessarily confined to what is first distinguished as holy; from the holy the profane can be changed, made holy. And this brings us back to the blessing of the seventh day. (Holy and profane are not the same as spiritual and secular, a distinction which does not come into the philosophy of the Hebrew scriptures.)

In ourselves the polarity of the seventh day can be discerned as between central stillness and outgoing action, a pair already noted. Since action is inevitable, if only because we cannot survive without it, it is the stillness than is most often to be sought. It is to be sought not only for its own sake, but also because our appreciation of it is integral with the fuller appreciation of our outgoing activity.

Here note may be taken of another polarity. Previously, on p.15 note was taken of good and evil in the works of the Creator. This polarity is also in ourselves, who are in the Creator's image, and is the subject of the post-biblical Jewish doctrine of the two impulses. According to this, each human being has a good and an evil impulse. The evil impulse is not, however, bad in its effects when under the influence of the good impulse. As is said in Midrash Rabbah*, the evil impulse is necessary for wholly good activities, such as marriage, having children, building a house, or practising a craft. The evil impulse is evil in effect only when the good impulse is not exercised with it. Therefore it is said that the Creator is to be worshipped with both impulses, the evil as well as the good. Further, it is the righteous and wise who, it is related in Talmud Bavli*, have the strongest evil impulse. Very near to this doctrine is William Blake*: 'Good is the passive that obeys Reason. Evil is the active springing from Energy'.

**

Thus the seventh day has an aim, an end, to which it points. This is outward in history and within the individual. The Hebrew scriptures combine these in their teachings about the perfection of the world. To pursue this matter would take us too far off the track, especially as it has been well put by Donald E. Gowan*. However, we do not need to be concerned with the last days to ask what is the implication of the divine purpose of the seventh day for human beings, co-creators in the divine image, here and now, and always. By so asking, it is possible to open up a field of the Creation story's meaning for human right action.

Unless with free will, unless able to choose, unless able to decide, we cannot be in the divine image, even imperfectly. Now it is only in a world which is, in some degree, predictable that one can decide effectually. If there were not repeatable and predictable relations between the movement of my hand and the mark made on the paper, how could I decide what to write, how could I give effect to that decision? If I could not be morally certain that the saucepan would stay in place rather than rise unpredictably to the ceiling or propel itself through the window, how could I sanely decide to give the sick man a hot meal or give effect to that decision? Human responsibility is possible only with some sort of natural determinism. Nature need not be wholly determinate, but a probable link of cause and effect is a necessity of effective action. There can be no free will in a universe without determinism. Yet although the conditions given by the Creator are determining, constraining, they are not wholly so, for there remains scope for us as co-creators (much more, perhaps, than we realise). Thus we exercise freedom within a framework of deterministic constraint. Clearly, we can decide most effectively how to move within that framework when we understand it. The better we understand the world, the greater our freedom, even to change the world that constrains us. The carver, the sculptor, create most freely when they know the grain of their materials.

Not only the seventh day, but later parts of the Creation story also, offer instruction for right action, but this instruction is not about what we ought to do, but about the scope available to us as co-creators, and about the consequences of carving the wood while ignoring the grain, as it were. The story tells us that the world is such that, if we act in certain ways or outside certain limits, we shall find our deeds self-frustrating, our purposes bent back on themselves. In its wholeness, the story of Creation does not say that there is an 'is' and an 'ought'. It presents the nature of the 'is' and leaves choice free whether to grow and find greater freedom, or whether to work against being in the divine image, which is our nature, and so diminish ourselves. Sometimes, when confronted by the unexpected, we say it is divine intervention, or that nature is truly indeterminate in some respects, or that our surprise is a measure of how far we have yet to go in understanding the world. These can be true, and may not be very different from each other. What is very different is to attribute the unexpected to 'luck' or 'chance' for, if we do so in all seriousness rather than for brief convenience, we abdicate our humanity.

Right action, then, is not defined by an arbitrary 'ought'. In the Creation story it is action in accord with the created order, action 'with the grain'. The combination of choice and constraint gives right action two aspects. There is the rule, wisdom, understanding (call it what you will, for the present purpose) which gives boundary conditions for action which is not self-defeating. There is also the creative activity which can be pursued freely and in indefinitely great variety within the boundaries given by the rule. We are unreasonable if we cry out against the boundary constraint; it follows from the predictability upon which our freedom depends. Here we arrive at an enrichment of the meaning of the two impulses. The impulse to observe the rules, to act in accord with the created order, is the good impulse. On the other hand, the impulse to create and act and exert energy, if it transgresses the boundary set by the created order, causes frustration, destruction, and suffering, and is therefore the evil impulse. Nevertheless the good impulse is not enough. It provides steering, but not motive power. To be co-creators in the divine image, because co-creators in accord with the given order of things, we need both impulses. In the book of the prophet Isaiah, the Creator claims authorship of both good and evil (Isaiah 45:7). Right action, in its fulness, is the action of those who, in acting, have brought the good and evil within themselves into an entirety.

To appreciate the universal meaning of the seventh day, it may be helpful to bear in mind the distinction between the creative episode and the institution. As an Israelite institution, the Sabbath (which is not merely a rest) is uniquely of one part of humankind. As a truth about the created order, however, the Sabbath is universal. It brings into one the inward and outward godhead. In it is the wholeness, without distinction, of the transcendent and the immanent, of our going out and coming in, of the systole and diastole of our being, of God in history and in our centre. The Sabbath is the end to which Creation points. We who are of the sixth day converge in the seventh day with the Creator, and in the convergence of Creator and co-creator is the completion of the Creation, outwardly in history, inwardly in each of us. The seventh day, the Creation's

35

Sabbath, may be considered alongside the words of St. Augustine of Hippo*.

> You have made us for yourself, and restless is our heart until it finds its rest
> in you.

The seventh day sets our aim and direction.

It draws us to the mystery that can be titled only by the name which cannot
be said. As the Tao Te Ching* puts it,

> The name that can be said is not the eternal name.

Among some peoples the name that cannot be said is the name that can be said
only as appropriate to its sacredness; the restriction for reverence is still there.
Therefore, underlying the Creation story, insofar as it speaks of human action
and being, is the implied instruction not to curse or belittle the name of God.
Now God has many names, and is represented in many ways in different languages and among various peoples. Nevertheless, each of the earth's peoples
can respect in its own way that which is beyond all things, and which is belittled by attempted reduction to words. It is the highest in value: other things
may be for the sake of yet others, but the highest is only for its own sake and for
the sake of everything. If it is all-encompassing, if it is the point on which converge all series of this-for-the-sake-of-that-and-that-for-the-sake-of-some-
thing-else, it is one's god.

Thus the name that may not be belittled need not be formulated in speech or
writing at all. Nevertheless, the beginning of right action is reverence for the
name. The atheist does not necessarily belittle the name. That of which the
name cannot be said may be known without a name, and what the atheist
denies may be an idol that others have misnamed 'God'. (Idols will come to our
notice when the Creation story comes to the matter of the unfinished city, after
the telling which speaks of nations.) Some atheists consciously revere that for
which the name can stand, but take representation of the divine to be misleading if it is personal. Others, who are not atheists, find the converse, that human
language is less misleading if the representation of the divine is indeed personal. To look reverently at the difference between a non-theistic philosophy
(such as Buddhism) and a theistic philosophy (such as that of the Hebrew
scriptures) is to worship; to argue polemically about the difference belittles the
name.

Those who speak much of God may belittle the name thereby, in that they
lack awe. Such may allow their lack of awe to nurture the notion of religion as
a department of life, distinct from the rest of life. Like them are those who will
question another about God in his heart, showing lack of respect for the godhead in its intimacy. Such people, with their questions, treat their neighbour
with as little respect as they would if enquiring into the intimate details of his
marital relationship. Thus they belittle the name, for reverence for the
divine name implies courtesy towards the divine image. Reverence is, of
course, compatible with familiarity, and may grow with it. Nevertheless, the

warmth that develops in the intimacy between Creator and created is not to be confused with the use of this or that name of God in harangue, pestering, or sectarian debate. These practices show only the mock familiarity which lack of experience may permit, and belittle the name that cannot be said.

What then of those that make man the measure of all things? Do they thereby scorn the divine name? Surely not, for the divine image is a way to the divine, and the humanist whose words are framed to reject God may be nearer to the truth of God than are some users of religious words. It is, however, just because we are created in the image of God, because of the divine in the human, that the use of people only as instruments, only as means to ends, is a failure to hold God in awe. It is a defamation of the name, and is exemplified by the attempt to make education aim solely at making someone fit to be used for the profit of others. The aim of education in accord with the order of Creation, is liberation inwards and outwards, in one's being and in society, to be male and female in the divine image, to have dominion, to be co-creator, and therefore co-author of history.

Because God is unity, and because God at the time of awe and in nature is God in each one's depth, respect for the divine name and for each other are one.

Created things are a universe of diversity and conflict. Their Creator is an unspeakable unity. At the surface of contact between Creator and created is the plane of mystery. We can find God at that plane, or even when turned towards it. There are many ways towards the plane of mystery. It may be through action, through compassion, through inner wrestling, through suffering, through stillness, and through pleasure; these are not all. Of these, perhaps suffering needs a few words, if only because reference has already been made to evil in the work of the Creator. When the deeds of others, beyond our influence, or other causes beyond our control or understanding, bring us pain, pain which arises from the very causality on which our freedom depends, then the acceptance of suffering can be a way of living according to the created order, so that suffering turns us towards the plane of mystery. (One's own accepted suffering, when due to the evil done by others, is brought into harmony with the created order when acceptance is a witness against the evil. Even when there is no human agency, and the acceptance is a cry against the evil, the Creator of evil can be worshipped in the howl of protest.) There are many ways in which we may be turned towards the mystic plane where Creator and created cleave to one another, and by which we may perhaps reach it. The awe of that meeting will not let us dishonour the name.

The meeting at the plane of mystery is not fusion. Fusion is infantile union. We grow out of this fusion as we differentiate from the matter of things. ('Matter', from the Latin *materia*, which is the *mater*, i.e. 'mother'.) The state of fused singleness is the beginning of existence, but union is the end of maturation. Thus we go from infancy towards being spouses. Of them it can be said that, at a plane of mystery, there is confrontation, the closest cleaving, between complementary creators. Also, the male and female in the universe, in society, in each person, unite in the process of perfection, holding opposites clear but in harmony, the person being thereby more exactly of his or her own sex. God, however, is complete; in our incompleteness we answer to different aspects of God, unless and until in our fulness we meet all the aspects which humanity is capable of meeting, and which are all one at the plane where meeting is made. For example, in the Hebrew scriptures God is represented as parent (Hosea 11:1) and as spouse (Hosea 2:21,22), both being of the same people. Parent and spouse each imply a different name of God. The name that includes all God's names is the name that cannot be spoken.

It is of the essence of God to be the Creator. Being the Creator is not, to use the philosophers' term, an accident; it is not an optional extra. To be Creator is part of the meaning of the unspeakable name. There is, however, no Creator without the created. Therefore created things are necessary to God. There is still the distinction between the ineffable unity and a universe of diversity and conflict, but they are unseparated at the mystic plane. Nevertheless, do we not separate ourselves from God when we hold cheap the name, and in other ways? Later, we shall find the Creation story telling of Cain, who says 'From your face I shall hide myself'.

The answer is in what the Creation story has already told us of the seven days. The Creator does not set things going and then leave them to run. What is made is named, given a function, or blessed; the Creator's part in the matter goes beyond mere bringing into being. This concern, which I have been calling adoption, expresses continuing care; it expresses love. Cain, as we shall see, may hide from God's face, but is reached by God's love, which protects him (4:15). Since humankind is in the image of God, we contribute to our fulfilling that image by our own loving. The divine image, however, is not just a possibility but, in any one respect, is to some degree an actuality. Loving is in us: in the way of a man with a maid, in the way of a mother with a suckling, in the fellowship of comrades, in the communion of human being with beast. Loving expresses the name that cannot be named. Those who, in economics, politics, entertainment, advertising, or other activity, attempt to predispose others towards constriction, distortion, diversion, or prevention of love's expression in motive and action, belittle and defame the name, and try to bring it about that others do the same.

For this respecting of God's name is precious. It is a necessary condition of freedom for all else. It keeps the eyes open and the ears unstopped, that they may be open to God, in whom we are and who is in us. It obviates a risk, the risk of not becoming ourselves, of withering unripened on the bough. It exposes us to a risk, the risk of a splendid and terrible adventure, the adventure of the open-ended Sabbath.

THE TELLING of the seven days of the Creation is followed by another Creation narrative. This second account is different from the first in style, content, and emphasis. The two are nevertheless related to each other. Although the second story, centred upon human existence and the human condition, lacks the cosmic concern of the first (except in a terse introduction), its effect, when the two accounts are taken together, is to expand on and interpret the sixth-day creation of humankind. It is to this second account of the Creation that I will now turn.

As has been seen, in the account of the sixth day of the Creation, humankind has four characteristics: to be in the image of God, to have dominion over the earth and its life, to be male and female, and to be fruitful and increase. These correspond to three relationships, between humankind and God, between humankind and the earth with its life and produce, and between male and female (from which stem fruitfulness and increase). Each of these relations in fact involves all the four characteristics; nevertheless, each most directly corresponds with one particular characteristic specified in the telling of the sixth day (except that the relation between female and male corresponds to two characteristics, as just indicated). The translation of the second account of the Creation, which now follows, is set out so as to form three columns. corresponding to the three relations just mentioned, but with a change of order of those three so that the text can begin in the first column. Thus the first column has matters bearing upon the relation between the human and the non-human creation, or between the human creation and God manifested in the non-human creation. The second column has passages relating the human creation directly to the Creator. The third column has material about human existence, whether as male and female or as the two unseparated.

It will be seen that the narrative passes repeatedly through the three columns in the same order. The cycles so manifested are not as distinct in the wording of the text as are the days and works in the first Creation narrative. Nevertheless, by dividing this account into passages according to relations corresponding to characteristics of mankind in the telling of the sixth day, one allows a perhaps unexpected pattern to emerge, as will be noted after the translation itself.

And now, just before the translation, it may be helpful to explain certain words. In the translation of the first Creation story, the account of the seven days, the English 'humankind' was used for the Hebrew *adam*. In what now follows, *adam* is rendered as a name, 'Adam', or 'the Adam' where the original Hebrew itself has the definite article. The word *adam* means the human species or a person, a human being of either sex. Except in this account of the Creation, *adam* is never a personal name in Hebrew (unless rarely and only very recently). The word 'man' is here used to translate *ish*, which is specifically male, answering to *ishshah*, 'woman'. The word 'ground' here translates the Hebrew *adamah*, and *adamah* can be heard and seen as a feminine form of *adam*, which is grammatically masculine, whatever the sex it represents. (Compare the French feminine 'une personne' which can refer to a male or a female.) It may be that the words *adam* and *adamah* are unrelated in their origins, but this has no bearing on any evident relationship which they have in the text. Concerning 'you', Hebrew distinguishes between the singular (English 'thou', 'thee') and plural (English 'ye', 'you'). However, the translation here follows modern English usage in having the word 'you' only. If 'You' means the plural it is spelt with a capital letter, while 'you' is singular in meaning, like the older 'thou'.

The translation is from Chapters 2 and 3 of Genesis, and continues that on pages 6 and 7. The verse numbers are indicated, as before, in the translation itself.

***

⁴ These are the generations of the heavens and the earth when they were created, in the day that the LORD God made earth and heavens.

*

⁵ No shrub of the field was yet
in the earth, and no herb of
the field had yet sprung up,
  for the LORD God had not caused
  it to rain upon the earth,

      and there was no human being
      (adam) to till the ground
      (adamah).

*

⁶ And a spring was rising from
the earth, and watered the whole
face of the ground *(adamah)* .
⁷ Then the LORD God formed the
Adam of the dust of the ground
(adamah),
  and breathed into his nostrils
  the breath of life

and the Adam became a living soul.

[8] And the LORD God planted a garden in Eden, eastward, and there he put the Adam which he had formed. [9] And out of the ground the LORD God caused to grow every tree good to look at and desirable for food, and the tree of life is in the midst of the garden, and the tree of the knowledge of good and evil.

[10] And a river goes out of Eden to water the garden, and thence it parts to become four heads. [11] The name of the one is Pishon. (It goes around the land of Havilah, where there is gold. [12] And the gold of that land is good; bdellium and the onyx stone are there.) [13] And the name of the second river is Gihon. (It goes round the whole land of Cush.) [14] And the name of the third river is Tigris. (It goes east of Asshur.) [15] And the fourth river is the Euphrates.

[15] And the LORD God took the Adam, and put him into the garden of Eden to serve it and keep it.

[16] And the LORD God commanded the Adam, saying 'Of every tree of the garden you may freely eat, [17] but the tree of the knowledge of good and evil, you shall not eat of it, for in the day that you eat of it you shall indeed die'.

18 And the LORD God said 'It is not good that the Adam be alone; I will make a help matched with him.'

[19] And out of the ground the
LORD God had formed every animal
of the field, and every flying
thing of the heavens, and he
brought them to the Adam to see
what he would call them, and
whatever the Adam would call it,
that was the name of each
living animal. [20] And the Adam
gave names to the cattle, to the
bird of the air, and to the
animal of the field. And for
Adam there was no help matched
with him.

[21] And the LORD God put a profound sleep upon the
Adam, and he slept.
And he took one of his ribs and
closed the flesh instead of it.

[22] And the LORD God built the
rib, which he had taken from
the Adam, to become a woman
(*ishshah*), and he brought her
to the Adam. [23] And the Adam said
'This at last is bone of my bones
and flesh of my flesh. She
shall be called 'woman' (*ishshah*)
because she was taken out of
man (*ish*)'. [24] Therefore
shall a man (*ish*) leave his father
and his mother, and shall cleave to
his wife (*ishshah*), and they
shall become one flesh. [25] And
they were both naked, the Adam
and his wife, and felt no
shame before each other.

*

[1] Now the snake was shrewder
than any animal of the field
which the LORD God had made,
and he said to the woman 'Did
God really say "You shall not
eat from every tree of the

garden"?' ² And the woman said
to the snake 'Of the fruit of
the trees of the garden we
shall eat. ³ But of the tree
which is in the midst of the
garden God said "You shall not
eat from it, nor shall You
touch it, lest You die"'

⁴ And the snake said to the
woman 'Indeed You shall not die.
⁵ For God knows that on the day
that You eat of it Your eyes
shall be opened and You will be
like God, knowing good and evil.'
⁶ And the woman saw that the
tree was good for food and that
it was a delight to the eyes,
and that the tree was desirable
for insight, and she took its
fruit and ate, and she gave also
to her husband (*ish*) with her,
and he ate. ⁷ And the eyes of both
of them were opened, and they
knew that they were naked,
and they sewed fig leaves together
and made girdles for themselves.
⁸ And they heard the LORD God's
voice moving in the garden in
the breeze time of the day, and
the Adam and his wife hid themselves
from the face of the
LORD God among the trees of the
garden. ⁹ And the LORD God called
to the Adam and said to him
'Where are you?' ¹⁰ And he said
'I heard your voice in the
garden, and I was afraid because
I was naked, and I hid'. ¹¹ And
he said 'Who told you that you
are naked? Have you eaten from
the tree of which I commanded
you not to eat?'

43

¹² And the Adam said 'The woman whom you gave to be with me, she gave me from the tree, and I ate'. ¹³ And the LORD God said to the woman 'What is this you have done?' And the woman said 'The snake deceived me, and I ate'.

*

¹⁴ And the LORD God said to the snake 'Because you have done this you are cursed more than all cattle and more than every animal of the field. On your belly you shall go and dust shall you eat all the days of your life. ¹⁵ And I will put enmity between you and the woman, and between your seed and her seed; it will bruise your head and you will bruise its heel.'

¹⁶ To the woman he said 'Much will I increase your suffering, and especially that due to conception, and in sorrow will you bear children.

And towards your husband is your desire, and he will rule you.'

¹⁷ And to Adam he said 'Because you listened to the voice of your wife and ate from the tree of which I commanded you, saying "you shall not eat from it", cursed is the ground because of you. With suffering shall you eat of it all the days of your life. ¹⁸ Thorns and thistles shall it bring forth for you, and you will eat the herbage of the field.

¹⁹ By the sweat of your face
will you eat bread until you
return to the ground, for from
it were you taken, since dust you
are and to dust will return.'

²⁰ And the Adam called his wife's
name Eve (*chawwah*) because she
was the mother of all living
(*chay*).

*

²¹ And the LORD God made for Adam
and for his wife garments of
skin, and clothed them.
²² And the LORD God said 'Behold,
the Adam is like one of us, to
know good and evil, and now,
lest he put out his hand and take
also from the tree of life and
live for ever...' ²³ And
the LORD God sent him from the
garden of Eden, to serve the
ground from which he had been
taken. ²⁴ And he drove out the
Adam, and caused the cherubim,
and the flame of the turning
sword, to dwell to the east of
the garden of Eden, to keep the
way of the tree of life.

¹ And the Adam knew Eve his
wife, and she conceived, and
bore Cain (*qayin*) and said
I have got (*qaniti*) a man with
the LORD'.

***

Thus the narrative runs in cycles. Each cycle deals first with the relation between the human and non-human creation, or God manifested in the non-human creation. Then, in the second column of the lay-out just used, it relates the human creation directly to the Creator. Finally, the third column has the last part of each cycle, which speaks first of human existence without sexual difference, and then the relation between the sexes.

45

There are nine cycles, preceded by a title. The first and last cycles function as prologue and epilogue. Between them are seven cycles on the creation of humankind. The seven cycles fall into three episodes, of three, two, and two cycles respectively. The completion of the ninth cycle is by means of a verse shared with the next section of the Creation story (Chapter 4, verse 1). The structure of the story of the Garden, then, may be represented by the table of Figure 3.

Chapters	Verses	
2	4	Title
2	5	A world without humankind (1 cycle)
2	6-25	The creation of humankind: the initiation of humanity (3 cycles)
3	1-13	The creation of humankind: the assertion of humanity (2 cycles)
3	14-20	The creation of humankind: the realisation of humanity begins (2 cycles)
3 to 4	21 1	Beyond the Garden (1 cycle)

Fig.3 *Summary of Cycles of Events in the Garden Narrative.*

These episodes are now considered, in the pages which follow immediately.

CHAPTER 11: *A WORLD WITHOUT HUMANKIND*

THE TITLE SENTENCE of the story of the Garden begins 'These are the generations of the heavens and the earth...' The expression 'these are the generations of...' *(eleh toldot)* is found elsewhere in scripture twelve times, ten in Genesis. From these examples we can learn two things about the phrase. The first of these is that it does not necessarily refer to a series of generations, but may mean 'this is the history (or story) of...' For example, in Genesis 37:2 we read 'These are the generations of Jacob'. What follows is not a genealogy, however, but the story of Joseph and the others of Jacob's sons. There is a narrative about characters in two generations, mainly the younger, not the setting out of a list of generations, as in 'the generations of Noah's sons' (Genesis 10:1), for example.

The second thing that we learn from other examples of the expression is that it always begins the story. Whenever we find the words 'these are the generations of...', they refer to what immediately follows. Some writers, such as Westermann* and Fokkelman*, take the sentence, 'These are the generations of the heavens and the earth when they were created', and attach it to the end of the story of the seven days. It then refers to what has just been written, not what follows. This, however, is not the plain meaning of what is before us; when a hearer or reader with a mind tuned in to biblical idiom meets this sentence, attention is directed to what follows.

The wording of the introductory sentence, referring as it does to 'the heavens and the earth', calls for some comment, since the story of the Garden seems to have little or nothing in it about the heavens. In the account of the seven days of the creation the cosmic content of the narrative narrows down stepwise until there is a concentration on the making of humankind, on which more is said than on any other created thing. Then the seventh day puts everything back into the widest possible context. In the story of the Garden, the sixth-day creation of humankind is presented with more particularity, and without direct reference to other works of the Creation except insofar as they may be relevant to humanity. If the Sabbath is the Creation's aim and end, according to Genesis, humankind is its centre. The story of humankind is said here to be the story of the heavens and the earth, so that the generations of humanity are the generations of the heavens and the earth, and the part implies the whole. The title introducing the story of the Garden makes

47

humankind the keystone and, as it were, the encapsulation of the Creation.

The Creation story converges on us, presaging perhaps later doctrine of the epitomising of the universe in the body, the macrocosm in the microcosm. Genesis is not in agreement with the perspective, common in the Twentieth Century, by which humankind is a frail and transient incident on a cosmically negligible body. If humankind is created in God's image and if God is Creator, then some characteristics of being Creator are human as well as divine. Thus, in some measure at least, we are co-creators with God. This is surely the peak of what a created being can be, to be itself creator. To see all the universe from a human viewpoint is, in the terms of the Creation story in Genesis, to view created things from their peak, accepting the perspective which this entails. Further, the philosophy of the Hebrew scriptures is concerned with responsibility and choice; astronomy has yet to yield even the slenderest behavioural basis for the supposition that galaxies make choices. Given what the text has said of the seven days, it is because the story of the Garden is about the creation of humankind that it can be introduced with the words, 'These are the generations of the heavens and the earth'.

So it is that the expression '...the generations of the heavens and the earth when they were created' continues with 'in the day that the Lord God made earth and heavens'. The usual expression is 'the heavens and the earth', and 'earth and heavens' turns it round. To put earth first is part of the convergence of the story of all things towards and into humankind. It may be added that the idiom 'in the day that...' means simply 'when...' in some contexts. One misunderstands the sentence if attention is narrowed on the word 'day' at the expense of the entire expression.

Although the expression 'These are the generations of...' may mean only 'This is the history of...' the word 'generations' nevertheless reminds the reader of humanity's reproduction. Here God is the progenitor, and it may be to the point to recollect that, in connection with the sixth day's work, it was noted that both male and female images (as well as much else) are needed in providing metaphors for God's activity (p.28). Nevertheless God, in the Hebrew scriptures, is a unity, and the polarisation of our descriptions into male and female is like the polarisation of a magnet, in which neither north nor south pole can exist without the other (cf p.33). We see the floating magnet, which is a compass, as north-pointing or south-pointing according to the focus of attention; similarly, our attention never grasps God's activities as a whole, even those which are evident, and we alternate between male and female metaphors for that which these scriptures present as the undivided parent of all things.

***

After the introductory title of the story of the Garden, the scene is set, without characters.

> ^{5} No shrub of the field was yet in the earth, and no herb
> of the field had yet sprung up,
> for the Lord God had not yet caused it to rain upon
> the earth,
> and there was no human being *(adam)* to till the ground *(adamah)*.

The word 'shrub' *(siyach)* refers to a wild plant, as does 'herb of the field'. Since there was no *adam* for the *adamah,* there were neither wild nor cultivated plants. Between mention of the non-human creation and of the human is the reference to God's rain, on which both depend. In terms of the telling of the seven days, this scene is before the making of plants on the third day, as well as before that of humankind on the sixth. However, as already noted in connection with the fourth day (pp. 18-21), the text does not agree with a reading which puts the products of the Creation after one another, as if necessarily strung out in time. If the description here of a world without humanity collapses together different stages in the telling of the seven days or even suggests a different sequence, it in no way goes beyond what the telling of the seven days can mean.

Thus we are left with three negative statements. There are no wild plants, essential to any non-human creation to which humankind can relate or on which it can subsist. There is no action of God to make possible either the human or the non-human creation to which humanity must relate and on which it depends. And there is no humanity to relate either to God or to the non-human creation.

CHAPTER 12: **THE INITIATION OF HUMANITY**

IN THE TELLING of the story of the Garden, as already set out (pp. 40-45) the initiation of humanity (p. 46) is presented in three cycles, occupying Genesis 2:6–2:25. In the first cycle (verse 6) the earth receives the water needed for fertility, and the breath needed for human life. In the second cycle (verses 8-18) the human being and the fertile earth are brought together by the Lord God. This cycle has, as an interruption, an indication (verses 10-14) of the whereabouts of the Garden. In the third cycle the Lord God brings about the human being's naming of beasts, and the ending of human solitude by the realisation of the human being as male and female.

***

The first of the three cycles has, on humanity's relation to the non-human creation, the watering of the ground and the formation of humankind from it. On humanity's relation to the divine, this cycle tells of the breath from God. Of humanity itself, there is the beginning of its becoming.

> [6] And a spring was rising from the earth, and was watering the whole face
> of the ground. Then the Lord God formed the Adam of the dust of the ground
> (*adamah*), and breathed into his nostrils the breath of life and the Adam be-
> came a living soul.

The word here translated 'spring' is commonly rendered as 'cloud' or 'mist'. Whatever the exact meaning, it was 'rising from the earth', and must therefore be of the lower waters. In the previous cycle it is said to be rain, which is from the upper waters, that is lacking. Rain, dew, and the water of rivers were all doubtless known to the writer as means of the soil's being watered; evidently, for the writer, all these sources are equally available to the Creator out of the Creator's own creation.

The close association of the Adam with *adamah,* 'ground', makes a point. They strike the hearer or reader as the masculine and feminine of each other. They are a couple. Here the *adamah* is the matrix, the mother material, from which the Adam is formed, ready to be made alive.

The word translated 'formed' is generally used for shaping, as by a potter, and requires material already created. The use of the word is without prejudice

50

to the need for a further act of creation, that referred to in the telling of the sixth day: 'and God created humankind in his image, in the image of God he created it, male and female he created them' (1:27, p. 7).

God, having watered the ground, and having formed something out of it, now acts directly on what has been formed, so that the Adam has the 'breath of life' and becomes 'a living soul'. 'Breath' translates *neshamah,* something that one has, while 'soul', as is usual in English versions of scripture, translates *nefesh,* something that one is. (In later Hebrew, one's *nefesh* can be something one has, but in scripture it is what one is, so that, for example, *nafshi,* 'my soul', is a way of saying 'I myself'.) Now the three words, 'breath' *(neshamah),* 'life' *(chayyim),* and 'soul' *(nefesh)* are all applied, in the Hebrew scriptures, to non-human animals as well as to human beings. That is to say, something more is needed to complete the account of the creation of humankind. This is obvious in another respect, that there is not yet in the story a fulfilment of 'male and female he created them'. The episodes of the story following this cycle do not come after the creation of humankind, but are integral with that creating.

***

Next, in the second cycle of the telling of how humanity is initiated, humankind *(adam)* and ground *(adamah)* are brought together by God as husbandman and husbanded. The ground, as female, is not only the matrix but now has another part to play, vis-à-vis humanity taking the male part. First, humankind is brought into relation with the non-human creation, as God plants a garden into which the Adam is put, to serve and keep it. Then humanity is brought into explicit relationship with the Creator through God's permitting and prohibiting the trees of which the human being may eat. Thirdly, the Lord God notes the Adam's lack of relation with any other human being, seeing it as not good.

[8] And the Lord God planted a Garden in Eden, eastward, and there he put the Adam which he had formed. [9]And out of the ground the Lord God caused to grow every tree good to look and desirable for food, and the tree of life is in the midst of the garden, and the tree of the knowledge of good and evil. ([10]And a river goes out of Eden to water the garden, and thence it parts to become four heads. [11] The name of the one is Pishon; it goes around the land of Havilah, where there is gold, [12] and the gold of that land is good; bdellium and the onyx stone are there. [13] And the name of the second river is Gihon; it goes round the whole land of Cush. [14] And the name of the third river is Tigris; it goes east of Asshur. And the fourth river is the Euphrates.) [15] And the Lord God took the Adam, and put him into the Garden of Eden to serve it and keep it.

[16] And the Lord God commanded the Adam, saying 'Of every tree of the garden you may eat, [17] but the tree of the knowledge of good and evil, you shall not eat of it, for in the day that you eat of it you shall indeed die'.

[18] And the Lord God said 'It is not good that the Adam be alone; I will make a help matched with him'.

The name 'Eden' is explained variously. Elsewhere in scripture (1 Kings 19:12) it is the name of an ancient Mesopotamian country. Also, the name is in practice identical with that of the Arabian city which we still call Aden. It is a word for a delight, or for a dainty to eat, and it has an abstract derivative *('ednah)* which is a word for sexual pleasure (Genesis 18:12). It is interesting that the Yemen, which stretches northward from Aden, was known anciently as Arabia Felix, 'Fruitful Arabia' or 'Fortunate Arabia', on account of its fertility.

The garden is the place for the Adam, who is to 'serve it and keep it'. For 'serve' *(avad)* one could use with equal exactness the English word 'work' or 'till'. The word 'keep' *(shamar)* generally implies guarding against those things that may endanger or threaten, rather than holding or retaining.

The expression 'in Eden, eastward' could mean in the eastern part of Eden, or simply that Eden is somewhere east of the narrator. However, the sentence 'A river goes out of Eden to water the garden' must mean that the garden is not 'in Eden' at all. This contradiction cannot be accidental. The hearer or reader is being unsettled by design, by art. The suggestion of mystery is heightened by the way trees are mentioned. Trees which are beautiful and which give good food are familiar. Yet next to them are mentioned two trees which are outside experience.

The Adam is forbidden by the Lord God to eat of the tree of the knowledge of good and evil. This is the only prohibition. All other trees are explicitly permitted, and the Adam may choose from them according to need, taste, opportunity, or convenience, as a bird might choose between cherries and plums from neighbouring trees. The tree of the knowledge of good and evil is, however, the subject of choice of another kind. This is the choice between obedience and disobedience to the Adam's very Creator, to that which contains the order of the universe and the order of the Adam's being. This is a human choice, not (in general, and as far as we know) a bird's. It implies a degree of freedom which is essential to being created in the divine image, for God is, as Creator, free.

The 'help matched with him' that the Lord is to provide for the Adam is what the Authorised Version translates as a 'help meet for him'. The Hebrew word *(ke-negdo)* can also be rendered as 'his opposite'. The meaning is clear, although hard to express. There is to be a partnership of two, opposite each other, neither above the other, complementary to each other. But where? In the Garden of Eden, it is clear, and verses 10-15 tell us where Eden and the Garden are. At least, they appear, at first sight, to be intended to tell us where it is. Closer inspection may help to elucidate what can, in fact, be learnt from the description, in verses 10-15, of the situation of Eden.

The first problem that strikes the reader trying to interpret the description of the situation of Eden and its garden, is the giving of a place to each name. To know that the Pishon flows round Havilah (verse 11) helps to locate either only if one knows where the other is. Some of the names are, however, more familiar. Let us begin, then, with those names of which the meaning is clear to us now, and must have been clear to Israelites at any time when the description could have been written. There are four such names here: Cush, Tigris, Asshur (whether the country Assyria or the city of Asshur), and Euphrates. Here is a sketch map in which these four names have been located and put in capital letters. (Names in lower-case letters, without brackets, are not in the description of Eden's location but are used now in this discussion, while the bracketed names are of other major geographical features.)

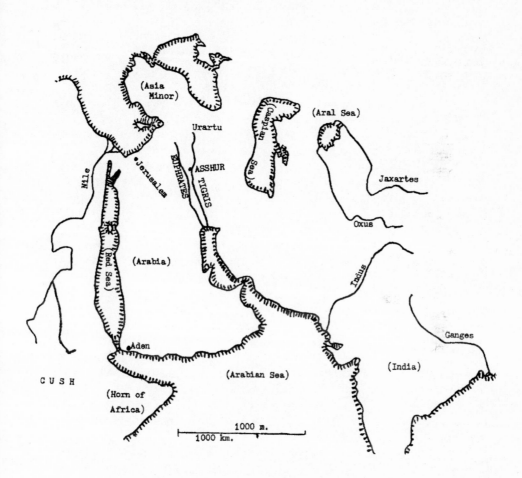

Fig.4. *Map to accompany the discussion of the location of the Garden of Eden*

Cush, in scripture, is what we now know as Ethiopia and Upper Egypt. Now, if a river divides into four, two of these being the Tigris and the Euphrates, how can there be another of the four going round Cush? Can the Nile have been thought to have a common origin with the Tigris and the Euphrates? Surely not. Some have said that Cush must be the land of the Cassites, east of the Tigris, but this still gives no river to identify with the Gihon that goes round Cush. Another interpretation is that Cush is the Cushan which the prophet Habbakuk (3:7) mentions in association with Midian; the Midianites lived to the north and north-east of the northern end of the Red Sea. Nevertheless, the identification of Cushan with Cush cannot be fitted to the scheme of the four rivers, given that the Gihon must originate from the same region as the Tigris and the Euphrates. Also, both the Cassite land and Cushan, even if either could also be called 'Cush' (and there is no evidence for this), present a further difficulty. In scripture 'Cush' is a usual name for an important region, and its plain meaning must surely be intended when there is no indication of any other meaning–and there never is. After all, plain 'Paris' does not mean 'Paris, Idaho' unless the context makes that likely.

Let us return to the four rivers themselves. What two rivers could have a common origin, or might be supposed to have a common origin, with the Tigris and the Euphrates? If we consider the Asiatic land mass, neither the Oxus (Amu-Dar'ya) nor the Jaxartes (Syr-Dar'ya), neither the Indus nor the Ganges, goes round Cush. What does go round Cush is the sea. Can the Gihon be ocean, like the Greeks' river of Okeanos? In this case, to fit the telling, the Tigris and the Euphrates must be thought of as originating at their mouths and stretching towards their source, while Eden and its garden are beyond the sea, which is itself the river that divides. Even if we suppose that it is intended that we understand that sea water waters the garden (2:10), Eden is itself consigned outside the known geography of any ancient people. Gihon is in fact the name of a spring just outside Jerusalem (1 Kings 1:33,38,45; 2 Chronicles 32:30, 33:14). If this is the river of our story, then the common origin of the rivers must be in the earth's far depths, where Eden and its garden must also be. Havilah may be somewhere in Arabia, as will be discussed in connection with the nations descended from Noah after the Flood. The river Pishon is said to go round Havilah, but locating the latter in Arabia does not help us to locate the river, unless it is an arm of the ocean. The Pishon may then be fitted to what was said of the Gihon being sea, with Eden beyond the ocean.

To put Eden far across the ocean or deep below the earth takes it out of ordinary biblical (or even modern?) geography. It may therefore be to the point to return to a remark made earlier. First we are told that 'the Lord God planted a garden *in* Eden' (2:8), and then that 'a river goes *out* of Eden to water the garden' (2:10).

So the garden is in Eden, and the garden is also outside Eden, wherever Eden is. The contradiction can hardly be accidental. Even if the statements came from two separate sources, they must have been seen and heard close together from the time that the sources were edited into one. Whether the contradiction is due to an originally single writing or to making one writing out of two, it can hardly be due to inadvertency. When all that our story says about Eden and its garden is taken together, what is found is not information but instruction. The instruction is: Do not ask what is the geographical location of Eden and the garden, for it is an inappropriate question.

***

In the third cycle of the initiation of humanity, the Adam is related to the non-human creation by the naming of animals, and directly to God by the Creator's bringing the Adam into being male and female. Thirdly, the man and woman so brought into existence are found in relation to each other.

> [19] And out of the ground the Lord God had formed every animal of the field and every flying thing of the heavens, and he brought them to the Adam to see what he would call them, and whatever the Adam might call it, that was the name of each living animal. [20] And the Adam gave names to the cattle, to the bird of the air, and to the animal of the field. And for Adam there was no help matched with him.

> [21] And the Lord God put a profound sleep upon the Adam, and he slept. And he took one of his ribs and closed the flesh instead of it.

> [22] And the Lord God built the rib which he had taken from the Adam, for it to become a woman *(ishshah)*, and he brought her to the Adam. [23] And the Adam said 'This at last is bone of my bones and flesh of my flesh. She shall be called "woman" *(ishshah)* because she was taken out of man *(ish)*'. [24] Therefore shall a man *(ish)* leave his father and mother, and shall cleave to his wife *(ishshah)*, and they shall become one flesh. [25] And they were both naked, the Adam and his wife, and felt no shame before each other.

The story of naming the animals has two relationships to the rest of the text. One of these is that it expresses the ordained dominion of the Adam over the non-human creation, since naming (or just knowing a name) represents knowledge and comprehension (that is, 'grasping'). The names are said by the Creator to be whatever the Adam says they are, indicating delegation to the one who, being in the image of the Creator, is also a creator and co-creator. This is not the only expression of the human over the non-human creation. There is also care for the soil and what grows: '...and put him in the Garden of Eden to serve it and keep it' (2:15). The word for 'serve', as already noted, can also be translated 'work' or 'till', but its connotation of 'serve' remains. We may compare the aphorism of Bacon* that 'nature is not overcome except by being obeyed'.

The other relationship of the story of the naming to the rest of the text is in its bearing on the fulfilment of 'male and female he created them'. The Lord God says that he will make a help matched with the Adam, because it is not good for the human being to be alone. Then the animals are brought to the Adam, but 'for Adam there was no help matched with him' (2:20). The fulfilment of having dominion without that of being male and female leaves the Adam poignantly lonely, having companions, but not a companion 'matched with him'.

The Lord causes a deep sleep to fall on the Adam. The single Hebrew word, *tardemah,* here rendered 'profound sleep', always means in scripture a sleep specially induced by God or one in which God is specially manifested. The other places where the word is found are Genesis 15:12, 1 Samuel 26:12, Isaiah 29:10, Job 4:13 and 33:15, and Proverbs 19:15; only in the last has the word *tardemah* no special divine cause or manifestation, and there it may be ironic. The Lord takes a rib from the unconscious Adam, closes the wound, and 'builds' a woman from the rib. To the Adam, after the 'profound sleep', the Lord God brings the woman (2:21,22). (Burns* argues that the woman is a man's dream figure, but this does not easily conform to what follows in the story.)

Since a woman has been formed out of the Adam, one might expect the residue to be a man. Not at all: the Lord God brings 'the woman' to 'the Adam' (2:22), not to 'the man' *(ish)*. (To avoid ambiguity I use, throughout this book, the word 'man' only for an adult male human being and never for 'person' or 'humankind'.) The Adam has been asleep and is therefore now aware less of an event than of a changed state and situation. This residual Adam bursts into a recognition of kinship and an acceptance.

> And the Adam said
> 'This at last is
> Bone of my bones
> And flesh of my flesh.
> This shall be called woman *(ishshah)*
> Because she was taken out of man *(ish)'* (2:23).

The residual Adam here sees himself as 'man' already, in a timeless manner. But the narrative is explicit that the residual Adam is not yet a man when the woman is brought to him. In fact the transformation to man here occurs when he first recognizes the woman as such. He calls himself 'man' only after he has uttered the word 'woman'. (This is the first occasion of either word in Genesis.) The man's use of the word 'woman' is not his assigning a name to her, but a recognition of the nature which is already hers, for the word 'woman' has already been used of her by the narrator. (The contrast with the naming of the animals is obvious; in that, the namer chose what to call each of them, and the choice determined the name. They, however, were not companions matched with him.)

What follows may or may not be part of the man's declaration.

> Therefore shall a man forsake
> His father and his mother;
> And he shall cleave to his wife,
> And they shall become one flesh (2:24).

(In his commentary on the Pentateuch, the mediaeval Rashi*, following Talmud Bavli*, hears this verse, with psychological shrewdness, as the Lord God's words prohibiting incest.) There is no mention of the woman's forsaking her parents. Is it assumed that the couple must form round her, or in her family, or is it assumed that the male is naturally the more mobile, or is it assumed that he would be more given towards incest than she would? Later in Genesis, stories of the patriarchs and matriarchs disagree with at least two of these explanations. If the husband is to join the wife's family, this does not blunt the understandable keenness of Jacob and his wives to get away from their father (Genesis 31:14-16), while it is unclear with which of the families of Esau's three wives he would have lived (Genesis 26:34; 36:23). Isaac does not seem mobile; his wife came to him (Genesis 24:58,62-67). Further, Terah's daughter-in-law Sarai and her husband are with his father's household in its movements (Genesis 12:31).

Whatever the anthropological or moral meaning of 'Therefore shall a man forsake his father and his mother', its primary bearing, especially in the present context, must surely be on human nature itself. Hence the word 'therefore', relating this statement to the residual Adam's recognition of sexual difference. The wording is plain: the man does not go from his parents to hers, but to her. She is presented as the self-standing partner.

If we set the formation of man and woman against the mention of their creation as male and female in the telling of the sixth day (1:27), we are reminded that the latter is concerned with human sexuality as distinct from sexuality in general. When, in the story of the sixth day, the male and female of humanity are mentioned, it is the first reference to there being two sexes, although the telling of the Creation has already spoken of the beasts, and one need not be a scholarly biblical critic to notice that the ancient Israelites must have been well able to tell a cow from a bull. Nevertheless, of animal life the story of the Creation tells of fecundity in general (1:22), but only of humankind does it tell of sexual difference.

Of humankind we are told: 'in the image of God he created it, male and female he created them' (1:27); being male and female then is a feature of being in the divine image. Male and female co-exist in the individual, in the couple (which is our sexual paradigm and which is able to be fruitful and increase, 1:28), and in society, for the word 'humankind' translates *adam*, which may be either singular or collective.

The Adam and his wife were naked and felt no shame before each other (2:25). The word *arom*, here translated 'naked', is not that used in scripture for sexual or quasi-sexual exposure. (The word with a sexual connotation is *ervah*, 'nakedness'.) The word *arom* ('naked'), used here, expresses the nakedness of poverty or deprivation. Evidently the couple are unashamed because they are innocent of what Ovid* calls 'the impious love of having'. As will be seen, this innocence is to be lost.

CHAPTER 13

THE ASSERTION OF HUMANITY

IN THE TELLING of the Initiation of Humanity (Genesis 2:6-25) relations have been opened between God and humankind, between humankind and the non-human creation, and between the sexes. Now, in the next two cycles, the story develops the three possible relationships so as to begin asserting just what is essential to being human. In the first cycle (Genesis 3:1-7a), the human couple each make a choice, a decision; in the other (3:7b-13) they have to face the decision they have made.

In the first of the two cycles the relationship with the non-human creation is with the snake, that with the Creator is in the snake's assurance to the woman, and that between woman and man in the shared eating of the fruit and in the shared sequel to the eating.

> [1] Now the snake was shrewder than any animal of the field which the Lord God had made, and he said to the woman 'Did God really say "You shall not eat from every tree of the garden"?'. [2] And the woman said to the snake 'Of the fruit of the trees of the garden we shall eat. [3] But of the tree which is in the midst of the garden God said "You shall not eat from it, nor shall You touch it, lest You die".'
>
> [4] And the snake said to the woman 'Indeed You shall not die. [5] For God knows that on the day that You eat of it Your eyes shall be opened and You will be like God, knowing good and evil.'
>
> [6] And the woman saw that the tree was good for food and that it was a delight to the eyes, and that the tree was desirable for insight, and she took its fruit and ate, and she gave also to her husband *(ish)* with her, and he ate. [7a] And the eyes of both of them were opened, and they knew that they were naked.

So the woman meets the snake who is 'shrewder than any animal of the field (i.e. wild animal) that the Lord God had made'. The word here meaning 'shrewd' (or 'prudent', 'subtle') does not in itself necessarily express disapproval of the snake. It is true that, elsewhere in the Hebrew scriptures, the word *(arum)* is used pejoratively (Job 5:12 and 15:5), but not always. Thus in the book of Proverbs it occurs eight times, always meaning prudent, as opposed to simple, in the getting of wisdom. Incidentally, *arum,* 'shrewd', is identical in form (except for the plural ending) with *arumim,* 'naked', which has just appeared in verse 25 of chapter 2. The pun is obvious to the hearer or reader, but the two words are related in neither meaning nor derivation.

Within the context of the Creation story, the explicit reference to the snake's having been made by the Lord God is merely stressing the obvious, unless a point is being made, namely, that it is important to the story that the snake is the Lord God's creature. We have already seen that, in the forming of the Adam from the ground, and in the bringing of animals for naming, the Creator, in making humankind, works through the non-human creation. The snake, specifically said to be made by the Lord God, must surely be seen as God's agent.

Here there is a tension in the story. The snake draws the woman's attention to the excellence of the fruit (3:1-5) already forbidden by God to the sexually undifferentiated Adam (2:16,17). There are two trees 'in the midst of the garden' (2:9), but what follows makes clear that the snake and the woman are talking about the tree of the knowledge of good and evil, the tree of which the fruit has been forbidden. The Lord God addressed the prohibition to the Adam as 'you' in the singular ('thou'), but the woman reports the Lord God as speaking to 'you' in the plural ('ye'), which is proper now that the duality of the Adam as a couple has been realised.

Since it is to the woman that the snake comes, it is she who is seen to be able to have discourse with an animal. The Adam's function expressed in naming the beasts, the function of rapport with animal life, is now shown to be of the female side. In chapter 3, verse 6, the expression 'with her' suggests that the couple had been together throughout the episode; if this is so we see the man as being in some way unable to enter into a conversation the report of which totally ignores him. The passage should be read attentively, and the force of 'with her' allowed its effect. The snake tells the woman that, by eating the fruit, the couple will come to resemble God in being able to tell good from evil (3:5), and there is no suggestion here or later that the snake is lying; on the contrary.

Previously the man has expressed his love for the woman: 'bone of my bones and flesh of my flesh'. Now the woman, finding the tree's yield good to taste, to sight, and for getting understanding, shares the newly found treasure with her man (3:6, the word *ish* meaning 'man' or 'husband', as context may require). The Creation story makes mutual affection a primal aspect of sexuality, together with conjugation and fulfilment of the command to 'be fruitful and increase', both of which come at a later point in the story (4:1). Now, as noted on p. 38, the Creator does not, in the telling of the seven days, just set things going and leave them to run, but names, blesses, and allocates functions, aspects of continuing involvement, expressing love. Humankind, made in God's image, also loves, and by nature, as is shown by the primal expressions of love between the man and woman in the garden.

To return to the conversation with the snake, the woman says that the Lord God forbade touching the tree (3:3), although he didn't; it is eating the fruit that has been forbidden. Since the woman is making forbidden that which is permitted, some, such as Rashi*, following Midrash Rabbah* and Talmud Yerushalmi*, see here a misunderstanding or a perverting of a precept, which error is the beginning of trouble. On the other hand it may be argued that prohibiting the touching of the tree makes eating the fruit less likely, that is, it is a fence around the precept. This has its dangers, however, as the third-century Hiyya is reported by Midrash Rabbah* to have said, 'You must not make the fence greater than what is fenced, lest it fall and destroy the plants'.

All this, however, assumes that the woman and man are wrong to eat the fruit. There certainly seems to be some danger in eating it, for the Adam is told (2:17) 'In the day that you eat of it you shall indeed die'. What sort of danger can this be, since the couple can and do eat the fruit without dying? The man is said (5:5) to die at the age of nine-hundred-and-thirty. Whatever is meant by 'In the day that you eat of it you shall indeed die', it cannot mean, with any respect for language, 'You shall die nine-hundred-and-thirty years after you have eaten it'. Nor can it mean 'You will lose your immortality'. There is not the slightest suggestion that the couple have been destined for immortality. Later indeed (3:22) it is explicit not that immortality is lost but that the Lord God prevents them getting it. Furthermore, 'In the day that you eat of it you shall indeed die' says something quite different from 'In the day that you eat of it you shall indeed become mortal, that is, certain to die at some future time'.

The matter of death will arise again in the story of the garden, but meanwhile it may be worth noting that, in Biblical language, 'shall indeed die' resembles a juridical formula which speaks of the weightiness of infringement. Thus although Leviticus 24:17 sentences homicide with 'he shall indeed be put to death' (mot yumat), without noting any exception, it is unlikely that the sentence could have been intended as universal (although this is what the words mean literally) since exceptions are specified by Exodus 21:12,13 and Numbers 35:22-25.

Nevertheless, the man and woman disobeyed the lord God. The garden was cared for and the beasts named in accordance with the divine will, but this was not fully voluntary, in that voluntary accord requires that there be an alternative. There is no obedience if disobedience is not a conceivable, a known, possibility. The word 'obedience' has no operational meaning until the act of disobedience has been performed at least once. ('Man can be truly *for* God only if he is morally independent of Him, and he can be thus independent only by being first *against* Him.'—John Hick*, original italics.)

The primary disobedience is not therefore just a liberating act; it is an essential of the creation of humankind, an essential of the sixth day's work. When choice has been experienced, then the knowledge of good and evil (given by the fruit), of better and worse, and the ability to make value judgments become possible. In this respect one becomes like God (just as the snake said), and it is in the image of God, the story tells us, that it is the work of God to make us. Thus the couple become co-creators of themselves.

The necessity of the primal disobedience for the creation of humankind does not make it an act wholly in accord with the divine order. It remains a contradiction of a divine injunction. However, the inescapability of choice between two evils is itself a feature of the human condition. It is not in the nature of the universe that we can go through life, even theoretically, with clean hands, but they become clean by repentance *(teshuvah,* 'return', in Hebrew; not cringing). The Creation, which includes us, is not an initially unflawed structure, rigidly maintained, for this might be unstable, but is a dynamic system in which flaws can be corrected by 'return',–cybernetically, as it were. In Talmud Bavli* repentance is said to be an essential of the Creation, created before the universe.

The first reported consequence of eating the fruit of the tree of the knowledge of good and evil is that the couple, instead of being naked and feeling no shame in front of each other (2:25), now know that they are naked. The new self-awareness involves the shame which previously they did not feel in front of one another. Shame is associated with self-awareness but, as Gabriele Taylor* makes plain, is not the same as guilt. Also, shame is not a necessary consequence of consciousness of having sinned, and it can be present without that consciousness. Shame is a feature of our humanity, and shamelessness can indicate a degree of dehumanisation. Alexander Pope* reminds us that shame is not necessarily connected with wrong-doing:

> Let humble Allen with an awkward shame
> Do good by stealth, and blush to find it fame.

Although the couple had been naked and unashamed, and now knew that they were naked, the primary association of this new-found shame is not with sexuality or with the body. As noted on pages 57-58, at the end of the last chapter, the word here translated 'naked' is not that used for nakedness with a sexual connotation (i.e. *ervah),* but is a term *(arumim)* associated invariably with privation, lack, or poverty. The couple's shame, shown in their awareness of being naked, is an aspect of a new-found consciousness of possessing nothing. With the knowledge of good and evil has come the notion of ownership.

***

In asserting the essential of being human, the story does not represent this essential as simply the disobedience. Integral with the disobedience is responsibility for it (3:7b-13).

> [7b] And they sewed fig leaves together and made girdles for themselves.
>
> [8] And they heard the Lord God's voice moving in the garden in the breeze time of the day, and the Adam and his wife hid themselves from the face of the Lord God among the trees of the garden. [9] And the Lord God called to the Adam and said to him 'Where are you?'. [10] And he said 'I heard your voice in the garden, and I was afraid because I was naked, and I hid'. [11] And he said 'Who told you that you are naked? Have you eaten of the tree of

which I commanded you not to eat?'

[12] And the Adam said 'The woman whom you gave to be with me, she gave me from the tree and I ate'. [13] And the Lord God said to the woman 'What is this you have done?' And the woman said 'The snake deceived me, and I ate'.

The couple have eaten of the tree of the knowledge of good and evil. They can choose, and can know right from wrong, better from worse. They can order things on scales of value, including but not only scales of moral value.

They hear the Lord God's voice stirring in the garden in the breeze time of the day (3:8). (Despite many translations, it is nearer to the original to say that the voice moved, than to say that the Lord God was walking.) The man is asked 'Where are you?' This is the start of a demand to answer for himself, as when a trial opens with the question 'Is the accused in court?' It is also a summons to look at where one stands, to be aware of the point at which one exists. God's creature out of the earth speaks to the woman; the voice in the day's breeze (the Hebrew word is the same as for 'spirit') is addressed to the man. The man pleads that he has hidden because he was naked on hearing the Lord God's voice.

Naked? Had they not covered themselves with girdles? The man's shame at being naked surely makes no sense if the shame is due to exposure. If, however, the weightiest connotation of the nakedness is, as already explained, privation, then a girdle of ephemeral plucked leaves does indeed make little difference. The Lord God makes it plain that, for the man to know that he is naked, he must have eaten of the forbidden tree (3:11).

The man tries to push the blame on to 'the woman whom you gave to be with me' (3:12). Note his detachment from her, contrasting with the earlier 'bone of my bones'. Also, the phrase 'whom you gave to be with me', harking back to the separation of female and male, is regressive in outlook towards the sexually undifferentiated state before that separation. Unless the female is accepted as a free-standing fact, there is a vitiation of maleness. So the Lord God asks the woman what she has done. She blames the snake. Their failure to take responsibility is incompatible with being in the image of God; there must be not only freedom of choice but also responsibility for the choice that is made. (The central importance, in this story, of the passing of blame was brought to my attention by Dr. A. Esterson.) 'Responsible' means 'answerable'. To whom, in this instance, are the man and woman answerable? To the voice which says 'Where are you?' This is the voice of the Lord that says 'Let there be light' (1:3), that deliberates within its infinite entirety 'Let us make humankind in our image, after our likeness' (1:26). Like Francis Thompson's* 'Hound of Heaven', it is never yonder, always here. It is heard in the voice of the Lord God's snake and in the breeze of the freshening day. The couple answered fully to the one but not to the other. The voice, however, is of the Unity. Partially heard, it is mistakenly heard; partially answered, it is inappropriately answered.

The failure to take responsibility is counter to 'in the image of God'. The change from 'bone of my bones' to 'the woman whom you gave to be with me' vitiates 'male and female he created them' (1:27), since the sexes are complementary, and each is fulfilled in itself only insofar as it regards the other. In two respects the couple fail to fulfil their humanity.

The man is now being called 'the Adam', the expression previously used for the sexually undifferentiated Adam, before there is man and woman. This name for the man will be discussed when the story introduces the woman's name.

CHAPTER 14: *THE REALISATION OF HUMANITY BEGINS*

THE CONSEQUENCES of the disobedience, and of the failure to take responsibility for it, are now worked out in two cycles. The first cycle bears especially upon the woman, the second on the man.

The first cycle tells about the cursing of the snake, and about the changed relation between it and the woman, and then about what the Lord God says of her relation to her children and to her husband.

> ^{14} And the Lord God said to the snake 'Because you have done this you are cursed more than all cattle and more than every animal of the field. On your belly you shall go, and dust shall you eat all the days of your life. 15 And I will put enmity between you and the woman, and between your seed and her seed; it will bruise your head and you will bruise its heel.

> ^{16} To the woman he said 'Much will I increase your suffering, and especially that due to conception, and in sorrow will you bear children.

> And towards your husband is your desire, and he will rule you'.

The curse on the snake, acting as it would seem in his capacity as God's creature, and presenting the woman with a choice, may appear harsh. However, this would not be the only example, in the Creation story, of the suffering of animals due to human behaviour. The wickedness of the generation of the Flood is, as we shall see, interpreted as a corruption of all flesh, and beasts share with human beings the calamity of the cataclysm. It has been said that the assigning to the snake a diet of dust is the worst of the curse, since the snake is enabled thus to find food anywhere and all the time, and so is condemned to live without challenge or effort, and without the stimulus which accompanies them; this I have been told, is of rabbinical origin, but I do not know what written source there may be for the comment. As far as the couple are concerned, the force of the curse is to vitiate the woman's relationship with the snake.

After the curse come the Lord God's words on two sufferings. The first is that conception and its consequences will bring sorrow; the reference is to children generally, and is not solely obstetrical. The second suffering is that the woman's desire for her husband will give him power over her. The two sufferings affect human characteristics, as they appear in the account of the sixth day; the first adds bitterness to 'Be fruitful and increase', the second to 'Male and female he created them'.

***

The second cycle tells first about the cursing of the ground and about the relation between it and the man, then about the Lord God's words on mortality, and finally about the man's realisation of his wife's nature.

[17] And to Adam he said 'Because you listened to the voice of your wife and ate from the tree of which I commanded you, saying "You shall not eat from it", cursed is the ground because of you. With suffering shall you eat of it all the days of your life. [18] Thorns and thistles shall it bring forth for you, and you will eat the herbage of the field.

[19] By the sweat of your face will you eat bread until you return to the ground, for from it were you taken, since dust you are and to dust will return.'

[20] And the Adam called his wife's name Eve *(Chawwah)* because she was the mother of all living *(chay)*.

There is here, to start, a curse on the ground. (The man, like the woman, is not cursed.) With this curse there is a vitiation of the man's relationship with the ground.

Then follow two sufferings. The first is that tillage will involve sorrow. The second is that the man is given consciousness, or a new consciousness, of his mortality. At the cost of some repetition, three points may be made about these words on death. First, it is not in accord with the plain meaning of what is said, to take this intimation of mortality as fulfilling 'In the day that you eat of it you shall indeed die' (2:17). Secondly, if there has been immortality up to this point in the story, why has there been no suggestion of so special a circumstance? Thirdly, when, as will be seen, the couple are prevented from gaining immortality, the wording is that to be expected if they might gain what they never had, not regain something lost. If this saying to the man is a death sentence, it is curious that it should be subordinate to a saying about toil; which would have the more severe implication? Here the new relationship with the soil, now cursed, is linked with the man's beginning and end in soil. Thus a return to the dust from which humanity has been taken (2:7) is used to tell the man not simply of death, but of the tragic cycle of death and birth. The sorrow is the new-found realisation of the wheel of death and coming-to-be, the very heart of tragedy.

Now the man calls the woman by her name, Eve. The names of the couple, as they appear in the story, may now therefore be conveniently reviewed. Before there is man or woman, there is simply 'the Adam', that is, 'person', 'humankind'. The Adam is related to the non-human creation in two ways, as a tiller (2:15) and as a namer of the beasts (2:19). After the Adam differentiates into female and male, the couple are referred to as 'the woman' and 'the man' (*ish*, a male adult, not *adam*, a human being). However, he has appeared as 'Adam', without the definite article, at the cursing of the ground (3:17), and will do so at the receiving of garments (3:21), at the begetting of his third son (4:25), and in his own genealogy (5:15). The woman's name is Eve *(Chawwah)* because, we are told, she is 'the mother of all living' *(chay,* a term which comprehends humanity and beasts alike, 3:20). There are beasts in the story before there is a woman, so that this is not only the familial motherhood of conception and bearing.

The word 'Adam', used as a name for the man, has two aspects, positive and negative. One of the characteristics of the primary, sexually undifferentiated Adam is this being's relation to the ground, *adamah*, which can be heard or read the feminine of the grammatically masculine *adam*. After the differentiation between male and female, the relation with the non-human creation represented by naming the beasts goes to the woman, who converses with the snake. The relation with the non-human creation represented by tillage goes to the man, the husbandman of the soil, *adam* to *adamah*. This is the positive aspect of the name Adam.

Concerning this positive aspect, we may remark the well-known male connotation of the plough. Correspondingly, the earth may be thought of as a woman. Thus Sylvia Townsend Warner's* poem 'The Rival' expresses movingly a farmer's wife's jealousy of the land. The sexual feeling of tillage comes to us when we speak of 'virgin soil', and in early rabbinical Hebrew the verb 'plough' *(charash)* is used for the man's activity in sexual congress.

There is, however, a negative aspect of the name. 'Adam' is a common noun, not (in Hebrew, unless recently) a proper name. In the Garden story, up to the awakening from deep sleep at 2:22, there is 'the Adam', with the definite article. (Singular personal proper names do not take the definite article in Hebrew; grammatically, they behave as though they already have it, so that adding it would make no sense.) The use of the word 'Adam' as a personal name suggests unfulfilled individuation. Indeed, it twice lapses back to 'the Adam', in common noun form, even after becoming the name of Eve's husband (3:21, 4:1).

Eve's name, representing her as 'the mother of all living', resembles 'Adam' in that it bears upon the relation of the named one to the non-human creation. Nevertheless, it is not a common noun, but a unique proper name. If it were merely a feminine form of *chay* 'life', it would be *Chayyah* ('animal') which, although now a personal name, is simply a common noun in classical Hebrew. The form *Chawwah* (that is, 'Eve') distinguishes it, within Hebrew as it actually exists in scripture and irrespective of etymology, from any common noun, although without disguising the meaning, since the sounds *w* and *y* alternate in Hebrew, as in the conjugation of verbs (as well as between Semitic languages, such as Arabic and Hebrew).

When Adam speaks Eve's name (3:20), the story is clearly stating that the name represents what she already is, irrespective of the naming. By contrast, when the Adam names the beasts (2:19), the wording strongly indicates the Adam's independence in determining what a beast is to be called. The contrast is explicit, since the story links the naming of the beasts with the differentiation into woman and man (2:20). In dominion, however, there is not the same companionship that is possible with 'a help opposite him'. The title 'the mother of all living' is given poignancy by the curse on the snake, which vitiates the woman's relationship with it. We may reflect at this point on her sorrow due to the children to whom she is, more literally, mother.

It has already been seen, at the awakening of the Adam, that the man first calls himself 'man' when acknowledging the presence of the woman, and he says 'woman' before he says 'man'. The woman, on the other hand, has not this implied dependency, and the story in fact speaks of 'woman' even before the Adam's awakening. Later, the man, somewhat impersonally called Adam, acknowledges the woman to be Eve, the name already proper to her nature. Thus, although the man depends on the woman for his awareness that he is male, she depends on him for neither her femaleness nor her Eve-ness.

***

It is now convenient to summarise certain features of the human condition, as presented by the story. The Adam is related to soil and to the beasts. With differentiation into male and female, working the soil becomes the male form of human interaction with the non-human creation, the female form being a relationship with the beasts. The now distinct male and female are linked by mutual affection. The whole of this can be represented by a triangle with male, female, and the non-human creation at its corners, the sides then corresponding to the relations between them (Figure 5).

In the figure, the three relations are indicated by double lines, with single, solid lines for the relations of the Adam in the sexually undifferentiated state. The broken lines and arrows show the change with sexual differentiation. The verse numbers relate the lines to the story itself. The English 'the' answers well enough to the prefix *ha-*; Hebrew has no indefinite article corresponding to the English 'a'.

The sides of the triangle are affected by the couple's failure to take responsibility. He attempts to conceal what he has gained, through the tree, from the earth, which is cursed on his account. She blames the snake, which is cursed on her account. He mars the relation between the sexes by blaming her as 'the woman whom you gave to be with me' although he had once acknowledged her as 'bone of my bones and flesh of my flesh'. (The word for 'bone', *etzem,* also means 'self' or 'substance', so that it carries a deep and intimate feeling.)

Beyond the triangle of vitiated relations are the four sufferings. The blessing of fruitfulness is to carry with it sorrow due to children; the wording (3:16) is wider in its applicability than simply childbirth. Secondly, marital love is to be refracted and imperilled through the power which a man has as a result of his wife's desire for him. Next, the man is to find that his task of getting subsistence is painful toil. Finally, the man is made aware of his mortality in a way that faces him with the tragic cycle of passing away and coming to be. (The man's sorrows are clearly connected with the curse on the ground, but the woman's are less readily related to the curse on the snake. Is there such a crude difference, or are the connections between the woman's sorrows and the curse on the snake subtle, becoming evident only with sufficient reflection?) Because children are also the father's, and because marriage is a matter for two, because women as well as men are concerned with getting subsistence, and because awareness of the cycle of death and birth cannot be confined to one sex, all four sufferings belong to both the woman and the man, even if each suffering affects them in a different manner, and with different degrees of immediacy, directness, or force.

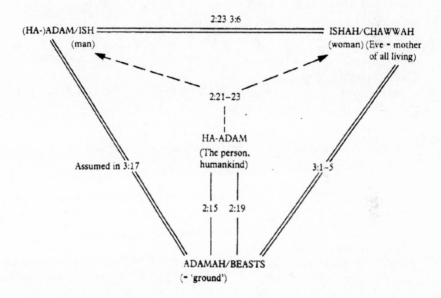

Fig 5. *relations between the male, the female, and the non-human creation.*

IN THE LAST CYCLE (3:21-4:1) of the narrative of the Garden of Eden, the consequence of the disobedience, and of the shirking of responsibility for it, begins to be worked out. First, the couple come into relation with the non-human creation in a new way, through God-granted ownership. Next, they are sent by the Lord God from the garden lest they eat of the tree of life. Finally they come together to make their first child (4:1, which also belongs to the next story, that about their son Cain). There is thus an entirely new development of their relationships with the non-human world, with their Creator, and with each other.

[21] And the Lord God made for Adam and for his wife (*ishshah*, 'woman') garments of skin, and clothed them.

[22] And the Lord God said 'Behold the Adam is like one of us, to know good and evil, and now, lest he put out his hand and take also from the tree of life and live for ever...[23] And the Lord God sent him from the Garden of Eden, to serve the ground from which he had been taken. [24] And he drove out the Adam, and caused the cherubim and the flame of the turning sword to dwell to the east of the Garden of Eden, to keep the way of the tree of life.

[4:1] And the Adam knew Eve, his wife, and she conceived, and bore Cain (*Qayin*), and said I have got (*qaniti*) a man with the Lord.

Although the garden has been said to be in Eden (2:8), the title 'Garden of Eden' is used only in connection with putting humankind into it (2:15) and, here, expelling humankind from it. Otherwise it is referred to as 'the garden'.

The Lord God's gift of garments (3:21) acknowledges the transformation of the couple to a condition in which there is felt a need to own. The gift answers to their own improvisation of clothing. Clothing is personal, and the Lord God's giving expresses approval for, or aquiescence in, owning what is proper to one's person, but has nothing to say about that which is not. Nor is there here any indication where the boundary might lie between property, in this sense, and improperty, that which is inappropriate to own individually, not being proper to the person.

Whether 'garments of skin' refers to their material or what they cover is not made plain. If the garments are made of skin, there may be a contrast with the appointing of green things as food (1:29,30). However, in the story, green diet is appointed for all animals also, which the writer must have known not to be the

70

case. Isaiah (11:7) looks forward to the era of the vegetarian lion, and it may be that the universal vegetarian diet of the sixth day of the Creation is intended to be a forward glimpse of the last days. On the other hand it may be that we are to understand the wearing of skins to be unconnected with the eating of meat, or that this is a special case. Also, the 'garments of skin' may be garments *for* the skin, even robes of honour, suggests Midrash Rabbah*. It is reasonable to conclude that very little can be inferred from the fact that the garments are 'of skin', except by speculating far outside what is given by the story itself.

The central part of this cycle, verses 22-24, certainly refers to the couple, and the term 'the Adam' must therefore mean not an individual, but have its general reference, humankind. Verse 23, with its reference to tillage, appears to make 'the Adam' name the man only, but recalls 2:7, in which the Adam is formed from the dust, and is still not sexually differentiated; in 3:23 and 3:24 the couple is meant, since neither the trees nor the expulsion is a matter for one only of them.

The tree of life, like that of the knowledge of good and evil, is planted by the Lord God (2:9) in the garden. God intervenes because humankind, like God, now knows good and evil, and is to be prevented from eating from the unforbidden tree of life, and so come to resemble God in gaining immortality also. The notion, sometimes met with, that it is here that the possibility of death enters the story, is contrary to the plain meaning of the words, that immortality is prevented. The expulsion from the garden is to the tilling of that ground from which humankind is taken (3:23), and to the dust of which it returns (3:19).

The way to the tree of life is then guarded. Are the cherubim and the flaming sword guarding the way to prevent its use, or are they guarding it to keep it open? The idiom 'keep the way' occurs elsewhere in scripture nine times, usually meaning 'keep *to* the way' (Genesis 18:19, Judges 2:22, 2 Samuel 2:22, 1 Kings 2:4, Malachi 2:9, Psalms 37:34 and 39:2, Job 23:11, 2 Chronicles 6: 16). This meaning does not seem to be relevant here, but three things may be to the point. First, in scripture the verb 'keep' (*shamar*) usually means to guard something from what might harm it. Secondly, the expression 'keep the way' never means to obstruct the way or prevent its use, but tends to be associated with that use. Thirdly, elsewhere in scripture the tree of life is mentioned as already attainable (Proverbs 3:13-18, in verse 18 of which 'the tree of life' is perhaps a better translation than the usual 'a tree of life').

The tree of life is, of course, a widespread image. It appears as the Christian cross and the Norse Yggdrasil, for example. A tree is associated with a revelatory perception of life in the story of the Buddha's enlightenment under the Bo tree. This in turn reminds us of the Coan plane under which Hippocrates, the father of medicine, taught the healing art initiated by Asklepios, the life-restoring beloved son of the god Apollo. The tree of life can loom large in the experience of shamans (Halifax*).

The story, then, says that humankind, having eaten of the tree of the knowledge of good and evil without taking responsibility for the deed, may not remain where they can eat of the tree of life. Nevertheless, the meaning of the writing seems to be that the way of the tree of life is open to those who can bring themselves to walk close to the terrible cherubim and the turning, flaming, sword. This is not a return, for they had not eaten of the tree of life, and to do so implies a differently experienced garden. Is this the way to resuming the shirked responsibility, and so to fulfilling the humanity which is the image of God? If so, perhaps this is what the Jewish mystics meant when they said that our fault is in eating of the one tree but not of the other.

***

Here we leave the nine cycles of the Garden of Eden.

NOW, IN GENESIS 4:1-17, the story continues with the son of Adam and Eve. Just as the first verse of what is now to be told has been taken also as part of the narrative about events in the Garden of Eden so there is a similar overlap between what is said about Cain, the killer, and what follows, verse 17 being appropriate in both. In the translation now following, spacing between lines has been used to break up the writing into episodes. The basis for dividing the text in this way will be presented after the translation itself.

4:1 And the Adam knew Eve his wife, and she conceived, and bore Cain *(Qayin)* and said 'I have got *(qaniti)* a man with the Lord'.

2 And she went on to give birth to his brother Abel. And Abel was the shepherd of the flock, and Cain was the tiller of the ground.

3 And it happened after some days that Cain brought, from the produce of the ground, an offering to the LORD. 4 And Abel, he also brought of the firstlings of his flock and of their fat parts. And the LORD turned his gaze to Abel and to his offering. 5 And to Cain and his offering he did not turn his eye, and Cain burned greatly with anger, and his face fell.

6 And the LORD said to Cain 'Why do you burn with anger and why has your face fallen? Is it not so that, if you do well, it will be lifted and, if you do not do well, a sin is a crouched beast at the doorway, its desire towards you, and you may rule over it?' 8 And Cain made an appointment with Abel his brother, and it happened that, when they were in the field, Cain rose up against Abel his brother, and killed him.

9 And the LORD said to Cain 'Where is Abel your brother?', and he said 'I do not know. Am I my brother's keeper?'

10 And he said 'What have you done? Listen. Your brother's blood cries out to me from the ground. 11 And now you are cursed out of the ground, which has opened its mouth to take your brother's blood from your hand. 12 When you till the ground it will not go on giving you its strength. A vagrant and a stray will you be in the Earth.'

13 And Cain said to the LORD 'My iniquity is too great to forgive. 14 See, you have driven me to-day from the face of the ground, and from your face I shall hide myself, and I shall be a vagrant and a stray in the earth, and anyone who finds me will kill me.' 15 And the LORD said to him 'For this reason, anyone who slays Cain will suffer sevenfold retribution'. And the LORD set a sign for Cain, lest anyone finding him should strike him. 16 And Cain went out from

73

the presence of the LORD, and dwelt in the land of Nod, east of Eden. [17] And
Cain knew his wife, and she conceived, and bore Enoch,...

There is no balance between the brothers in the attention paid to them. Cain is
at or near the centre in every episode of the story. All we are told of Abel, which
is his occupation, appears as distinction from Cain, rather than the independent portrayal of a character. While Abel lives, his part in the story is passive, as victim; only the blood of his slain body takes any initiative. Because of
the difference in the way we are told about the brothers, the telling is less about
the victim or the killing then about the killer. Cain is the theme.

In connection with the very scanty information about Abel, it may be to the
point to notice that his name, *Hevel* in Hebrew, means 'vapour' and that which
is vain or transient. Even if this is not a true explanation of the origin of the
name, its evident meaning must have been noticeable when this tale was first
framed, just as *Adam* and *adamah* must always have been heard as a masculine and feminine pair, although not necessarily related etymologically. Further note will be taken of the meaning of Abel's name, in connection with
psychological aspects of the tale.

Together with this emphasis on one brother's character, deed, and words,
there is a second striking literary feature of the narrative. This is the echoing
of the story of the couple in the Garden of Eden. God challenges Cain 'Where is
Abel your brother?', just as he challenges the Adam with 'Where are you?'
When we hear 'You are cursed out of the ground', addressed to Cain, we are led
by memory to receive it alongside God's words to Cain's father, 'Cursed is the
ground because of you'. The cherubim which kept the way of the tree of life
were caused to 'dwell to the east of the Garden of Eden'; Cain 'dwelt in the land
of Nod, east of Eden'.

***

These two features are indications pointing to the pattern of the story of the
killing. If we give attention to the person of Cain, and if we are alert for echoes
of the story of Cain's parents, the tale of the killing of Cain's brother falls into
the seven episodes, as indicated already in the spacing of the translation.
These seven episodes correspond with the nine cycles of the story of the Garden
of Eden, since the story of Cain has no equivalent of the cycle about a world
without humankind, and since Cain, as a single character, has a single episode
to set opposite his parents in the two cycles of the realisation of humanity.
Later it will be shown that comparing the two stories helps to elucidate the
natural history of Cain's sin. Meanwhile the episodes may be defined by comparison with the earlier story, as in Figure 6.

***

2:6,7.........The Adam is made.	4:1.........Cain is conceived and born.
2:8-18......The Adam is to tend the garden, is promised a companion, and is forbidden the tree.	4:2..........Cain gets a brother. He tends the ground.
2:19-25.....The animals are named. The couple is made.	4:3-5......Relation of the brothers to the produce of the earth and of one brother to the other.
3:1-7a......The couple disobey.	4:6-8......The Lord offers two choices. Cain makes a third, and kills his brother.
3:7b-13.....They are confronted. 'Where are you?' They shirk responsibility.	4:9.........Cain is confronted. 'Where is Abel, your brother?' Cain shirks responsibility.
3:14-16.....The curse on the snake. The woman's sufferings. __ with _____ 3:17-20.....'Cursed is the ground because of you.' The man's sufferings.	4:10-12...'You are cursed out of the ground.' Cain's sufferings.
3:21-24;4:1...God protects and expels. Cherubim are caused 'to dwell to the east of the Garden of Eden'. The couple have a child.	4:13-17a...Cain is expelled with the Lord's protection. Cain 'dwelt in the land of Nod, east of Eden'. Cain has a child.

Fiig. 6. *Table comparing the story of Cain with that of his parents.*

The details of each episode contribute to understanding the whole.

First episode. The love between the man and the woman receives a blow when the man blames 'the woman whom you gave to be with me'. Now they come together to make a child: 'And the Adam knew Eve his wife'. The biblical use of 'know' *(yada')* for sexual congress gives the act a particular kind of intimacy. The word 'know' in the Hebrew scriptures encompasses more than knowing that something is so, more than being acquainted with somebody. It represents

75

a total, unanalysable knowing. Thus the book of Proverbs (12:10) says that 'the righteous knows the soul *(nefesh,* 'life', 'person', 'self') of his beast'. (The translation 'regardeth' is really too weak, a rare lapse in the 1611 bible.) So, despite blaming her, 'the Adam knew Eve, his wife'.

Yet all is not well between them. The expression 'I have got a man with the Lord' is like nothing else in scriptural birth stories and genealogies. The word translated 'with' *(et)* means 'accompanied by', not 'by means of'. Eve claims her place as co-creatrix with the Lord. The verb *qaniti,* 'I have got', is one that implies not only possession but, often, making or authorship. One is not faulting a mother's acknowledgment of divine accompaniment if one asks why such enthusiasm for the child's origin excludes mention of the father. Perhaps one can attach too much importance to this, but the question remains why Eve calls the child a man *(ish).* This is the word for a human adult male, and can mean 'husband'. It is not a normal word to use for an infant boy. Eve sees her son, from the outset, as a male adult. Perhaps this lends point to the exclusion of Adam from the parental triad God-mother-father. Where there is something odd between mother and son, may we not suspect something odd between mother and father? The tendency of this episode is to alert the reader or hearer to the possibility of unhappiness in the child's life. (For this way of looking at Cain, I gratefully acknowledge the influence of a seminar by Dr. A. Esterson at Leo Baeck College, London.)

Second episode. Cain gets a brother and becomes a tiller of the soil. The word for 'till' *(avad)* is the same as that for 'serve' when 'the Lord took the Adam, and put him into the Garden of Eden to serve it and keep it'. The brother has another occupation. In what has been told us of Cain's parents, the ground and humanity are related to each other; we are now further told that differences of calling and division of labour also belong to the human condition, and that variety of work is part of the divine order.

Third episode. The expression translated 'And it happened after some days' means, in scripture, the continuation of a story. Here it can act only to arouse awareness that this is not the beginning, since we are not told what happens before. The offerings which each brother brings are a natural means of expression according to the work of each. The specification of Abel's offering as of his best ('firstlings', 'fat parts') is taken by some to mean that Cain was less selective in what he brought. However, the actual text does not say this, and only in the description of Abel's offering, when Cain's has already been noted, is there any reference to details of what was offered. The telling conspicuously omits any reason why the Lord turned to Abel's offering only, or how Cain knew this. What we are given is a difference in the way the Lord looked at the brothers, without explanation, and it is to Cain's reaction to the difference that our attention is directed.

The episode bears upon two relationships. First, the offering by each brother confirms his relation to the Lord and to the earth. Secondly, the consequence of the offerings is a reaction by Cain affecting relations between the brothers. What was said of the couple bears upon the relations between two people of opposite sex, and between those two people and the non-human creation. Now we have another relationship, between two people of the same sex but of different occupations and consequently of different ways of life.

Fourth episode. The couple in the Garden of Eden have two possibilities: obedience to the Lord God, and disobedience. To Cain, however, it is from the Lord that two possibilities come, for his choosing. First, 'If you do well, it will be uplifted' (or 'there is uplifting'). That is, if Cain does well, he will change his attitude, and no longer have a fallen countenance. Secondly, 'If you do not do well, a sin is a couched beast at the doorway, its desire towards you and you may rule over it'. That is, if Cain does not do what is good, he retains his attitude, and a sin waits for him. Nevertheless, even then the sin need not prevail. The word here translated 'couched beast' *(rovetz)* means an animal that is docile, or stable, or hard or dangerous to rouse or shift, or laden, or firmly settled. It is exactly contrary to a beast which is threatening or ready to spring. The phrase 'its desire towards you' echoes what was said to the woman in the Garden of Eden: her husband could rule her because she desired him,–'and towards your husband is your desire'. Therefore it follows that, for Cain, 'you may rule over it'. Cain can do well and change his attitude, or he can do badly, not changing his attitude, and find a sin awaiting him. Nevertheless he can, even then, master the sin. Cain, however, neither avoids the sin nor overcomes it. He kills his brother.

The sentence which I have here translated 'And Cain made an appointment with Abel his brother' can be rendered as 'And Cain said to Abel his brother...', without specifying what he said. In either case, it comes between the Lord's advice and the killing, and suggests that the murder was premeditated.

Fifth episode. Just as the Lord God asked the Adam 'Where are you?', so Cain is now asked 'Where is Abel, your brother?' Both shirk answering for what they have done. Adam blames his wife; Cain says 'I do not know. Am I my brother's keeper?' The one avoids responsibility for his deed, the other for his deed and for his brother. The man in the Garden of Eden will not answer for an essential of his being made; his son will not answer for having destroyed another created being like himself. Adam says that his wife gave him the fruit, which is half the truth; Cain said that he did not know where his brother was, which is wholly a lie.

Sixth episode. Cain cannot, by lying, however, avoid the consequence of what he has done, for the earth receives the blood of the victim and the Lord hears the cry of the innocent, a cry to the Lord. The result of this requires the intervention of no living human being. Cain has acted against the divinely appointed order of created things. Therefore the earth, which has received the victim's blood, will no longer give the killer its 'strength', that is, its yield, and will no longer give him an abiding home.

Cain is cursed: his father and mother were not (even if the snake and ground were cursed because of them). Cain is not to have the ground's yield; his father could have it, although with toil and frustration. Cain is without a place on earth, while his parents are expelled only from the Garden of Eden, with its tree of life.

The terms translated 'a vagrant and a stray' *(na' wa-nad)* do not imply a nomadic existence, but movement hither and thither, as of one hunted and hounded. The contrast is not between migrant and settled life, but between either of these and having no place at any time. Nomadic peoples are not 'vagrants and strays' in the sense of the words in this passage, even if they are migratory. The nomad has more than one place, perhaps many: Cain is to have none.

Seventh Episode. Now Cain recognizes what he has become. 'My iniquity is too great to forgive' translates what may also be rendered as 'My punishment is too great to bear'. The words translated 'iniquity' and 'forgive' have each some ambiguity. However, the point is plain: Cain is faced with the intolerable. There is, of course, a sense in which a killing must always be unforgivable; none can forgive an injury except the one injured, and the victim of a killing is no longer available to offer forgiveness.

Cain says 'See, you have driven me to-day from the face of the ground'. Previously, however, the story has made the effusion of innocent blood the cause of a curse out of the ground, with being a vagrant and stray as one of the effects of the curse. That is to say, Cain's being driven from the face of the ground is shown by the Lord to be a natural consequence of the killing, not the result of the Lord's social intervention. Is Cain right then in saying that the Lord has driven him from the face of the ground? It could be said that Cain is refusing to acknowledge the point that the Lord has made to him. However, he sees what is to happen to him as predictable when he says that anyone who finds him will kill him. In fact, we seem to have here an example of explanation such as is found elsewhere in the Hebrew scriptures. Sometimes there is no sharp distinction between a natural consequence, according to the pre-ordained order of created things, and a divine action particular to the occasion. To say that the ground rejects Cain, as a predictable result of the killing, and to say that the Lord has driven Cain from the face of the ground, are not two distinct explanations of his condemnation to be a vagrant and a stray.

There is another manner of explanation, also. 'From your face I shall hide myself.' Cain is saying that his vagrancy is due to his attempt to avoid the face of the Lord; it is driven from within himself. It is implicit that this hiding cannot be achieved, else the vagrancy would be temporary, which is hardly compatible with the whole tenor of the story, which presents a total transformation of Cain's state. As for the pervasive philosophy of scripture, it has already been noted (pp. 16 and 17) that there is a general assumption of the universal presence of God; and references were given to a few scriptural examples expressing this. The reader wishing to look up further examples may find them in Psalm 139:7-12 and Amos 9:3,4.

Now there is an explicit and unambiguous intervention by the Lord. Cain says that his being a vagrant and a stray is a state in which 'anyone who finds me will kill me'. The punishing result of Cain's deed would thus lead to a further effect, resulting from abhorrence of the shedder of blood. The Lord therefore undertakes to effect retribution on Cain's behalf and sets a sign for Cain, so that it is known that he may not be attacked. We may see this action of the Lord's in various ways, as limiting punishment, for example, or as stopping a chain of killings of killers. What, however, is clear is that the Lord is protecting Cain against a possible consequence of his deed. We cannot know what was the sign set for Cain but, as in the story of the seven days, the Lord is shown as one who does not simply appoint the way things are and then leave them to run.

The Judge having spoken, 'Cain went out from the presence of the Lord'. This is a legal formula, marking the end of a trial, the trial which opens with the accused being asked 'Where is Abel, your brother?' The form of a trial has, as already noted, been used in the telling of events in the Garden of Eden. The land of Nod is unknown geographically. The name 'Nod' means 'wandering aimlessly'.

Before Cain's parents are expelled, God gives them garments, respecting their condition of being ashamed of their nakedness. Before Cain is expelled, the Lord gives him a sign, respecting his condition of being 'a vagrant and a stray'.

The blessing to be fruitful and increase is fulfilled in the couple and in the killer alike. It is not a conditional blessing.

CAIN FAILS TO AVOID or overcome the sin which he therefore goes on to commit. The telling does not use the word 'sin' *(chat'at)* in describing the deeds of Cain's parents. The word is first used in connection with Cain himself. Now scripture does not define 'sin', any more than it defines 'cow' or 'rain', although it uses both words. If, however, we compare Cain's sin with what happens in the Garden of Eden, we may be able to distinguish some of the characteristics of sin, something—as it were—of the natural history of sinning.

The couple in the Garden of Eden are loving to each other at first. Even when the man blames the woman there is no conflict; she says no word against him, but blames the snake. There is no suggestion that they are anything but together in all things. Cain, however, is set against his brother to the extent that he cannot bear his brother to be more approved of than himself. *It is an essential feature of Cain's sin that it starts from lack of fellowship.*

The couple in the garden disobey the Lord God in order to discover freedom to choose. Cain, however, is offered alternatives by the Lord. Cain's sin is not a necessary consequence of exercising freedom. Indeed, the consequence of Cain's sin restricts his freedom. *Cain's sin is not necessary in order to have alternatives from which to choose,* even if it is itself one possible choice.

The couple disobey the Lord God. The matter is between them and their Creator and, as explained already, their very disobedience can be seen as an act of cooperation in the Creator's work. Cain not only goes outside the Lord's word, but kills a human fellow-creature, made in God's likeness. *Cain's sin is an offence against the divine ordering of created things.*

The man and the woman pass on the blame. What each says is not in itself a falsehood, even if it is less than the whole truth in a situation in which nothing less than the whole truth is appropriate. When Cain avoids responsibility, he tells a downright lie. The killing leads to total falsehood. *Cain's sin is a spreading corruption.*

In the Garden of Eden the snake and the ground are cursed, not the man and the woman, although the curses affect the human condition. Cain, on the other hand, is cursed out of the ground whose mouth receives the victim's shed blood. *Cain's sin harms him because it is reflex to his being.*

In the Garden of Eden the couple become excluded from one possible way of existence, and go back to their native soil ('the ground from which he had been taken'). Cain, however, has no place on earth, all will be against him, he cannot face his Creator. *Cain's sin separates him from the earth, from people, and* (but for the Lord's compassionate intervention) *from his Creator,* from whose face he feels bound to hide himself.

In the Garden of Eden the couple begin to know suffering, but in the sense that they come to know what it is to be human like the rest of us. Cain has, and laments, the burden arising specifically from his sin, and this burden he finds more than he can bear. *Cain's sin is an intolerable burden to the sinner.*

These are the characteristics of Cain's sin, which is, as the first sin within the story, a pattern of sins in general. It shows their circumstances, nature, and consequences. A sin is not, in this philosophy, the infringement of an arbitrary rule. It is action contrary to the order of created things, and is therefore a concern of the Creator. Insofar as it affects other created beings, it is a concern of one's fellow-creatures.

***

The effects of Cain's sin are primary and secondary. The primary effects of Cain's killing his brother are told as inevitable, relentless. Although the first effect is to attract an enquiry by the Lord, the Lord says that innocent blood cries to him. The bloodshed itself starts a train of consequences. Cain is cursed out of the ground which has opened its mouth to receive his brother's blood. In all this there is emphasis on what follows naturally and, if the Lord's intervention is not, in this sense, a natural event, it is still hard to suppose the Lord's ignoring the cry of an innocent victim, given the Hebrew scriptures' persistent theme of the Lord as protector and vindicator of the defenceless and the wronged. Up to the end of the Lord's pronouncement of Cain's destiny there is a strong emphasis on the development of the matter according to assumed rules of cause and effect.

Secondary effects take off, as it were, from the development of the primary effects. Cain's intensely personal cry of despair, and his lament over his destiny, evokes a personal response from the Lord, who protects him and cuts short a potential continuation of bloodshed. Cain enjoys the blessing of progeny, by which we know that his sin has not in every respect separated him from human society and divine care.

Thus the totality of the primary and secondary effects, considered together, is the general relentlessness of the consequences of Cain's sin, and the limitation of these consequences by the Lord's care for his creature. The relentlessness is an aspect of the predictability necessary for the freedom to be morally responsible for one's actions. The limitation exemplifies that which transcends cause and effect, and without which Cain's sin would lead to his destruction.

***

81

One may see in Cain's murder of his brother an expression of the rivalry between those of arable land and those of pasture. To put this rivalry at the centre of interpretation is to miss the relationship between the narrative and that about Cain's parents. Since the couple in the Garden of Eden speak to us archetypically of the human condition, we may expect the same of the brothers. The particularities of social setting are then no more than tributary to a more general, more comprehensive matter.

The social aspect of the story of Cain's killing Abel may be put thus. The brothers were of the two basic occupations of inland peoples, and differences of occupation, giving differences of interest, may contribute to conflict or cause it. The story of the Garden of Eden is concerned with, among other things, humanity as a couple, male and female. The story of Cain is about siblings, and about people of different occupations and ways of life. Later, as will be seen, the Creation story brings to consideration people of different nations also.

This is not, of course, the only ancient mythology with a story of rivalry culminating in fratricide. Further, we can find other peoples among whom the murderer is a placeless vagrant, whom any may kill, but who can gain asylum under divine protection. All these possibilities of comparison may contribute to an understanding of the sources of material that might have been used in the making of our story. The story itself must, however, be interpreted in relation to its content and context as we now have it. The primary meaning of a story is what the story says it is, even if the art of the story makes alternative meanings possible. If outside material helps to provide meaning where none can be discerned, or if it is suggestive of interpretations consistent with the actual text, then it can be of literary usefulness. Otherwise the part it plays is historical and antiquarian, but not necessarily elucidatory. We do not gain a better understanding of *Macbeth* by using other sources on the history of Scotland to amend the play or say what it is 'really' about. The relevant historical context of the story of Cain is Israelite history at the time when the story acquired the form in which we know it. The difficulty is that, even if we were to know what that time was–knew, that is, according to the discipline of historical research,–we probably would not know the relevant particulars of the social or other history of the time. The origin of the material of the story and of the story itself has little bearing on its meaning.

The social meaning of the story of Cain and his murder must be sought within our material. Cain's killing is told within a narrative which presents, as the telling of Creation, a comprehensive philosophy. This philosophy is shown in the Hebrew scriptures to have certain implications, some of which we describe as 'social'. Indeed, the Creation story itself will have something to say about the nature of human society. Thus Cain gains a social context. To seek this context when we have met only one couple and two brothers, however, seems a trifle impatient.

***

One couple and two brothers, even if meagre as a social setting, are sufficient to provide a family background. If we go over Cain's story with an eye to his parents and brother, we may be able to add to our understanding of his sin. When the man blames the woman, the words he uses mark a change from when he awoke and declared 'bone of my bones'. When Cain is born, Eve speaks of herself as co-creatrix with the Lord (which she is) without mention of her husband. The meaning of this is not clear, and one should not make too much of it, since it may not be in itself significant. When, however, the mother calls her new-born son *ish* we have to notice something odd between mother and child. The word *ish,* as already noted, can represent a man or a husband, but never a boy-child, only an adult male. It is difficult not to suppose that the failure to take responsibility in the Garden of Eden has led to some loosening of the bonds between wife and husband, so that the mother has some free valencies, unsatisfied attachments, as it were, to direct towards her boy. (Midrash Rabbah* suggests that Adam is the 'man', whom the birth will win back, but would *qaniti,* 'I have got', then be *le mot juste?* I doubt it.)

A parent's love, if fully developed, rejoices in the child's eventual maturation, with the inevitable fledging, the separation that this entails. Love between spouses looks forward to permanent companionship. I make the point here only to clarify that these are distinct modes of loving. If the two ways of loving are different, then one cannot substitute for the other without the substitution itself having some effect. If Eve's love for Cain has some of the character that is appropriate to her love for Adam, how might Cain be affected?

The bond between spouses is exclusive. Biblical stories of men with more than one wife (there are not many) emphasise rather than contradict this; think of sad Leah (Genesis 29:23-35). The bond between mother and son, in its full development, is not exclusive, for there are father, brothers, sisters, and all the wider world for which parental care is a training. If Eve looks to Cain, from the start and in his growing, as a 'man', the man she has got, her man, the jealousy that Cain might feel towards his brother is to be expected. It is intolerable that Abel should do something better than he does, be more commended by their Creator than he is. It preys on Cain's mind; his fallen countenance stays fallen.

Abel, as noted, has no active part in the story, and his name, *Hevel* in the original, means 'vapour' or something insubstantial. If Cain projects the unacknowledged in himself on to his brother, which is possible because he fails to meet his real brother, then the Abel he sees is indeed vapour and insubstantial. When we create an enemy by projecting on to another the unacknowledged in ourselves, the other is not so much a fellow to us as an absolute enemy whom it is always justifiable to hurt or destroy. In a manner of speaking, we cease to see our offence against the enemy as sinful because we do not see the enemy as a real fellow human being. Cain, having kept his fallen countenance, cannot overcome the sin which is therefore present, since his perception of Abel prevents an appreciation of his brother's human worth and of the consequent enormity of the sin itself. Indeed, how can one sin against a mere vapour?

Killing, however, is real. It makes the victim real, flesh and blood, flesh and shed blood. Cain's lie to the Lord, his evasion on being questioned, shows him on the run from reality, looking for somewhere to hide. But the Lord makes him acknowledge what the ground and his brother's blood are saying. Cain, unable to continue his pretence of ignorance, fears the consequence of his deed (4:13,14). At last the mother's boy, her 'man', has no choice but to face reality. (Such mother 'love' is no love, for love has respect for the needs of the loved.)

Because of Cain's father the ground is cursed, but Cain is himself cursed out of the ground. A failure to fulfil one's humanity is one thing; a sinful deed goes further. Yet the one leads to the other. Cain alone, however, must take responsibility for his own deed, though the roots of our actions be not all in ourselves.

***

The natural history of Cain's sin, then, shows features of three kinds. First, there are those characteristics of sinning which are shown up by comparison between Cain and his parents. Secondly, there is the two-stage process of sinning: not correcting oneself (not lifting the fallen countenance), and then not overcoming the sin which presents itself because one has not corrected oneself. Thirdly, there is predisposition or the occasion of sin, not due to the sinner, which does not, in the story, diminish the sinner's responsibility. Characteristics of this third kind, together with the Lord's mitigation of the consequences of Cain's sin, reminds us not to be too simple in our view of sinning. Rather, it is an aspect of the art of the terse and compact narrative that it demonstrates the untidiness of its subject: the interplay of circumstance, personal responsibility, and divine mercy.

AFTER THE STORY of Cain and Abel, the biblical account of the Creation continues with Cain's descendants (Genesis 4:17-26). The family is presented in two ways, as a line of ancestors and descendants, and by descriptive notes and stories about particular people. The lineage forms a continuous thread, to which the other material is attached, or from which it sprouts. It is to this other material that attention will be paid now, immediately after the translation. It will be convenient to look at the family line later, when that of Seth is considered.

¹⁷ And Cain knew his wife, and she conceived, and she bore Enoch, and he was the builder of a city, and he called the name of the city after the name of his son, Enoch.

¹⁸ And to Enoch was born Irad,
And Irad fathered Mehuyael,
And Mehiyael [sic] fathered Metushael,
And Metushael fathered Lamech.

¹⁹ And Lamech took for himself two wives; the name of the one was Adah and the name of the other Zillah. ²⁰ And Adah bore Jabal; he was the forebear of the tent-dweller with cattle. ²¹ And the name of his brother is Jubal; he was the forebear of all who handle lyre and pipe. And Zillah, for her part, bore Tubalcain, the sharpener of every bronze or iron tool, and Tubalcain's sister is Naamah. ²³ And Lamech said to his wives:

'Adah and Zillah, hear my voice,

Wives of Lamech, give ear to my saying,

Because a man have I killed at my wounding,

A young one at my being bruised.

²⁴ For sevenfold shall Cain be avenged, but Lamech seventy-sevenfold'.

²⁵ And Adam knew his wife again, and she bore a son and called his name Seth (*Shet*). 'For God has set *(shat)* a seed'—another instead of Abel, for Cain killed him. ²⁶ And to Seth, him also, was born a son, and he called his name Enosh. Then calling on the LORD's name began.

This passage introduces city-building, and the origin of pastoral life, of instrumental music, of the smith's craft, and of calling upon the Lord's name. The initiatives are attributed to two lines, Cain's accounting for all but one, and Seth's for calling on the name of the Lord. It may be convenient to set these out on a family tree, as in Figure 7. It is not clear whether we should attribute both tillage and shepherding to Adam, or only the former. In either case they are reintroduced in the story of Cain and Abel. In Figure 7 the letter 'W' is used to stand for women who are assumed but not named.

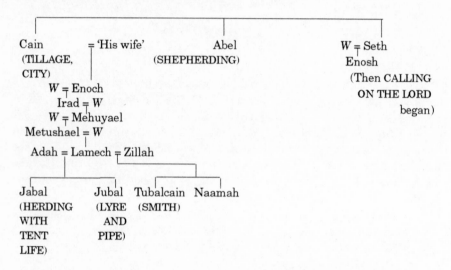

Fig. 7. *Family relationship between the authors of inventions*

The reader who wonders who married Cain and Seth, and whether they married their sisters, is referred to Ginzberg's* review of Jewish legends. On Cain's wife, more will be remarked shortly.

From Enoch to Metushael there is a series of names, giving a family line. In a genealogical series, stated without trimmings, the Hebrew scriptures normally provide a line of male names only. This is because, in many societies, and presumably in that in which this story arose, a genealogical lineage established rights of tillage and pasture, which were necessarily male occupations among the Israelites, as among others, whether there was female involvement or not. Thus, even when a genealogy was not used for this purpose, it was still a string of fathers and sons, since this had become the standard form of genealogies.

The initiatives by human characters amplify the notion of humankind as co-creator. In classical mythology Hephaestus brings metal working from heaven to earth, and the god Saturn teaches agriculture to the Italians. The Israelites, by attributing these arts to human agency, give a greater dignity to humanity. Inspiration needs somebody to be inspired, even if the inspiration is of divine origin.

***

86

This short passage has a number of interesting points. It may throw light on the meaning of the whole if these points are considered in turn.

First, I would revert to the question who Cain's wife is, since she is mentioned explicitly. When the story was first told or written in the form in which we have it, the matter of the origin of Cain's wife could hardly have gone unnoticed. The omission of a clue to the answer is therefore a deliberate feature of the telling. Thus we are reassured that to enquire whether, for example, Cain's wife is his sister can have no bearing on the purpose of the story. It is as though, on hearing that two is equal to one plus one, the listener were to enquire 'Do you mean two elms or two goats?' Some questions bore rather than illuminate. The interpretation of a painting, and the appreciation of it as it is, are not helped by scribbling in the spaces left by the artist. Better it is to see the spaces in relation to the rest of the picture, to see them as integral with the work as a whole.

The city which is built (verse 17) is not simply a set of structures for people to live in. A city in the Hebrew scriptures is a political unit, sometimes with its own king, having fields, orchards, and vineyards outside its walls, and likely to be self-sufficient in the necessities of life. To be the 'builder of a city' is not simply to lay stone on stone. It is to initiate a complex social organisation.

Concerning this city, some have argued that the text must here be corrupt, and that 'after the name of his son' should read 'after his name'. With this change the builder would be Enoch himself, not Cain. (Enoch's name, *Chanokh*, may be connected with *chanakh*, 'dedicate', also 'train', 'educate'.) The appeal to the ear of *boneh* ('the builder of') with *beno* ('his son') suggests, however, that 'his son' is not due to a scribal error. In either case, whether the builder is the farmer or the farmer's son, the close dependence of civic life on agriculture is implicit. The invention of tillage makes possible the invention of the city.

The story has already shown that the curse on Cain does not abrogate the blessing to be fruitful and increase. The enrichment of human life by the inventiveness and effort of Cain's family does not itself necessarily bear upon this matter but, if Cain is the builder of a city, the intention of the story seems to be that the curse on Cain does not prevent his making a contribution to civilisation. Can the meaning be that the one condemned to be 'a vagrant and a stray' on the ground out of which he is cursed is driven to seek, perhaps successfully, perhaps unsuccessfully, something that promises to separate his life somehow from the hostile earth? If this, in turn, means that city-building is being associated with Cain as a killer nowhere acceptable, have we here a tradition about the origin of city life comparable with the story that Rome was built to accommodate all who wanted to move in, irrespective of origin and personal history (Livy*, who says that this had been the ancient policy of the founders of cities)?

In verse 18 the names Irad, Mehuyael (of which Mehiyael is a variant), Metushael, and Lamech have been squeezed to the pips by scholars trying to extract meaning. Two of the names, Irad and Lamech, are probably not Hebrew at all, and none of the four have any obvious meaning for the listener or reader, although the element -*el* means 'God'. The impression of foreignness, to a Hebrew-speaker, given by a name such as Lamech, reinforces the universality of the telling of the Creation stories, which are concerned with the human condition. (The passages, later in the scriptures, about those people whose language is that of the scriptures themselves, rest on this universal philosophy, and cannot be understood without it.)

Although only a few characters in the Hebrew scriptures have more than one wife each, there is nothing remarkable, in the context of the book of Genesis, that Lamech should have two wives. It may, however, be suggestive to distinguish his children according to their mothers.

Adah's sons are orginators of nomadic herding and instrumental music. It is not clear whether we are to see the herding as a re-establishment of Abel's occupation, or whether we are to understand Abel's shepherding and Jabal's keeping of cattle as distinct. The word *ts'on*, 'flock' used of Abel's beasts, refers specifically to sheep, but the *miqneh*, 'cattle' of Jabal can include sheep with oxen and other beasts. Jubal's music is of the two anciently recognized kinds, string and wind. We may recollect the Greeks' contrast between Apollo's rational lyre and the orgiastic flutes of Dionysus, and there is a distinction, even if not exactly that in Greece, between the instruments' use in ancient Israel. The plucked string instrument, but not the pipe, entered Temple worship. Among the many uses of the flute, on the other hand, was music in prophecy (1 Samuel 10:5, where there are string instruments also), in popular celebration (1 Kings 1:40), and in worship outwith that in the Temple (Isaiah 30:29, which has lyres also). The association, through Adah, of instrumental music with herding in particular is not explicable with certainty, but may represent a tradition that instrumental music first arose among herdsmen, or that it is typical of herdsmen above all others.

Zillah's son Tubalcain is a smith. Smiths in ancient times, like tinkers down to the twentieth century, resembled herdsmen in being often nomadic. The word *nechoshet,* here translated as 'bronze', can mean copper also, and is commonly represented as 'brass' in the older translations. It is not surprising that bronze should be mentioned before iron here, since iron replaced bronze only slowly, and since, in the Hebrew scriptures, iron tends to be associated with things unpleasant, from ugliness to oppression and fighting, as Sawyer* has shown. However, iron came into use for sharp-edged implements and weapons more quickly than for other purposes, since its initial superiority over bronze was in the sharpness of edge and point of which it is capable. Thus the Philistine champion Goliath had bronze armour but an iron spearhead (1 Samuel 17:7) Nevertheless, Tubalcain was a sharpener of bronze as well as iron tools. This suggests that our story goes back not to the established iron age, but to the early days of iron-working, perhaps the 13th century B.C.E., when, archaeologically, Israel first emerges in Canaan (Coote and

Whitelam*), but our final version may incorporate this bronze-sharpening as an older fragment. The point is not to date the text, but to note how difficult it is to see its origins in the 'dark backward and abysm of time'.

Naamah stands as the culmination of Cain's line. She is part of the family pattern, in that Adah and Zillah alike have two children, and the second child of each is introduced rather similarly: 'and the name of his brother is Jubal', 'and Tubalcain's sister is Naamah'. Because Naamah is felt by the reader to belong to the pattern, it is arresting that she differs from her brother and half-brothers in that nothing is said about her. The effect is a kind of austerity, a pregnant silence, leaving the story of Cain's line open-ended, as it were, while we wait, with Naamah the focus of our waiting. It will be possible to speak further of her later, in connection with Noah.

In Lamech's boasting to his wives, in verse 23 and 24, he tells them that he has avenged himself, going beyond what the Lord has deemed necessary to protect Cain. Lamech arrogates to himself the retribution which has been the Lord's, and takes it on himself to exceed what the Lord would do. Further, Lamech reacts to an injury, while the Lord spoke to Cain conditionally about retribution, so as to protect. This bragging of lawless bloodshed is perhaps to be related to what has been said of Lamech's children. Does the placing of the boast in the telling, immediately after naming further increases in human skills and powers, make it into a comment on them? May this not be the overweening pride that follows success? In any case, we are not told the circumstances of the incident referred to in the boast; the point is simply that Lamech is proud of being a murderer, and in his pride brags to the women.

***

After telling of Cain's family, the narrative turns to Cain's brother, Seth. The presentation of the birth of Seth echoes that of the birth of Cain.

Birth of Cain	*Birth of Seth*
'Now the Adam knew Eve his wife, and she...bore...'	'And Adam knew his wife' again, and she bore...
The mother names the child.	The mother names the child.
The explanation of the name refers to the Lord.	The explanation of the name refers to God.

The hearer or reader is led by the similarity to make a comparison. It is true that certain features of these birth stories are common in the Hebrew scriptures, but the birth story of Cain is the first in Genesis, and the next is that of his brother, only eight verses later. They stand together, not lost in a mass of stylised similar examples. (The statement on Abel's birth carries no story.)

Instead of 'the Adam' we have 'Adam', putting the emphasis on its use as a personal name. This is because, as will soon be seen, it is to stand in a genealogy. (The naming of Cain's and Seth's parents has been discussed on pages 66-68.)

Correspondingly, the name 'Eve' is omitted on the second occasion, in accordance with the form of the genealogy which follows immediately; the restriction of formal genealogy to male names has been discussed on page 86.

The change of name for the Creator cannot be due to a change of writer. The source critics themselves attribute the two birth stories to one writer, 'J'. Even if there were two sources, however, the difference in meaning between the unpronounced name YHWH, 'Lord', and the title *Elohim*, 'God', would remain. The four-lettered name, the tetragrammaton, while associated with immediacy and awe, is intensely personal. On the other hand *Elohim* is also a word for 'judges' or 'rulers', and represents the Deity as the world's creator and judge. The change in naming of the Creator corresponds to the contrast between the intimacy of 'I have got a man with the Lord' and the cool 'God has set a seed', in which the speaker, Eve, does not mention herself.

The text gives Eve a particular reason for choosing the name Seth (*Shet*), but *shet* can mean 'foundation'. As the story will continue, the aptness of this meaning will also become evident.

The name Enosh, in verse 26, means 'humankind', just as does the name Adam. Enosh is not, except in this story, a Hebrew personal name; the same is, as already noted, true of Adam (except in the most modern usage). The effect of the equivalence of the two names will be looked at when Seth's descendants are considered.

In the sentence 'Then calling on the Lord's name began' (verse 26), the word 'then' clearly refers to the birth of Enosh. There are two contrasts. First, the listener or reader will recall Cain's 'From your face I shall hide myself'; calling upon the Lord's name is the opposite of hiding oneself from the Lord's face. Secondly, we have just heard Eve call the Deity 'God', having previously said 'Lord' in the earlier, parallel story. Now, at the birth of Enosh (the new 'humankind'), the name translated 'Lord' returns, and as the subject of comment. The word *huchal,* here translated 'began' can also mean recommenced. As Cassuto* points out, biblical Hebrew may have a single word for an action performed for the first time and for its repetition, so that *banah,* for example can mean both 'build' and 'rebuild'.

90

THE ACCOUNT of the Creation continues, in Chapter 5 of Genesis, with a genealogy giving the ten generations from Adam to Noah. In this passage as now set out the numbers have been translated more literally than good English requires; this is in order to make a point later about the form of the numbers. To bring out the recurrent pattern in the descriptions of the generations, the ending of each line has been made to correspond with the punctuation given by the musical tropes used in reading the Hebrew.

¹ This is the book of the generations of Adam.

In the day that God created humankind (*adam*),
In the likeness of God he created it,
² Male and female he created them,
And he blessed them and called their name Humankind (*Adam*),
In the day when he caused them to become created.

3 And Adam lived thirty and a hundred years
And fathered in his own likeness, after his image,
⁴ And called his name Seth.
And the days of Adam after he fathered Seth were eight hundred years,
And he fathered sons and daughters.
⁵ And all the days of Adam which he lived were nine hundred years and thirty years,
And he died.

⁶ And Seth lived five years and a hundred years
And fathered Enosh.
⁷ And Seth lived after he fathered Enosh seven years and eight hundred years,
And he fathered sons and daughters.
⁸ And all the days of Seth were twelve years and nine hundred years,
And he died.

⁹ And Enosh lived ninety years
And fathered Kenan.
¹⁰ And Enosh lived after he fathered Kenan fifteen years and eight hundred years,
And he fathered sons and daughters.

[11] And all the days of Enosh were five years and nine hundred years,
And he died.

[12] And Kenan lived seventy years
And fathered Mahalal'el.

[13] And Kenan lived after he fathered Mahalal'el forty years and eight hundred years,

[14] And he fathered sons and daughters.
And all the days of Kenan were ten years and nine hundred years,
And he died.

[15] And Mahalal'el lived five years and sixty years

[16] And fathered Jared.
And Mahalal'el lived after he fathered Jared thirty years and eight hundred years,
And he fathered sons and daughters.

[17] And all the days of Mahalal'el were five and ninety years and eight hundred years,
And he died.

[18] And Jared lived two and sixty years and a hundred years

[19] And fathered Enoch.
And Jared lived after he fathered Enoch eight hundred years,

[20] And he fathered sons and daughters.
And all the days of Jared were two and sixty years and nine hundred years,
And he died.

[21] And Enoch lived five and sixty years

[22] And fathered Methuselah.
And Enoch walked with God after he fathered Methuselah three hundred years,
And he fathered sons and daughters.

[24] And all the days of Enoch were five and sixty years and three hundred years
And Enoch walked with God and he was not, for God took him.

[25] And Methuselah lived seven and eighty years and a hundred years

[26] And fathered Lamech.
And Methuselah lived after he fathered Lamech two and eighty years and seven hundred years,

[27] And he fathered sons and daughters.
And all the days of Methuselah were nine and- sixty years and nine hundred years,
And he died.

[28] And Lamech lived two and eighty years and a hundred years
And fathered a son.
And he called his name Noah (*Noach*), saying 'This one will comfort us (*yenachamenu*) from our works and from our hands' toil, which is from the ground the LORD cursed'.

[30] And Lamech lived after he fathered Noah five and ninety years and five

hundred years,
³¹ And he fathered sons and daughters.

And all the days of Lamech were seven and twenty years and seven hundred years,
And he died.

³² And Noah was five hundred years old,
And Noah fathered Shem, Ham, and Japhet.

As explained on p.86, a biblical genealogy is a series of male names, with no women. The effect here is to make a readily felt distinction from the preceding lineage, that of Cain, which is presented not only as a genealogy but also with narrative, so that the account of that family includes mention of women. The general effect is that the telling of the history of Seth's line, after that of Cain's, seems masculine to the extent of making a point. Later this difference between the two lines and the story's accounts of them will be taken up again.

The numbers in this genealogy are given in ascending order, units before tens and tens before hundreds. In scripture this way of writing numbers is characteristic of lists and statistics, as opposed to telling about characters and events. Thus the form of the numbers agrees with the formal genealogical style. The one exception, Adam's total life-span, will be noted soon, below.

Each generation is similarly described, with six elements, which are, in order

- length of life before fathering a son,

- the fathering of the son and his name,

- length of life after fathering the son,

- 'and he fathered sons and daughters',

- total life-span,

- 'and he died'.

The regularity of the pattern, generation after generation, each described according to the same formula, shows up those features of the story which do not conform to the pattern. Such features will now be considered in the order in which they appear.

***

'This is the book of the generations of Adam.' The expression 'These are the generations of...' always introduces a newly begun section of scripture. The word 'book' indicates that the earliest form of this passage, as far as the story-teller is concerned is written; he does not consider himself to be reproducing what has thus far been oral. The change from 'the Adam' to 'Adam' has been discussed already in certain respects, and is also functional in this particular context. The plain 'Adam', having therefore the form of a personal name, is appropriate to a genealogy.

In the second verse, however, *adam* is referred to by 'them' or 'their' and therefore means not an individual but 'humankind'. The force of bringing Adam, represented as an individual, into the lineage of *adam,* and as its first member, is to bring out and declare the family relationship of humankind and its unity of origin. Since the Creation story is about the world as it is, however, unity of origin in the story has implications beyond any question of origin.

In verse 1 the phrase 'In the day that…'means simply 'when'. This is normal in scripture and outside it, in Hebrew of the biblical periods. The expression has already occurred with this sense in Genesis 2:4, at the beginning of the story of the Adam and the couple in the Garden of Eden (pages 40 and 48).

In the first two verses there are four echoes of earlier parts of the Creation narrative. 'The likeness of God', 'male and female he created them', and 'he blessed them' are each repeated from the creation of humankind on the sixth of the seven days, while 'In the day when he caused them to become created' *(be-yom hibar'am)* harks back to 'when they were created' *(be-hibar'am)* in Genesis 2:4, at the opening of the story of the Garden of Eden. The source critics, noting the continuity between the telling of the seven days and this presentation of the generations from Adam to Noah, attribute both to a single author, who is other than that of the passages between them. For us, however, the art is in the writing as we have it. In this way the passages between are firmly integrated with the opening of Genesis and with what is said of the line through Seth. Whatever the origins of the text, it comes to us as something to be taken as a whole.

One effect of this sandwich structure, and it need not be due to multiple authorship, is that Seth's birth is given twice. At the end of the story of Cain's killing his brother (4:25), it is said that Eve bore Seth and named him. Now, in 5:3, Adam names Seth. The mother names the child on bearing him, the father in association with fathering him. (Naming by the mother is commoner in scriptural stories of begetting and birth.) There are two points of view. For the mother, who has lost her son Abel, the newly born child is God's gift of another seed. Adam's naming of his son is in the context of future lineage. The female context is one of restoring foundations, the male context is of the restored foundation in relation to continuity. Eve's naming is given, by the writer, intimacy and warmth. Adam's naming, because of its setting, has a certain formality.

If the passage now under consideration is compared with the account of Creation's sixth day, of which it has echoes, there is one striking new feature: God names humankind. Now we have seen that naming can have either of two imports. Adam names the beasts at discretion, but calls the woman 'woman'. after the story has said that this what she is, and calls her 'Eve' because she already has the nature that 'Eve' represents. In the naming of humankind, this passage and the telling of the sixth day's work speak of humankind, using that term (i.e. *adam*) before the act of naming is mentioned. The implication is that God, in naming humankind, is recognizing the nature which it already has as a result of God's creating it. The naming is a recognition, like Adam's naming of Eve. As such, it is proper to the dignity of being made in the image of God.

It is somewhat arresting to read that Adam 'fathered in his own likeness, after his image'. The wording is that used in Genesis 1:26 (p. 7) where God says 'Let us make humankind in our image, according to our likeness', except that the words translated 'image' and 'likeness' are reversed in their order. The echo is striking to the reader or listener. Adam is said to do for Seth what God does for humankind. The effect is to emphasise the place of humankind as co-creator. Or to put it the other way round, the transmission of the human form between generations is made a model or analogy for the genetic relation between God and humanity.

In all this passage, with its genealogy, Adam's 'nine hundred years and thirty years' is the only number in descending form, that is, with the hundreds before the tens. This is in keeping with the inclusion of narrative details about Adam within the bare genealogical form. Later members of the lineage have narrative details woven into the genealogy, but the account of Adam is exceptional in the exalted style of its opening, in verses 1 and 2.

The five generations from Seth to Jared, which now follow, are given according to the regular pattern, with its six elements. About Jared's son, Enoch, however, there is additional information. First it is said that 'Enoch walked with God', and then that 'Enoch walked with God and he was not, for God took him'. This last sentence replaces the generally recurring 'And he died'. The word for 'walk' here is that used for 'move' when 'they heard the Lord God's voice moving in the garden' (3:8). The expression 'walked with God', in verse 22, must refer to righteous living, since this its undoubted meaning later, when it is used of Noah (6:9). When 'walked with God' is said the second time, in verse 24, it must still imply righteousness but be considered also in its coupling with 'and God took him'. The statement 'and he was not' need, in itself, mean no more than that he died, but the entire expression 'and he was not, for God took him' represents a death not like that of other people, a death within God's special care. The terseness here perhaps leaves more unsaid than is said. Abundant legend and homiletic about Enoch has explored ways of making the unsaid explicit. The curious reader can find non-scriptural material in Ginzberg*, and in books attributed to Enoch and named after him, but written after the scriptural books.

The notice of Lamech's life has inserted into it a sentence (verse 29) on the naming of his son Noah. The explanation and name are not in agreement, as has been noticed for centuries. Noah's name could be more easily referred to the verb *nuach,* 'rest' while the word *yenachamenu,* 'he will comfort us', might suggest a name such as Menachem or Nachman. For this reason there is a legend that Noah was also called Menachem (Ginzberg*). The reference, in verse 29, to the curse on the ground, because of Adam, and to relief from it, looks forward perhaps to the Lord's saying to Noah that he will no more curse the ground 'because of the Adam' (8:21). More generally, Lamech's prophecy makes the point that, as humankind passes through its generations, even the drawbacks of the human condition are not necessary causes for hopelessness.

***

The enormous life-spans in this lineage surely require some comment. Except for Enoch, all the ten from Adam to Noah live between seven-hundred-and-fifty and one thousand years. In a later section of the Hebrew scriptures we find a run of patriarchs, matriarchs, leaders, and teachers, from Abraham to Moses and Joshua, whose ages at death lie between 110 and 180 years. Between Noah and Abraham, that is, between these two groups, is a series of ages diminishing somewhat irregularly to provide a transition. After Moses and Joshua life-spans are such as we are familiar with to-day, David's seventy years being typical; Psalm 90:10 also takes this as a normal age at which to die. So we have four groups: up to and including Noah, then a transitional group followed by a patriarchal series of centenarians, and finally those whose ages would be ordinary in twentieth-century lands fortunate enough to be free of famine. Figure 8 sets out these groups with the named individuals in the order in which they appear in the scriptural story. Shem is presented as intermediate between two groups, to both of which he may fairly considered to belong.

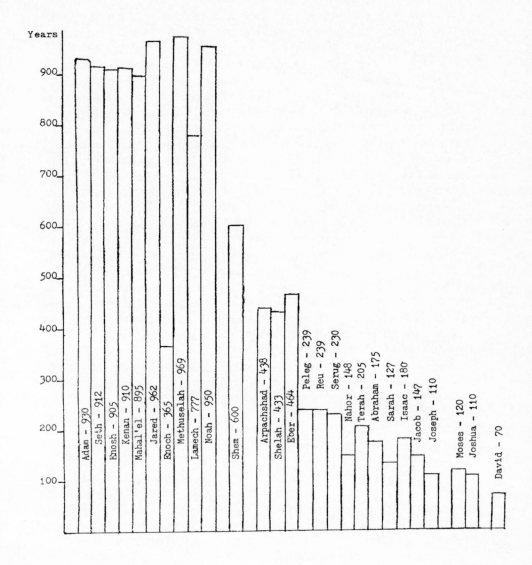

Fig. 8. *Life-spans before and after the Flood*

To take the groups in reverse order, there is no need to comment on that of which David is typical. The individuals from Abraham to Joseph have life-spans comparable with those of twentieth-century centenarian communities, such as the Hunza of northern Kashmir, the Avkhazians of Soviet Georgia, and the people of a cluster of villages in Loja Province, Ecuador. (One source for these is David Davies*; since he wrote, the communities of the Ecuadorian centenarians have been disrupted by road-building.) Even in these centenarian communities life-spans like those of Abraham and Isaac are not to be expected, however. Passing through the intermediate group, back to Noah, we come to those whose ages at death are given in the scriptural passage under consideration. These are said to have lived to ages unknown among mammals, whether human or not.

One mode of comment on the long lives of the antediluvians is to take them as a borrowing from Sumerian and Babylonian stories. This does not get us much farther. The differences between the Hebrew and the Mesopotamian Creation and Flood stories means that, if the Israelite writer (or writers) used Sumerian or Babylonian material, there was selection and creative incorporation of the material into something new, not indiscriminate borrowing. The Israelite account, if it presents us with borrowings, still leaves us to ask why this or that was borrowed. Further, the similarities are only partial. Although some Mesopotamian versions, but not all, have ten generations up to the Flood, the names do not correspond with the series in Genesis, and the Sumerian and Babylonian accounts have lists of kings, not simple ancestral lines, as in the Hebrew scriptures. What is more to the point is that life-spans are grossly different. The Hebrew text has ages of less than a thousand years at death, while the antediluvian kings in the Sumerian and Babylonian accounts each live for tens of thousands of years. Comparison of the Hebrew scriptures with other writings may help us to historical conclusions about style and form, but they do not explain why the ages reached in the line from Adam to Noah are what they are.

Cassuto* has tried to show that the ages, taken simply as numbers, can be related by rules which involve multiplication and addition. However, the rules must be considered as loosely applied or needing subsidiary rules to deal with exceptions. By taking the numbers not from the Hebrew but from an old translation, such as the Greek Septuagint, no better patterning becomes evident. It is my own opinion that there is no arithmetical relationship, which has the elegance to be convincing, between the life-spans in this genealogy,

Nevertheless there are two observations that can be made about these late fatherings and, more particularly, long lives. First, they suggest a world which was 'other', a world to which our experience of humankind cannot be applied in its everyday concrete particulars. Secondly, it is general in the Hebrew scriptures that longevity is associated with righteousness. This is not to say that the righteous never die young nor the wicked old. Rather, righteousness is often enough coupled with dying old for the two to be felt as appropriately belonging together. By using longevity to suggest otherness, the telling indicates at the same time that the generations from Adam to Noah are to be considered as, in general, righteous.

***

Most members of this lineage have similar life-spans. The exceptions are Enoch, Lamech, and Shem. (Ham's and Japhet's ages at death are never stated, but Shem's is given in a later passage.) Of the other eight lives, the longest, that of Methuselah, is only 8.3 per cent longer than the shortest, that of Mahalal'el. It is evident that all these eight life-spans are much of a much-ness, and are all somewhat short of a thousand years. All are in the nine-hundreds, leaving aside Mahalal'el's 895 years.

A period of one thousand years is used twice in the Hebrew scriptures to represent a period of the greatest length of imagined experience. Ecclesiastes (6:6) meditates on one who lives among transient things: 'were he to live a thousand years twice over he would not see good'. Note how the manner of expression, 'a thousand years twice over' rather than 'two thousand years', makes the thousand-year period the unit of discourse. Psalm 90 (at verse 4) says to the Lord 'For a thousand years in thy sight are like a day which is already yesterday'. It is as though the men from Adam to Noah are being given the longest life-spans short of that thousand years which is the limit of imaginable experience. Fantastic figures are thus still humanly imaginable, still within the proverbial thousand years. Like the inventors in Cain's line, these are human.

At this point it may be convenient to have the life-spans set out in a chart as in Figure 9 overleaf. In the chart each life line is broken by the age at the son's birth, while the number under a life line is the total of the years of life.

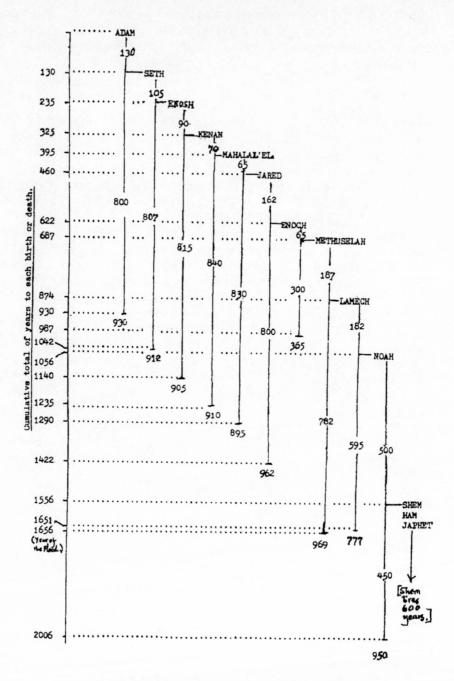

Fig. 9. *Time-chart of the generations before the Flood.*

If, on this diagram, a ruler is laid on the beginnings of most of the lives, and another on their ends, then two can be seen to be approximately parallel. This is to say in another way what has already been pointed out, that eight of the members of the lineage have approximately similar life-spans. Against this regularity, certain individuals have peculiarities to which attention can now be given.

If seventy years, David's life-span, is taken to be normal, as in the Psalms (90:10), Adam's years are short of a thousand by just this amount. A legendary comment on this is that Adam gave up the seventy years needed for David. The number of years of Jared's life after fathering Enoch is the same as the number in Adam's life after fathering Seth. Enoch's years equal in number the days in a year. Thus, although Enoch has a much shorter life that any other member of the series, there is a suggestion that it has completeness in some special respect. Methuselah dies in the year of the Flood. If, as already suggested, longevity is to be associated with righteousness, we may suppose, in the light of biblical passages yet to be considered, that the intention is to represent Methuselah as dying just before the Flood, not being drowned in it. Lamech's 777 years can hardly be unrelated to the importance of the number seven, already met with in the days of the Creation. The years of Lamech's life before fathering Noah equal in number the whole days in half a year. Noah has his sons much later in life than do his forebears. The wording seems to suggest that Noah fathered three sons in the same year. However, it is later made plain that the sons are not triplets (10:21). This should be a warning against deforming meaning with a certain kind of literalism. Shem, at six hundred, has a shorter life than any of Seth's line born before the Flood (except Enoch). This might be seen as related to his double aspect; he is antediluvian by birth, and also is ancestral to nations which repopulate the earth after the Flood.

At this point, of course, the Flood itself has not yet appeared in the scriptural narrative. It is, however, convenient to anticipate, while hoping that anticipation will not cause difficulty.

IT IS OBVIOUS that the names of Cain's descendents and of Seth's resemble each other. Not only do two names, Enoch and Lamech, appear in each genealogy, but others resemble each other more than can reasonably be attributed to coincidence: Metushael and Methuselah (*Metushelach* in the Hebrew), for example. Modern commentators generally explain these resemblances by source criticism. That is to say, they suppose that a single ancestry of mankind appeared in two versions, which were later put together. This is an historical explanation, but it is not adequate from a literary point of view. Since the resemblances between the two lines must always have been obvious, what possible intended meaning could there be in combining them so that, for example, there are two Lamechs with apparently different characters? To conclude, perhaps quite reasonably, that we have two Lamechs because we have two sources, does not explain why the two sources should have been combined in a way that presents two distinct lineages with obviously similar names.

The writing flaunts a combination of the similarity of the names with the distinctness of the lines. Let us take this as a challenge, and confront the challenge by setting out the lineages as in Figure 10, so as to preserve their distinctness while emphasising the similarities. (Where, in Figure 10, the customary English differs from the Hebrew form of the name, an approximation to the latter is added, in brackets.) The big 'X' between the lineages indicates the exchange necessary if each pair of similar names is to lie in one generation. The double line between Naamah and Noah is broken, to indicate that their being spouses is not in scripture, but comes from other tradition; this will be discussed later. As the figure shows, the line from Adam to the children of Adah and Zillah has fewer generations than that from Adam to Noah, but Noah is in the same generation as the last of Cain's line if one places Adam opposite his grandson Enosh. It is this manoeuvre that pairs similar names within each generation. 'Adam' and ' Enosh' are similar in meaning, and in three of the generations the correspondences Qayin-Qeynan, Metushael-Metushelach, and Lamech-Lamech appear.

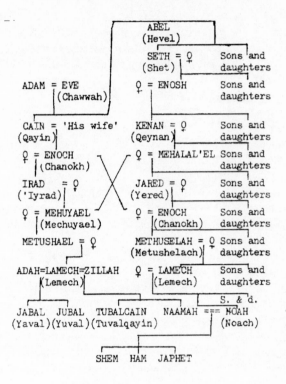

Fig. 10. *The two lines from Adam*

The tension between distinctness and resemblance may perhaps be felt more strongly if the generations are each taken in turn, beginning with that of Adam and Enosh.

Both 'Adam' and 'Enosh' mean 'humankind' or 'person'. They are common words, with these meanings in Hebrew, scriptural and down to the present day. Nowhere are these words found in classical Hebrew as proper names, except for the one example of each here in the Creation story. It may of interest to compare the origins of Adam and of Enosh, according to the Creation story.

The Adam (i.e. humankind) is made in the likeness of God, who names him.	Seth is gendered in the likeness of one of his parents and is named by both, being 'set' there, as his mother says, by God.
From this total Adam arises the individual Adam.	Seth fathers Enosh.

103

Cain (*Qayin*) and Kenan (*Qeynan*) are forms of one name. The meaning of *Qayin* is not certain, despite Eve's pun on it. Some refer it to a weapon or tool, others to the smith that makes them. The text makes no special comment on Kenan, but he follows Enosh, just as Cain follows Adam.

The name 'Enoch' (*Chanokh*) strongly suggests 'dedicate' (*chanakh*), but the matter is unclear, since the name is not obviously a part of the verb. In Cain's line Enoch's name is given to a city. In Seth's line the Enoch is noted for righteousness ('walked with God') and closeness to God at death ('walked with God, and was not, for God took him'). One Enoch is associated with action, but without indication of the moral worth of the action. The other Enoch is commended ethically, but without the mention of any specific action.

Irad (*'Iyrad*) has a name opening with the gutteral sound, indicated by the letter *ayin* (shown here by the inverted comma), which Jared (*Yered*) lacks. Nevertheless, the similarity seems beyond coincidence, and one of the sounds anciently represented by the *ayin* was quite light. Neither name has an obvious meaning, although *yered* might remind one of *yarad*, 'go down'. However, *'Irad* is probably not of Hebrew origin, and the other name need not be so either.

Mehuyael (*Mechuyael*) and Mehiyael (*Mechiyael*) are two forms of the same name, both occurring in the text. The ending -*el* would mean 'God', but the meaning of the rest of the name is not strikingly obvious if one is thinking in Hebrew, and the name could be from a related language. Mahalal'el's name, on the other hand, could be understood in Hebrew to mean 'the praiser of God'. If this is so, then we have, as with Enoch, a suggestion of piety in the line through Seth.

In Metushael and Methuselah (*Metushelach*) the element *metu* can mean 'the man of...' in Akkadian, the language of Babylonia and Assyria, in which *sha*- can mean 'of' (as in some Canaanite dialects). In this way Metushael's name could mean 'the man of God'. This is quite speculative, however. A similar treatment of *Metushelach* would give 'man of Shelach'; Shelach occurs in the Hebrew scriptures as an individual, and perhaps the name of a nation (Genesis 10:24, 11:12-15, 1 Chronicles 1:18,24).

The difference between Lamech who boasts of violence and Lamech who prophesies a change in the human condition is conspicuous in the story. Once again, there is piety in Seth's line. The children of the boaster, however, are credited with useful arts such as are never mentioned in connection with the descendants of Adam through Seth. The names Adah and Zillah (*Tsillah*) may mean 'ornament' and (musical) 'ringing' respectively, referring to beauty seen and beauty heard.

The names of Jabal (*Yaval*) and Jubal (*Yuval*), as well as the first element in the name of Tubalcain (*Tuvalqayin*) may perhaps be connected with *yevul*, the noun for 'yield' or 'produce'. On the other hand, *Yuval* may originally have had some relation to 'Jubilee' (in fact, a ram's horn for blowing, by which the Jubilee year was signalled, Leviticus 25:9), since Jubal is 'the forebear of all who handle lyre and pipe'. 'Naamah' is a female name apparently based on *na'im*, 'pleasant', 'lovely', 'sweet-sounding'. (The name 'Naomi' has a similar connotation, for the same reason, giving rise to Naomi's way of expressing her grief, in Ruth 1:20.)

Noah's name is explained in the text itself (5:29), and comment on the explanation has been made on p. 95.

As already remarked (p.88), the use of non-Hebrew names in a Hebrew Creation narrative is in accord with the character of the story as universal in its bearing on the world and on the human condition.

The scriptural text does not name Noah's wife. There is a tradition (given, for example, by Rashi* on Genesis 4:22) that Noah was Naamah's husband. As far as the scriptural story is concerned, Naamah has the last name in the account of Cain's descendants, and is mentioned without comment just after information has been given about several other characters, including Naamah's brothers. The effect is of open-endedness, with the reader left to wonder who Naamah is, apart from her family relationships. Now we find that a view of the two human lines that gives the greatest possible pairing of. similar names in single generations, brings Naamah and Noah, himself the climax of the story of the line through Seth, into the same generation. Later, a positive reason for scripture's not naming Noah's wife will be given, but this must wait until after the story of the Flood has been considered.

***

Having put the two lines of Adam and Eve's descendants side by side, and having then examined them generation by generation, it is now possible to see in what respects the lines differ. Comparisons between the two lineages, each taken as a whole, can fall into three groups, those in the fields of activities, of relationship with the earth, and with sexual polarity.

Cain's sin and Lamech's glorification of vengeful violence can be set against the piety of the Enoch or Lamech in the line through Seth. In this way one can be represented as a family of wrong-doers, the other as a family of the righteous. This is the distinction that has long been made by commentators. There is, however, a catch in this generalisation, as there usually is in life when we group people into baddies and goodies. The catch is simply this: Cain's descendants are active in many inventions, and to generalise that this family's activities are bad is to suggest that these inventions are bad rather than good. It is true that the city, nomadic herding, metallurgy, and instrumental music might be used to further what most would regard as unrighteous purposes. What classes of human invention cannot be so used?

The overall picture of Cain's line is of action. A city is built, and herding, metallurgy, and music are pursued. Nevertheless Cain is a murderer and his descendant Lamech boasts of violence. There is a ferment of action, sometimes destructive, but by no means invariably. Action, however, is just what does not come into the account of the line from Seth to Lamech, just as there is no mention of righteousness in the account of the line from Cain to the children of the other Lamech. Cain's family are depicted as rich in human urges which, unguided, are variable in outcome. Seth's family are described as having commendable principles but no urges for them to guide. The. activities of the two human lines are complementary.

This complementarity is close to the rabbinical doctrine of the good and evil impulses. According to this, each human being has both, and needs to make the good impulse prevail. The two impulses are not, however, opposed to each other. The evil impulse is not effectively evil in the presence of the activity of the good impulse. Indeed, the evil impulse is required for necessary and wholly good activities. Therefore it is said that God is to be worshipped with both impulses, the evil as well as the good, and that the wise and righteous have the strongest evil impulse. This point has already been made on p. 34, where reference was made to God as author of good and evil alike, discussed on p. 15.

What we have here is not an opposition of good and bad, but a division between good and bad in the sense in which they are equally necessary for completeness, for the fulfilment of the image of God. This is a tension that is relaxed, not when good overcomes evil, but when good and evil are one in wholeness. William Blake* wrote of 'the Antediluvians who are our Energies'.

***

Thus the two lines differ in their activities. They differ also in their relationship to the earth.

Cain tills, Abel shepherds, Jabal herds cattle, and Tubalcain works the yield of the earth's ores. These are people of the soil. In contrast to Cain's family history, what we are told of Seth and his descendants touches ground only when Lamech prophesies about his son, and that is not what one would call a hands-on kind of earthiness.

The third difference between the lines is in their sexual bias. In that each is presented as a genealogy, its very form introduces a male framework. However, on this framework the two family histories are differently constructed. In the account of Seth and his descendants there are no women, so that the formal maleness of the genealogical form is left to male emphasis. The difference begins with the birth stories. Cain's birth story includes his mother and father, both by name (4:1). Seth has two birth stories; in the first (4:25) the mother's name is not given and in the second (5:3) she is not mentioned at all. After the births of Cain and Seth, the account of the latter's family has not a single reference to a woman. In Cain's family it is to his wives that Lamech boasts, and in Naamah that the lineage culminates. The arts which are mentioned in connection with Cain's line each arise from the initiative of a man, but this cannot be otherwise since, at the time of writing, these arts were certainly all male occupations. Nevertheless, every initiator of an art is the son of a named mother. Given the formally determined character of a genealogy and the distribution of occupations between the sexes, the story of Cain's family makes women nevertheless important, while that of Seth's family consistently excludes them.

THE FAILURE of Adam and Eve to take responsibility, Cain's sin against his brother, his rejection by the ground, and the manipulation of the ground by one human line while the ground is of little recorded concern to the other—all these are divisions. It is possible to argue that they arise each from the previous one, as when I speculated how Cain's character might be traceable to Eve's attitude to him, which can be related in turn to her relationship with Adam, due to the manner of his failing to answer for himself. However, the series of divisions is there, whether we make one the cause of the next, or whether we do not. If we do, then perhaps Cain's building a city on the ground, Jabal's grazing it, and Tubalcain's working of its ores, are a manipulative reaction to the rift due to Cain's being cursed out of the ground. In any case, the text has brought the story to a point at which there is a line of earthy activity stemming from Cain.

Correspondingly, it may be said that Seth is born as a substitute for a murdered brother who can remain only as a memory. (Recognized as a substitute, rather than for himself, 4:25, he would be necessarily an idealised character in his mother's eyes.) Whether or not one views Seth in this way, the story of his descendants emphasises an unearthy, unapplied, righteousness. The contrast with Cain's line is there, however we may or may not interpret clues in the narrative as suggestions about how the difference arose.

The voice of God's earth creature, the snake, came to the woman. The voice in the breeze time of the day came to the man before the woman, although the story suggests that they were present together. If the earthy is to be associated with the female and the unearthy with the male, the distinction is reinforced by the absence of female characters in the story of Seth's line, and their importance in the story of Cain's.

Those things that can be constructive when complementing each other need not be so when separated. If there is piety in Seth's line, on what does it act? If there are urges and actions in the story of Cain's line, what is there to prevent their being manifested in behaviour such as Lamech boasted of?

Against this background of split humanity, the Hebrew scriptures take up their story in Chapter 6 of Genesis.

[1] And it came to pass, when humankind began to increase on the face of the ground, and daughters were born to them,[2] that the sons of God saw the daughters of humankind that they were good to look at, and they took for themselves wives of whomever they chose.

[3] And the LORD said 'My spirit shall not abide in humankind for ever, for they are indeed flesh, and their days shall indeed be a hundred and twenty years.'

[4] The Nephilim were on the earth in those days (and afterwards also) when the sons of God came into the daughters of humankind, who bore sons to them. These are the mighty ones of old, men of renown.

[5] And the LORD saw that the wickedness of humankind was great in the earth, and that every devising of the thoughts of their heart was only evil, continually. And the LORD was sorry that he had made humankind upon the earth, and it grieved his heart.

[7] And the LORD said 'I will wipe out humankind, which I have created, from the face of the earth, from human being to beast, to creeping thing, and to the flier in the sky, for I am sorry that I have made them'.

[8] But Noah found grace in the eyes of the LORD.

The wording of this passage has a quality of strangeness. Who are these sons of God? They are represented here as perhaps different from humanity. If they are from some older telling, why are they here, without the context of their own story? Or was this context well known and orally transmitted when this written narrative first had its present form? Again, who are the Nephilim? At the only other scriptural mention of them (Numbers 13:33) their name is used for giants, reported by the dishonest members of the reconnoitring party of the Israelites approaching Canaan.

Stranger perhaps is the feeling that may be excited by a reversal of the Creation, or at least of its later works. The mention of one human being alone, Noah, as an exception casts a small-centred beam that throws the Lord's dark resolution into relief.

To say that these things are from older material does not explain what they are doing brought together in the story as we have it. The partial reversal of the Creation is a major theme in the Flood story which follows. The mention of the sons of God and of the Nephilim puts that Flood itself into a context of strange things in 'the dark backward and abysm of time'. We are reminded to ask ourselves what kind of discourse this is, we are reminded that the rules for judging it true or false need not be those applicable to archival history or analytical chemistry, and we are reminded to understand before we oppose or dismiss. We may, even if rarely, respond inexpressibly with something between a thrill and a shudder.

Unavoidably, a writing in such a style has phrases and statements which come to understanding only after we direct our consideration. Before reviewing the general pattern of the passage, therefore, attention will be given to a few of the possible difficulties.

***

The first difficulty is in elucidating who 'the sons of God' are. Five explanations have been put forward. (1) Some have taken 'the sons of God' to be angels. However, in the Hebrew scriptures, and especially in the Pentateuch, the five first books, an angel is just what the Hebrew word for 'angel' (*mal'akh*) means, 'a messenger', 'one sent'. An angel comes in human form, and can be a human being with God's message, a prophet (e.g. Isaiah 44:26). If a *mal'akh* is probably not human then it is always singular, as in 'the angel of God'. The biblical (not later) notion of an angel does not include heavenly beings, also biblical, such as cherubim and seraphim. The matter is difficult, but there is no use of 'sons of God' in scripture when the meaning is certainly 'angels'. The slight possibility of this meaning remains, perhaps, although it would here imply heavenly beings of a particular sex, otherwise unknown in the Hebrew scriptures. (2) The phrase 'the sons of' can, in biblical Hebrew, mean 'beings of the general kind of'. This would make 'the sons of God' themselves gods, as in non-Israelite Canaanite writings. This meaning is very difficult to accept alongside everything else in the Creation story, and in the rest of the Hebrew scriptures, which presents and assumes God as solitary,. single, and supreme. The 'sons of gods' (*b'nei elim*) in Psalm 29:1 are not divinities, as can be seen from the use of the same expression in Psalm 89:7(6); in the latter they may be astronomical bodies worshipped by non-Israelites. (3) The scriptural book of Job, 1:6, has 'sons of God' as members of God's heavenly court, who attend him. (4) It has been suggested that 'sons of God' means the righteous, and that the righteousness of Seth's line was lost by miscegenation with Cain's. This is against what the writing says. The term 'daughters of humankind' has no connotation of unrighteousness whatever, and it will be seen shortly that it is the 'sons of God', not the 'daughters of humankind', who are presented by the story as unrighteous. (5) The Hebrew word for 'God' (*Elohim*) can mean 'judges' or 'rulers'. It has been proposed that 'the sons of God' are those with status and power, and that 'the daughters of humankind' should be understood as 'the women of the common people'. This explanation has at least the merit that it is compatible with the sexuality and unrighteousness (soon to be discussed) of 'the sons of God'. The difficulty is that, although the Hebrew words for 'God' and 'humankind' (*adam*) can bear these meanings, such meanings do not occur elsewhere in the Creation narrative of the first eleven chapters of Genesis. Who would have included a single switching of usage, without any aid to the reader, in the middle of a story, unless more interested in confusion than communication?

The purpose of the phrase 'sons of God' may not be in its definable meaning, which could have become lost or irrelevant (if not unacceptable) on incorporation into this narrative. The purpose which stares out of the text is the distinguishing of 'the sons of God' from 'the daughters of mankind', as two groups. There is no doubt that the telling is of unequal pairings, in which women become brides whether they will or no, as chosen by males to whom they look good. There is abuse in that one sex imposes its will on the other, without necessary reciprocity. By representing this as socially possible, without suggesting the direct violence of rape, the telling is able to speak of marital and sexual abuse without the complication of abuse of another kind. Such socially possible abuse requires inequality of power, uncorrected by law, an inequality which the story therefore represents or implies. 'The sons of God' function in the narrative to provide this inequality. The terms 'inequality' and 'abuse' I use here without judgment. In verses 1-4, taken alone, the forced marriages are neither approved nor condemned.

The statement, in verse 3, that 'my spirit shall not abide…', clearly reaffirms human mortality, adding to the reaffirmation an explicitly stated lifespan. As noted in the comments on the line from Adam though Seth to Noah, 120 becomes a typical age at death in the patriarchal period, with a transition towards this, giving intermediate ages, after the Flood. In verse 3, as in the telling of the seven days of Creation, 'And the Lord said' implies the effect spoken of; what is spoken is the word of power.

As already noted, the term 'Nephilim' is used to name giants of some kind, but they need not have been known as contemporary beings when this writing was new. Here they are procreated through the forced marriages with which this passage opens. Whereas giants in some cults are divinities, and whereas intercourse between sons of God (in some sense) and human women would in some cults cause the birth of heroes, the Nephilim are among those condemned for their wickedness, and are a component of a regrettable outcome of the Creation. Is this coincidence, or is one purpose here to present alternative values to Israelites who knew what various non-Israelite philosophies and practices taught, to turn other people's mythologies upside-down so as to put the 'mighty ones of old, men of renown' in their place?

One of the most pregnant statements in our passage is 'the Lord was sorry', which might also be translated 'the Lord repented', or 'changed his mind'. This statement occurs in several narratives in the Hebrew scriptures, although in one place, for example, we read of the prophet Samuel telling Saul that this what a human being does, but not the Lord (1 Samuel 15:29).

Two usages of scriptural Hebrew may throw light on the Lord's repenting of doing something. First, it is normal in scripture to use terms from human life as metaphors in speaking of God's actions. The 'hand of God' (e.g. Exodus 3:20) is no more a hand of flesh than is Moab a place where God washes when it is 'his washpot' (Psalm 60:10, v.8 in English versions). It has already been remarked that characteristically female or male activities are attributed to God, although the divine unity precludes the pairing characteristic of sexuality in human and other species. Thus, it is proper to bear in mind that there is likely to be an element of metaphor in God's regretting, for want of a better way of describing it in language adapted to human purposes. Secondly, in scriptural Hebrew, especially when the subject is God, a mental verb often implies the consequent action. When we are told that God hears the cry of the lender's victim, we understand that God acts because of hearing it (Exodus 22:26, v.27 in English versions). When God remembers Noah (Genesis 8:1), there is no suggestion that he had forgotten him; God's behaviour is that appropriate to remembering. That the Lord, in the passage now under discussion, is sorry, certainly includes the implied action that follows from the regret, although this action is then specified. It must be specified, since the statement about regret cannot sufficiently define the consequence of regret in action.

The statement that 'it grieved his heart' takes the matter further. The word for 'and it grieved (him)', *wa-yit-atsev,* is a part of the verb corresponding to the words expressing the woman's sorrow (*etsev*) and the man's suffering (*it-savon*) in the story of the Garden of Eden. Is it being said here that God suffers? That is certainly the plain meaning. When God makes humankind in his own image, he thereby gives it some measure of power and choice. Thus God is the author of an ability to go against his own nature or purposes. Human choice, to the limit of its freedom, can be for or against human and divine nature. When it is against them, that of humankind which is of God denies itself. Nevertheless, what God has, as it were, delegated into humanity is still God, and its impairment by self-contradiction can therefore be spoken of as a source of divine suffering. So not only was God 'sorry that he had made humankind', but also 'it grieved his heart'. This is not to say that the divine and the human are not distinct here. Their distinctness is repeatedly explicit and implicit in the Hebrew scriptures. It is, however, by speaking of them as distinct that the way is prepared for considering their connectedness. There is a ravine bridged by inseparability.

God's suffering in the face of human wickedness is the other side of the coin shown us by Edinger*, when he points out that, in the Israelite scriptures, God has a need of Israel's righteousness. Correspondingly, the Creator has a need for human creativity, for the world of created things waits for the furthering of its creation by the co-creator, who is such because in the Creator's image. This gives alchemy some of its meaning. As Jung* writes,

> For the alchemist, the one primarily in need of redemption is not man, but the deity who is lost and sleeping in matter.

***

Having looked at some difficult and critical expressions in the passage being considered, it is now possible to look more generally at the story it tells.

At the start, humanity is represented in a new way. Up to this point, in the Creation narrative as a whole, the telling has been in terms of individuals. Even if a character has been portrayed so as to tell about what is general, or even if an individual has been archetypical of a sex or occupation, the subjects of the story have nevertheless been named persons, not society in general. (An exception is Cain's concern about the hostility of people in general, but this serves the story of Cain rather than to say more about those people. However, as will be shown, these potentially threatening people can be compared with the generality of humankind when the nar-

111

rative turns frankly to society.) It is true that more general than individuals are the 'sons and daughters' which are fathered by the members of the line from Adam to Noah through Seth, but nothing is said about them, and they serve largely to prepare the reader for what follows, since this requires that 'mankind began to increase on the face of the ground'.

This increase sets the scene. Now we read of 'the daughters of humankind', and 'the wickedness of humankind', not of this or that person. In the passage as a whole, except for the concluding statement about Noah, people are mentioned only collectively or in the plural. The subject is now society and the state of society.

The first thing to be said of humanity, seen socially and fulfilling the blessing to be fruitful and increase, is that there are forced marriages. Only one marriage has so far been the subject of narration, that between the primal woman and primal man. This begins with the newly wakening husband lovingly accepting the bride brought to him by the Lord. As soon as the woman finds the tree to be, in her own perception at least, 'good for food', a 'delight for the eye' and 'desirable for insight' she shares her treasure with her husband. There is mutual affection arising from a divine initiative. Now, however, 'they took for themselves wives of whomever they chose'. In this there is no mutuality, even if its later development remains a possibility. Since these marriages are forced not by the sporadic power of one individual over another, but by power which differs between groups, the forcing expresses a social relation between the groups. If 'the sons of God', as a group, are able to take wives 'of whomever they chose', each of the 'daughters of humankind' must, by implication, have no power effectually to refuse whoever may choose her.

The forced marriages touch on many matters. The union of the sexes tends towards three fulfilments. It permits each sex to be more fully itself, and so further the end 'male and female he created them'. Next, since the Creator's deeds can be described as being both male and female in type, although issuing from one fount, the union of the human sexes furthers creation in the Creator's likeness. Thirdly, marriage provides the social frame within which to 'be fruitful and increase'. It follows that a statement about marriage, such as that about the sons of God and the daughters of humankind, is not just about some detail of living. Within the context of the Creation narrative the story of the forced marriages bears widely upon the essentials of human existence.

Now follows the Lord's saying that the human life-span will be a hundred and twenty years. This is, as already noted, a typical age at death in the scriptural account of the patriarchal period, with a decrease towards it setting in after the Flood. Already in the Garden of Eden the Adam has an intimation of mortality. Now there is an indication of life-span. To know that one is mortal is part of being human, whether the knowledge is regarded as intuitive or socially acquired, and is complementary to awareness of one's instinct, shared with other species, to preserve oneself. To know one's natural life-span is necessarily and more fully social, since it becomes known by observation of each other, and by transmission of observations. (Of course, 'And the Lord said "My spirit shall not..."' does not necessarily mean that 'the Lord said' to anyone in particular, but that the Lord so determined. The life-span of one hundred and twenty years is that which, in the scriptural narrative, will obtain after the formation of the nations, that is, after humanity is fully itself.) The statement about length of life can be taken with 'when humankind began to increase', in that the one points to humanity's social character, for which the other is one of the necessary conditions.

We next learn, after what proves to be an interruption of the story of the forced marriages, that they yielded distinguished offspring. Only men, however, are mentioned; 'mighty ones' (*gibborim*) are warriors or other males, and the 'men' of renown are also adult males (*anshei*). The mothers are without choice and the daughters of no note.

In all this matter of the forced marriages, there is the indication of a social condition, but no judgment about that condition, not at least thus far in the telling. The fixing of the length of life is not a punishment, since it amplifies with additional information the earlier statement on mortality (3:19), '...and to dust will return'. There is no explicit disapproval of the forced marriages and, if we go only by the telling thus far, the change from mutuality to coercion might appear to be intended as a consequence of 'when humankind began to increase'. Any judgment on the forced marriages within the story itself will be come apparent when they are considered within the context of the whole of this passage.

The judgment, the evaluation, of the general state of humankind comes soon and is clear, however. We are told that 'wickedness...was great in the earth'. Unqualified, the term translated 'wickedness' (*ra'*, 'evil') refers to actual events, deeds in this case. The state of mind accompanying the deeds is, however, also noted: 'every devising of the thoughts of their heart was ceaselessly evil'. There is not only wickedness, but also a continuing inner drive towards it.

A person may choose to do this or to do that, to further the Creation or impede it. In any case a change in deeds may still be possible. The expression 'ceaselessly', on the other hand, indicates fixity in the actuating totality of the person. ('Ceaselessly' translates *kol ha-yom*, 'all the day', which is in classical Hebrew found only in elevated and emotional speech, as Benno Jacob, cited by Westermann*, points out, so that it here gives intensity.) Non-human creation is also to be bereft of beast, creeping animal, and flying animal. Humankind, in having dominion over other living things, has a function in their existence. Only humankind has been said to be wicked, yet beasts also are to be wiped out. This is therefore not primarily retribution to punish the guilty, even if it is that also. What the Lord says he will do is a correction of the Creation, motivated by divine regret.

Humankind causes the Lord to be sorry that he has made it, and a human being who does not contribute to that sorrow is notable. 'But Noah found favour in the eyes of the Lord.'

***

The question arises what, if any, is the connection implied by the story, between the forced marriages and the general wickedness of humankind; are we to understand the one as an example of the other? In order to approach a possible answer to this question, let us look at the pattern within this passage about humanity awry.

Just before this passage, Noah's genealogical entry was broken off (5:32, compared with other entries, just before). At the end of the passage (6:8) Noah is again the subject. We have therefore a narrative unit, delimited by its context. This unit falls into two parts. Verses 1-4 are about the condition of the world, verses 5-7 evaluate and judge of those conditions. The second part answers the first in some detail. Before looking at the detail, it will be convenient to have the translation set out again, but now with the two parts opposite each other (Figure 11).

¹ And it came to pass, when humankind began to increase on the face of the ground, and daughters were born to them,

⁵ And the LORD saw that the wickedness of humankind was great in the earth,

² that the sons of God saw the daughters of humankind that they were good to look at, and they took for themselves wives of whomever they chose.

and that every devising of the thoughts of their heart was only evil, continually.

³ And the LORD said 'My spirit shall not abide in humankind for ever, for they are indeed flesh, and their days shall be a hundred and twenty years'.

⁶ And the LORD was sorry that he had made humankind upon the earth, and it grieved his heart.

⁴ The Nephilim were on the earth in those days (and afterwards also) when the sons of God came into the daughters of humankind, who bore children to them. These are the mighty ones of old, men of renown.

⁷ And the LORD said 'I will wipe out mankind, which I have created, from the face of the earth, from human being to beast, to creeping thing, and to the flier in the sky, for am sorry that I have made them'.

⁸ But Noah found grace in the eyes of the LORD.

Fig.11. *Parallel structure in Genesis 6:1-8*

When the hearer meets 'the wickedness...was great (*rabah*)' in verse 5, there is an appeal to the hearer's memory of 'began to increase (*le-robh*)' in verse 1. The effect of the two audibly related words is enhanced because terms related to *rabh*, 'much', 'great' (and these are all related to amount or size), although very common, have not been heard since the story of the seven days (*rebhu*, 'increase'). Again, there are only two references to human mental states, to choosing in verse 2 and to evil thoughts in the latter part of verse 5. If we allow these pairs to guide the way in which we hear or read verses 5-7 in relation to verses 1-4, other parallels or contrasts become noticeable. To read that 'the LORD was sorry that he had made humankind upon the earth' in verse 6 recalls and, in part, contrasts with the Lord's granting a particular life-span in verse 3. It may be added that, if we take these two together, and note the manner in which verse 5 introduces the judgmental part of the story, it is evident that we are being told of things not to be taken as simultaneous; rather, that the evil deeds and thoughts develop on the way to the story's climax.

Finally, of the pairs across the two halves of the passage, the last is that of verses 4 and 7. The latter says that the Lord determined that humankind was to be wiped out. Verse 4 has however concluded 'These are the mighty ones of old, men of renown'. What, in the view of conventional story-telling, is success, is in a divine view utter failure. The 'mighty ones' provide a fine conclusion to the story of the forced marriages. What a decline in mood there is from this to the other conclusion: 'I will wipe out mankind...for I am sorry that I have made them'.

When the second part of the passage is read or heard as parallel with the first, other connections and resonances appear. To return to the paired themes already mentioned, if the first in each pair be termed the calling theme, and the second the echoing theme, the pattern as already described may be set out as in Figure 12 overleaf, which shows also chiasmatic themes, to be noted immediately.

Ch. 5, v. 32—NOAH: GENEALOGICAL ENTRY BROKEN OFF

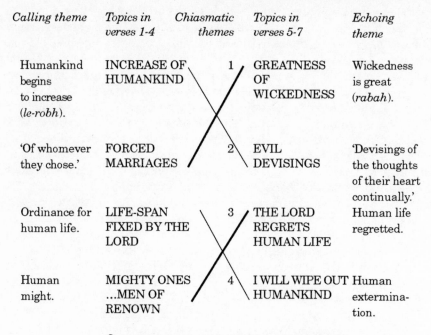

Calling theme	Topics in verses 1-4	Chiasmatic themes	Topics in verses 5-7	Echoing theme
Humankind begins to increase (le-robh).	INCREASE OF HUMANKIND	1	GREATNESS OF WICKEDNESS	Wickedness is great (rabah).
'Of whomever they chose.'	FORCED MARRIAGES	2	EVIL DEVISINGS	'Devisings of the thoughts of their heart continually.'
Ordinance for human life.	LIFE-SPAN FIXED BY THE LORD	3	THE LORD REGRETS HUMAN LIFE	Human life regretted.
Human might.	MIGHTY ONES ...MEN OF RENOWN	4	I WILL WIPE OUT HUMANKIND	Human extermination.

v.8—NOAH: SEEN WITH FAVOUR BY THE LORD

Fig. 12. *Poetic pattern in Genesis 6:1-8*

A chiasma is a crossing, taking its name from the Greek letter *chi,* which has the shape X. In descriptions of Hebrew poetry, the term 'chiasma' is used when, in a pair of lines of poetry, the first half of each line has some correspondence with the second half of the other. Here, instead of lines of verse, there are pairs of themes. The chiasmatic themes are shown in the figure by numbered lines. Thus the first chiasmatic theme links the first verse of the second pair (i.e. verse 2) with the second verse of the first pair (i.e. the beginning of verse 5), and so on, as in the figure. The four chiasmatic themes, then, as numbered, can be described as follows.

1. These are the two statements in this passage explicitly concerned with human action, with deeds.

2. These two statements are about unlimited quantity: 'increase' and 'continually'.

3. These are about the same subject, human actions or achievements, from two viewpoints, human and divine.

4. These are about duration of life, life-span and extermination.

How may this complexity of structure present itself to the reader or listener? Even if the modern reader finds it improbably intricate, there are two possibilities to be borne in material. One is that in the culture in which this passage arose such material was known by heart and frequently repeated, so that internal subtleties would be more readily realised than by a modern westernised reader. The second possibility is that the passage was among that material used for intensive study under an experienced teacher who would bring out what was not obvious, and that it was designed for such use. Examples of both can be found in other cultures, and still in modern Jewry.

This short passage on humanity awry is, then, a compact and carefully wrought work. It is comparable in this respect with some English poetry of recent centuries, but not with servile journalism or the conveyor-belt production of unchallenging novels. It can give up its meaning only if it is read for what it is, for which modern reading habits are not ideally suited.

***

Within the structure of this passage on humanity awry, the forced marriages receive a condemnation which is not explicit in the wording when they are mentioned. There would appear to be a relation between 'of whomever they chose' and the wicked thoughts, the only two human mental states mentioned, one in the account of the world's condition, the other in the evaluation of that condition and the judgment on it. With this there is also a direction of attention to the relation between the forced marriages and the greatness of the wickedness of humankind. Therefore, one might be led to take the forced marriages as an example of the state of humankind as it came towards the condition referred to when it is said that 'the wickedness of humankind was great in the earth'.

Here a difficulty arises. The offenders are 'the sons of God; the 'daughters of humankind' are the victims. What have the latter done wrong, and are the sons of God to be included with the humankind whose wickedness is great? To this there is a double answer. First, the association of the forced marriages with general human wickedness is intelligible if they are symptomatic of the state of society, since the passage, as explained, breaks new ground in the Creation narrative by its emphasis on human society rather than on individuals. Secondly, a comparison of verses 3 and 7, and consideration of the wording of verse 5, indicates that the passage is to be understood as showing a process, not a single condition, in the first part at least. The forced marriages have offspring who are 'men of renown', and then the story tells of general wickedness. That is, the forced marriages lead indirectly to the wicked condition.

Whichever we choose of these routes of association between the forced marriages and the condition that merits destruction of all life, there is no doubt that the marriages are presented as a key to the general state, the manifestations of which are wickedness of action and of heart. The marriage of male and female

117

is the Creation story's first relationship between individuals, the pointer, as it were, to all social relations. The change from mutuality to force may be considered as an archetypal social deviation therefore, for we are concerned here not with a couple but with society. In order to see why this is, we may reflect on Cain's killing of his brother.

Cain knew that everybody would be against him, the killer, and he needed the Lord's protection from other people. Here, on the other hand, we meet with a general condition, so that the evil-doing, instead of causing revulsion, is referred to as having become normal. The social context of Cain's murder and of the forced marriages is different; it is the difference between public hostility and the public acceptance that is implicit in the passage under discussion. The social character of the forced marriages is also implicit in that one group can do as it will with another group, without the latter's consent, since they 'took for themselves wives of whomever they chose'.

The boasting Lamech (4:23,24) indicates an earlier stage in the development of this social state. Although he speaks very much as an individual, he gives, for his killing, a reason which would make such behaviour more general. We are not told, nor can we infer, that Lamech behaved in the manner of humankind generally, but he took it for granted that he would have at least the approval of Adah and Zillah.

If we compare the world approaching the Lord's decision to wipe out human life, with the world of Cain's sin, and even perhaps that of Lamech's boasting, we do not see that individuals had just become wicked. Earlier, Cain's deed was certainly not righteous. Also, there is no evident certain intention of the story to convey that sins became more numerous, that Cain's contemporaries and those about to perish in the Flood differed only statistically, in the crime rate, so to speak. What is new is that the offence lacks social disapproval and expresses a particular social relationship. Therefore we are dealing with the wickedness of mankind, not simply the aggregate of wickedness of independently wicked individuals. Cain's sin was one man's sin, even if there was a predisposition to it already given to Cain. When individuals were great in their wickedness and evil in the devisings of their hearts, so that the Lord was about to wipe them out, the individual wickedness lay within and was part of a social wickedness which was more than the sum of its parts.

The reader familiar with the Hebrew scriptures will not be surprised. Throughout them we find commendation and condemnation of the righteousness or unrighteousness of nations, and sometimes of other corporate groups, although individuals are always responsible for their own actions.

CHAPTER 22: *THE WICKEDNESS OF HUMANKIND*

'AND THE LORD saw that the wickedness of humankind was great in the earth...and the Lord said "I will wipe out humankind",' (6:5,7). What is this wickedness? I have suggested, in the previous chapter, that the clue to this is in the statement that they 'took for themselves wives of whomever they chose' (6:2). I would like now to go backwards and forwards from that suggestion. I mean, by going backwards, returning to the reason why taking 'wives of whomever they chose' is essential to understanding 'the wickedness of humankind'. Now, however, I want to do this without reference to the detailed structure of the passage. In this way I can show that the conclusion does not depend on the structure as I have presented it, so that nothing further is affected if the reader does not accept the structure. By going forward,—and this is my principal concern,—I mean going beyond the point reached so far, and exploring what characterises this 'wickedness'.

Clearly we have here a thoroughgoing condemnation of humanity. We are helped to understand the condemnation by its lying within a sharply delimited passage, which gives it its context. This passage about the state of the world interrupts the story of Noah, so that the beginning and continuation of that story sharply mark off the beginning and end, respectively, of the account of human wickedness, which account is thus, as it were, stood between bookends, rather than left to flop all over the mantelpiece. Within this unit (6:1-7) there is only one human activity or action mentioned specifically and said to have been carried out. This is the marriages between 'the sons of God' and the 'daughters of humankind'. Since 'the sons of God' (whoever we take them to be) took wives 'of whomever they chose', the women had no say in the matter and, in effect, one group could, in forced marriages, make another group do what it wanted.

Although the forced marriages are the only deeds provided by the context of the wickedness, it may be that they are not necessarily to be seen as identical with that wickedness. Not only are the forced marriages not specifically picked out for condemnation but, more importantly, 'the wickedness of humankind' is unlikely to be deeds in which 'the daughters of humankind' are the victims, while the perpetrators have their membership of humankind much less clearly represented, if they are indeed human at all. This is a matter of the words used, whatever they represent. The interpretation of 'the sons of God' as a human social class is, as already noted, not wholly satisfactory, but it makes better sense

119

than any of the other interpretations.

It may be that the wickedness is that of the Nephilim, 'men of renown', who may then be seen by a reader or listener to develop the tendency set in train by the oppressive begetting of them. Whether the forced marriages constitute or exemplify the wickedness (which, as just said, may not make good sense), or whether they represent the tendency out of which the wickedness, perhaps exercised by the Nephilim, has its springs, the thrust of the passage as a whole is to say that the forced marriages indicate the characteristics of the wickedness.

As already noted, these marriages indicate in two respects a social condition. First, one group is, in a particular activity at least, able to exert unrestrained power over another. Secondly, this exercise of power is not said to excite any public reaction, as Cain feared, and the Lord implicitly confirmed, his sin would do.

***

To take up the forward exploration from this point, what further social implications do the forced marriages present? One implication is that since group oppression is here sexual oppression, the ordering of sexual relations is shown as an aspect of social relations. Whether or not one wishes to note especially the sexual aspect of the matter, there is also a social aspect, and both aspects are borne upon by the one question: what are the conditions among humankind for the oppression of one group by another? (The question remains, even if, in the archetypical model activity, the oppressors are not human.)

When one person oppresses another it may be that there is no third to intervene, or that the third who might intervene does not do so. When whole sections of humanity oppress one another, the same is true, but with one difference. The systematic character of the oppression means that, if there is a third who does not intervene, this third fails to intervene not though an ephemeral contingent lapse, which is a possible explanation when instances of oppression are sporadic, but by unwillingness to act or though weakness. Unwillingness makes the third no longer a true third, but an accessory of the oppressor; weakness that prevents effective action means that, in practice, there is no third, since what might be that has no function in preventing oppression or bringing relief from it.

Put otherwise, the systematic oppression of one section of humanity by another implies that there is none to whom the oppressed can go for judgment. 'The wickedness of humankind', whatever else it was also, was a lack of judgment between people.

What if judgments are correctly given in accordance with oppressive law? This possibility needs the wider context of the Creation story for its consideration. In the discussion of the seventh of the days of Creation, the implication was drawn that the scriptural story means that one may not belittle or fail to respect the name that cannot be said. The being that the name is of is the being

120

in whose image we are. Respect for the name entails respect for humanity. Law which oppresses humanity is not law in accord with the created order.

Thus we have the principle constraining laws, the laws themselves, and the judgments which implement the laws. Therefore judgments cannot be considered fruitfully in isolation, but only with respect to what underlies them—also, what goes beyond them. The levels at which judgments present themselves if they are to fulfil the requirements of respecting the divine image and safeguarding against oppression can be taken as four, but this is for convenience only, and no more is claimed for the four levels. First, the laws and the methods of making laws must respect the unspeakable name and all that the name stands for. Secondly, what exactly is the law must be made known in order that victims and potential victims may know how to obtain redress. Thirdly, judgments must be independent and impartial, or they are instruments of oppression, either by the oppressor or by the previously oppressed. Fourthly, judgments must be readily available to all, and they must be effective in that the obtaining of them is not by-passed by procedures not subject to these rules, and in that their outcome is neither unimplemented, nor falsely interpreted.

If we take 'the sons of God (*Elohim*)' to have the sense, already discussed, when *elohim* is translated as 'judges' or 'rulers', then oppression by *elohim* indicates the deepest corruption.

The Creation expresses condemnation of conduct in two ways, through the ordering of created things and though God's word. The story of Cain's sin speaks against the killing, and does so though the curse from the ground and the hostility of people to the killer, while the Lord does not directly punish but exercises mercy in order that there shall be justice. On the other hand a rule of conduct may arise from what God says and does. Concerning the seventh of the Creation days, it has already been argued in the chapter about that day, that God's Sabbath entails the rule: you may not belittle the name that cannot be spoken, the divine name. The Lord's judgment on the 'wickedness of humankind' entails a second rule: you shall have judgments among you.

ABOUT ONE QUARTER of the Creation narrative is devoted to the Flood. The Flood story is itself complex, but it has a unity and shape of its own. In order to show the general pattern of the Flood story, it has to be taken as one piece. On the other hand, it may not be convenient for the reader if comments and explanations are held back until after so long a stretch of translation. The Flood will therefore be considered in four divisions: 'Before the Flood', 'The Waters Rise', 'Dry Land Emerges', and 'After the Flood', together with a further chapter of comment. The three sections in each division, giving the twelve (with an introduction) into which the whole story is presented, are not arbitrary. After all are considered they will be seen to have an obviously patterned relationship to each other.

In the translation the breaks between lines correspond to the punctuation heard in the musical tropes of the original Hebrew. As in the story of the Garden of Eden, 'You' and 'Your' are given a capital letter if they translate the plural, and a lowercase initial letter when singular, that is, when 'you' and 'your' mean 'thou', 'thee', 'thy', or 'thine'. In the book of Genesis the Flood story runs from 6:9 to 9:17, this first division going as far as 7:5.

Introduction

9a This is the history of Noah.

(i) The just one, and a corrupt world seen by God

9b Noah was a wholly righteous man in his generations:
with God did Noah walk.

10 And Noah fathered thee sons, Shem, Ham, and Japhet.

11 But the earth was corrupt in God's sight,
and wickedness filled the earth.

12 And God saw the earth and, behold, it was corrupted,
for all flesh had corrupted its way upon the earth.

(ii) God's covenant with the just one

13 And God said to Noah 'The end of all flesh has come before me,
for wickedness has filled the earth because of them

and, behold, I am destroying them with the earth.

¹⁴ Make yourself an ark of gopher wood.
Cabins shall you make in the ark,
and you shall pitch it inside and out with pitch.

¹⁵ And this is how you shall make it:
three hundred cubits long the ark,
fifty cubits its width,
and thirty cubits its height.

¹⁶ A light shall you make for the ark and to a cubit shall you complete it
above,
and the doorway of the ark shall you put in its side;
with lowest, second, and third decks shall you make it.

¹⁷ As for me, I am bringing the Flood, water upon the earth,
to destroy all flesh in which is the spirit of life
from under the sky.
Everything on earth shall perish.

¹⁸ And I shall establish my covenant with you,
and you shall come into the ark,
you and your sons, and your wife, and your daughters-in-law, with you.

¹⁹ And of the living, of all flesh, two of each shall you bring into the ark,
to keep them alive with you,
  male and female shall they be.

²⁰ Of the flying thing according to its kind and of the beast according to its
kind,
of every moving thing of the ground according to its kind,
two of each shall come to you to be kept alive.

²¹ And as for you, take for yourself of every food that is eaten,
and you shall collect it for yourself,
and it shall be for food for you and for them.

²² And Noah did it:
according to everything which the LORD God commanded him, so he did.

(iii) The Lord orders the saving of life

^{7:1} And the LORD said to Noah
'Come, you and all your household, into the ark,
for it is you that I have seen righteous in this generation.

² Of each clean beast you shall take seven pairs, a husband and his wife,
and of each beast that is not clean, two, a husband and his wife,

³ also of each flying thing in the sky, seven pairs, male and female,
to keep alive seed on the face of all the earth.

⁴ For in seven days' time I will make it rain upon the earth for forty days
and forty nights,
and I will wipe out from the face of the earth all existing things that
I have made.'

⁵ And Noah did according to all that the LORD had commanded him.

It may be helpful to note some of the peculiarities of expression before considering the substance of what is said. The introduction refers to the entire Flood story; immediately afterwards attention is drawn to Noah's sons. 'History' here translates *toldot,* literally 'generations', but often meaning simply 'history'. As already explained on pages 47 and 93, 'These are the generations of...' (or perhaps translated 'This is the history of...') always opens a section of narrative in the Hebrew scriptures, introducing the subject.

In verse 12 the word 'behold' (*hinneh*) is idiomatic, used after a verb of perception to indicate that what follows is the perception, rather than the thing perceived as anyone might see (or hear etc.) it. The earth's corruption, the story says, was seen by God. We are not told whether others, such as the corrupted ones themselves, saw the earth that way.

In verse 13 the expression 'The end of all flesh has come before me' can be taken as 'The reason for the end has come to me judicially, and the end is what I pronounce'. Where, as in this verse, the term 'destroy' occurs in the Flood story, the Hebrew word is the verb *shachat* which appears in a different grammatical form with the meaning 'corrupt', as when 'all flesh had corrupted (*hi-shechit*) its way', so that 'destroy' and 'corrupt' come to the ear as related.

Concerning the dimensions of the ark, it may be mentioned that the cubit (*ammah,* 'arm', 'forearm') is originally the distance from the elbow (Latin *cubitum*) to the tip of the middle finger. In practice the cubit of the Hebrew scriptures may be taken as about equal to half a metre.

***

The story of the Flood opens with a stylistic ambiguity appropriate for a tale of destruction which is part of the Creation. In verse 9b the Hebrew has the word order 'with God walked Noah', so that Noah's name opens the first half of the statement and closes its second. Thus, although, to the ear, this half-verse is contained, the next verse points outward through mention of the begetting of offspring. Any sense of outward thrust, however, is then smothered by verses 11 and 12, in which 'corrupt' occurs three times, and which, in this respect, contrast with the sketch of Noah in verse 9b.

The state of the earth is emphasised by the contrasts which echoes evoke. 'And God saw the earth and, behold, it was corrupted': compare, from the seven days of the Creation (1:31), 'And God saw all that he had made and, behold, it was very good'. 'And wickedness filled the earth' (verses 11 and 13): compare 'increase and fill the earth' (1:28). Also, 'All flesh had corrupted its way' recalls, within this same passage, 'With God did Noah walk', one's 'way' being what one takes in one's 'walking', a very frequent metaphor, in the Hebrew scriptures, for conduct.

Previously, in reading how humankind had gone awry, we learnt of the Lord's resolving to bring destruction to the earth. Now this resolution is communicated to Noah. The Creator speaks to the co-creator. Throughout the Hebrew scriptures there is a polarity between two modes of the unspeakable: God terrible, majestic, and beyond any human imagining, and God needing humankind and human righteousness. Reciprocally, there is evoked in human beings the inseparable fear of God and love of God. Noah is presented as someone confidently intimate with God, who is at the same time God of creation and destruction, ruler of all things.

The reader will notice that the command to build the ark comes before the intention to bring the Flood is communicated. Giving the reason is secondary to the expression of God's will. Having the command and information out of their logical order might suggest that it was the obedience that opened Noah to receive the information.

In verse 18 the words 'I will establish my covenant with you' are not a promise to make a covenant but to fulfil one already made; this is the meaning of 'establish' in such a context. Noah's obligation under the covenant is to build the ark as instructed, and to take into it those designated by the Lord. The Lord's part is to bring the Flood and, by implication, ensure the effectiveness of what Noah does and therefore the safety of those in the ark. Noah's fulfilment of his obligation is indicated by the words 'And Noah did it' (verse 22). The Lord, about to fulfil what he has promised, says 'I will establish my covenant with you'.

***

In verses 11 and 13 reference is made to the wickedness in the earth. This seems to duplicate what was said—when humanity goes awry, that 'the Lord saw that the wickedness of humankind was great in the earth' (6:5). In fact, however, the word for 'wickedness' is now different. Previously it was *ra'*, which means 'evil'; now the word is *chamas*, which has a strong connotation of violence. Indeed, in most places where the word is found in the Hebrew scriptures the meaning is violence in particular rather than wickedness in general. If this is linked with what has already been said of the wickedness of mankind before the Flood, the oppression which characterises society is manifested specifically in violence. This is hardly surprising since oppression generally requires either violence or the threat of violence. The Lord has condemned the wickedness (*ra'*) of humankind, and the social implications of this have been explored and a conclusion concerning judgments reached. Now God condemns the violence (*chamas*) which fills the earth. What does this condemnation offer as positive instruction? Is there a precept implied by the condemnation? If so, what?

First of all, it may be said that the social character of the wickedness condemned previously is not a limitation on the nature of this violence. The oppression of group by group generally requires violence or the threat of violence, but the violence is necessarily the action of individuals and bears upon individual victims. That is to say, when the wickedness is specified as violence the personal aspect of its social nature is brought out. More than this, within the passage now under consideration violence is presented so generally as to permit it to be seen as social or individual, or both.

Violence has two presentations, direct and indirect. Direct violence is against the mind and body of the person. Indirect violence is against those things which a person may legitimately consider his or her own, or against those things that a person needs for life, 'life' here including health and all that is for the fulfilment of being in the image of God. This means that some theft; being of what is needed for life, would then be a form of violence. In this category of taking as violence there is included, of course, deprivation which is unconnected with ownership, since there can be violence by depriving someone of the enjoyment of that which is not a possession. Just as deprivation, by theft or otherwise, can be violence against somebody, the converse may also be true, that direct violence against the person can be a deprivation,—of health or liberty, for example.

In order to find a single term for direct and indirect violence against a person, it may be helpful to realise how difficult it is to think of direct violence that deprives the victim of nothing. The English word for violent deprivation is 'robbery', which the Oxford English Dictionary defines as 'the action or practice of feloniously seizing, by violence or intimidation, property belonging to another'. If we extend this beyond property to anything of one's person that one has enjoyment of and that outside oneself which one enjoys and which is necessary for life, and if we drop the word 'feloniously', by which we are restricted to a technical term within the legal system, then 'robbery' is a good enough English word to amplify, without addition or subtraction, the notion of 'violence' implicit in the Hebrew *chamas* which, in the story, specifies the 'wickedness' *(ra')* because of which humankind is to be wiped out.

Since robbery is violent, not all theft is robbery. It so happens, although the words do not come into the Creation story, that Hebrew has a distinction something like that in English, with *genevah* for 'theft' and *gezel* for 'robbery'

In this discussion of violence the use of the word 'life' to include all that is for the fulfilment of the image of God, leaves it to be asked just what is for that fulfilment and what is not. Since the question can be answered within the philosophical framework of the Creation story only when the story can be taken as a rounded whole, the matter will need to be raised later, when the entire Creation narrative has been reviewed. Meanwhile, just as the Lord's condemnation of 'wickedness' (*ra‘*) was seen to imply the precept to have judgments in society, God's condemnation of 'wickedness' (*chamas*) in the passage now under consideration implies a precept forbidding violence or, in the wider sense just discussed, robbery.

***

Suddenly, and all together, four strange words occur in verse 14. The first of these is *teva*, translated 'ark'. The reader familiar with the Hebrew scriptures or translations of them should be warned that the word for 'ark' when the Ark of the Covenant is spoken of, is quite different. The word *teva* is used for this ark, which Noah builds, and for the ark in which the infant Moses was placed among the reeds on the water of the Nile (Exodus, chapter 2). It is a special word, which in all the Hebrew scriptures has only these two uses, and both of them associated with rescue on water. However, it is certain from the way the word comes to be used in Hebrew after scriptural times that it represents a chest or box, not a navigable vessel. In the flood story in the Babylonian epic of Gilgamesh, on the other hand, the words used are of shipping and navigation. If those who first heard the Flood story in Genesis knew the Babylonian account, the difference would have no doubt struck them; it could have reinforced the strangeness of the word *teva* as a habitable vessel, and would have emphasised the trust in God shown by Noah, for 'with God did Noah walk' (verse 9).

The ark is to be built of gopher wood. We have no idea what species of tree the gopher might be. If we look at the older translations it seems that there was no agreement what gopher was, even two thousand years ago. One cannot help but suspect that this was a rare word even at an earlier date, therefore.

In the same verse the word *qen* is used for a cabin. This is in fact a normal word for 'nest', and is otherwise unknown as a term for 'room', 'cabin', or the like. Nevertheless the meaning is clear, so that one is forced to accept a word in a sense which may be not only unusual but unique.

Also otherwise unknown in the Hebrew scriptures is the word for 'pitch', *kopher*. This may well be related in origin to the Akkadian *kupru*, which means 'pitch' in the Mesopotamian flood story. At all events, it is a most unusual word in Hebrew.

That these words all come close together must charge the passage with a particular strangeness for the listener or reader whose literary language this Hebrew was. The strangeness is reinforced by the word for 'Flood'. Throughout the Flood story the word *mabul* is used for the Flood itself. This is not a word for an inundation, a disastrous amount of water. It is the proper name of this Flood, and in the Hebrew scriptures it is found outside the Flood story of Genesis only once. This in Psalm 29:10, where it appears to refer, nevertheless, to Noah's Flood. Cassuto* suggests that *mabul* is derived from the Hebrew and Canaanite *yabhal*, which is usually found with the meaning 'to carry along', but which has a form meaning 'watercourse', and which is apparently related to an Arabic word meaning 'to pour with rain'. Whether this is or is not so, the word *mabul* means only this particular Flood. The naming of the Flood, like some of the words used in the story, lets it be known that this is not just a known natural catastrophe which happens to be unique in extent, severity, and consequence. It is of its own kind, without lesser examples of the same, and not to be compared with any other event.

***

In verse 18 of chapter 6 God orders Noah, 'you shall come into the ark', but in the first verse of chapter 7 God says 'Come, you and all your household, into the ark'. What was a command has become inviting and so more intimate. Has Noah come closer to his Creator by building the ark and thus fulfilling in part his side of the covenant? This is how some might see it. More definitely, the change in distance conveyed by the wording is accompanied by a change in the name used for the Creator, who is now referred to as *YHWH* ('LORD' in the translation), instead of 'God', the Hebrew of which (*Elohim*) can mean 'judges' or 'rulers'. Even if, as has often been argued, these two designations of the Creator (and there are many more) correspond to different materials incorporated in the scriptural text we have, the two names are different in connotation, drawing attention to different aspects of the Godhead. (Later, the Hebrew scriptures lead into an introduction to the mystery of the name *YHWH:* Exodus 3:13-15, 6:2-3, but it is very difficult to translate Exodus 6:1-3, and English versions are usually misleading.) The way in which the names 'God' and 'LORD' are used in the Creation story becomes clear if the parts of the story are taken severally.

In the telling of the seven days, the Creator of all things is 'God'. In the garden the 'LORD God' is still Creator of the universe, but is now seen also in a personal relation to humanity. Cain is confronted, person to person, by the 'LORD', who protects him.

When Cain is born, Eve speaks intimately of her Creator: 'I have got a man with the LORD', but there is more distance, as well as a change of name, when she says of Seth's birth 'God has set a seed'. However, when Enosh is born, 'calling on the LORD's name began', a personal process. In the genealogy from Adam to Noah, though Seth, 'God' is mentioned and there is an obvious reference to the sixth of the seven days (5:1-2) the telling of which has the same usage. The 'LORD' is mentioned by Noah's father in connection with the curse on the ground, which was put on it by the 'LORD God' in the story of the couple in the garden.

The 'LORD' regrets having made humankind when he sees its wickedness, and this could hardly be said of 'God'. When this verb 'regret' (*nicham*) is used to signify regretting or repenting of an act or intention, and when the subject of the verb is the Creator, he is called 'LORD' (YHWH) 25 times (20 distinct occasions) and 'God' (*Elohim*) only twice, both on the same occasion (Jonah 3:9,10).

Now, in the Flood story, 'God' commands Noah to go into the ark, but the

'LORD' invites him. Later, it will be seen that the 'LORD' shuts him in, accepts his offerings, and withdraws the curse on the ground with leniency towards the bad in humankind. On the other hand, in this same Flood narrative, we read of 'God' in connection with judgment, punishment, covenants, and law-giving. Thus, throughout the story of Creation, so far, the two ways of naming the Lord God correspond to two aspects of the divine character. Three warnings must, however, be given. First, we have here tendencies, not precisely definable functions. Secondly, the distinction which can be made in this early part of Genesis need not hold for all the Hebrew scriptures; it may do so, but that needs further examination. Thirdly, differences in what the names signify do not mean that they cannot be used also in historical analysis of the text. That is another matter. (Rudolph Otto* has said that in *Elohim* the rational preponderates over the numinous, in *YHWH* the numinous outweighs the rational.)

***

There are two commands to Noah concerning the saving of animals. In 6:19 he is told to bring two of each kind, male and female, and in 7:2,3 to take seven of each 'clean' species. The actions prescribed for Noah are not quite the same. Of all animals in pairs it is said 'you shall bring' (literally 'cause to come') but, of pairs with sevens, 'you shall take' them. 'Take' here translates the Hebrew verb *laqach,* which implies acquisition or taking hold, not causing to come. The clean beasts will appear later in the story. In scripture the distinction between clean and unclean species of animal refers to the use of them as human food. So, when the animals are mentioned in the least numbers necessary for their own survival, they are brought, caused to come. When their function as human food comes into the story, they are taken. Such is the double nature of the relationship between human beings and beasts. The regulation of this relationship will come later into the Flood story.

Since this early part of Genesis is the 'primal history' of the Israelite scriptures, it is proper that the characters in it do not necessarily conform to rules of conduct later appearing as specifically given to Israel. In 7:3 the wording may imply that all birds are clean to eat, but the Israelites are restricted in the birds they may eat (Leviticus 11:13-19). The implication is clear: that the distinction between clean and unclean animals is of universal validity, but that Israel was enjoined to observe that principle in a particular way.

ALL THINGS BEING prepared, the Flood begins (7:6-24). Again, the narrative falls into three sections, or episodes. Here again, the breaks between lines correspond with the Hebrew musical marks.

(iv) Entering the ark

⁶ And Noah is six hundred years old,
and there was the Flood,
water upon the earth.

⁷ And Noah, and his sons and his wife and his daughters-in-law with him,
went into the ark
because of the water of the Flood.

⁸ Of each clean beast
and of the beast
which is not clean,
and of each flying thing,
and of all that creeps upon the ground,

⁹ two by two they came to Noah into the ark, male and female,
as God had commanded Noah.

(v) The start of the water and God's closing of the ark

¹⁰ And after seven days
the water of the Flood was on the earth.

¹¹ In the six-hundredth year of Noah's life,
in the second month,
on the seventeenth day of the month,
on this day all the springs of the great deep broke out,
and the windows of the sky were opened.

¹² (And the rain was on the earth
forty days
and forty nights.)

¹³ On this very day came Noah,
and Shem and Ham and Japhet, the sons of Noah,

and Noah's wife, and his three daughters-in-law, with them, into the ark,

¹⁴ them and every animal after its kind, every beast after its kind,
and every creeping thing that creeps on the earth, after its kind,
and every flying thing after its kind,
every bird of every kind.

¹⁵ And they came to Noah, to the ark,
two by two, of all flesh
in which is the spirit of life.
¹⁶ And those coming, male and female, came of all flesh,
as in God's commanding him,
and the LORD shut him in.

(vi) The water prevails

¹⁷ And the Flood was forty days upon the earth,
and the water increased and bore up the ark,
and it was lifted from off the earth.

¹⁸ And the water prevailed and increased greatly upon the earth,
and the ark went on the face of the water.

¹⁹ The water, it prevailed greatly indeed on the earth,
and so were covered all the high mountains
which are under all the skies.

²⁰ Fifteen cubits upward
did the water prevail,
and the mountains were covered.

²¹ And all flesh moving on the earth perished, bird, cattle, and beast,
and every creeping thing that creeps on earth,
and all humankind.

²² Everything with the breath of the spirit of life in its nostrils,
whatever is of dry land, it died.

²³ And he wiped out all that existed on the face of the ground, from
human being to beast, from creeping thing to flying thing
of the sky,
and they were wiped out from the earth,
and there was left only Noah and those with him in the ark.

²⁴ And the water prevailed on the earth
a hundred and fifty days.

In the account of what happened before the Flood we were told twice, curtly, that Noah, having received commandments, carried them out. Now, in verses

6-16, Noah's obedience is set out more explicitly, echoing the commandments themselves. In this telling of just what Noah does, verses 13-16 expand with particularity what is in verses 7-9. These two statements, together with the earlier ones, telling simply that Noah did as commanded, form a crescendo. In this way there is emphasis on Noah's obedience and reliability, as well as the developing repetitions which give the resonance becoming to epic narration on a great theme. For the account of Noah's obedience to echo the commandments which he has already been said to have carried out, it is not necessary to repeat every particular. The ark's people and animals are now mentioned, but not the food for them. The animals, clean and unclean, come in their twos, but there is no mention of Noah's taking clean beasts and birds in sevens; the aspect noted in this repetition is animals being saved, not animals being of use to humankind.

In verse 6 Noah's age is given and, as will be seen from verse 11, the age must be that at his next birthday. There is an obvious difference between these two verses. At the first mention of Noah's age it is part of the flow of story-telling, but at the second it is used to give a date, and it is the date which is part of the story. In the Flood story, dating by Noah's life may recall to the reader the custom of using reigns to number years, as elsewhere in the Hebrew scriptures, in English law, and widely among ancient peoples. With all, except those in the ark, about to be wiped out, it is not surprising that Noah's is the life used for numbering years. Later, when all the Flood story's indications for dating have been seen, the manner in which the dating provides a chronology will be reviewed.

In order to put together all the Flood story's dating, it is necessary to bear in mind what is meant by saying that 'the rain was on the earth forty days'. 'Rain' (*geshem*) is falling rain, not rain-water. These forty days are given as the time in which rain was falling. In this period the 'fountains of the deep' and the 'windows of the sky' let out the lower and upper waters, respectively, which meet in the Flood. There is a reference here to the separation of upper and lower waters in the first chapter of Genesis, with the implication that the Flood is, to some degree and in some manner at least, a reversal of the fundamental character of the created world. The Flood story cannot be understood except as part of the Creation story.

The 'windows of the sky' in verse 11 are perhaps one of the nudges the story gives the reader to hint what sort of story it is. This was written, of course, many centuries before windows were glazed. In fact the word for 'window', *arubah,* used here represents a lattice. To open a lattice, which has spaces in it, to let water through is a curious image. Elsewhere in scripture *arubah* is never a barrier except once in Malachi (3:10), where its being opened lets through blessings, and once in Isaiah (24:18), where there seems, however, to be an echo of the Flood story itself. It is true that the standard dictionary of scriptural Hebrew, that of Brown, Driver, and Briggs, gives to *arubah* the possible meaning 'sluice-gate'. This is not, however, an independent witness to the meaning, since it depends on what the authors have read into the Flood story, with support from no other source. In this connection it is noteworthy that the Second Book of Kings (7:2, 19) has rain coming because celestial *arubot,* 'windows', are made, not because they are opened. The image of water held back by lattices has a mysteriousness which must surely be intentional. There is some resemblance to the way in which miracle and mystery are suggested when some old European stories have someone going to sea in a sieve.

In verses 17-24, telling how the water prevails, there are two major themes: rising water and extermination, in verses 17-20 and 21-23, respectively, with a further reference to water in verse 24. In the first four verses the three statements of increase, and the repetition of the words 'water' and 'earth', convey the relentless increase of the water, until the ark could float freely above the highest mountains. The next three verses have a similar device. There are three statements of extinction, piled upon each other, but differently expressed, giving a cumulative effect which conveys the utter totality of extermination. The first part is capped, in verse 20, with words on the water's depth, the second with words (verse 24) on its duration. Against this devastation, the terse remark about those in the ark, at the end of verse 23, is related to the rolling words about the Flood in a way that conveys a sense of the ark's isolation. As for the water itself, one needs only to imagine water fifteen cubits deep (verse 20) over the highest mountain tops to realise that the Flood is not just the extreme form of the disastrous inundations known to human experience. In this connection it is relevant to note that the only mountains specified in the Flood story are those of Ararat, mentioned later, which rise to heights of the same order as those of the highest Alps.

THE STORY of the Flood does not pause to tell what was happening in the ark, nor does it relate anything about the world while the waters were at their full depth for 150 days (7:24). So terrible an event requires at its climax a terrible silence. It is the silence of the earth's death, to which all possible words are inappropriate. The waters have risen; now the story speaks of their subsiding. Again, there are three sections, or episodes, all in chapter 8 of Genesis.

(vii) The water subsides

¹ And God remembered Noah
  and all the animals, all the cattle
  with him in the ark,
  and God made a wind to pass over the earth,
  and the water abated.

² And stopped up were the springs of the deep
  and the windows of the sky,
  and the rain from the sky was held back.

³ And the water returned from off the earth, toing and froing,
  and the water diminished
  from the end of a hundred-and-fifty days.

⁴ And the ark came to rest in the seventh month,
  on the seventeenth day of the month,
  on the mountains of Ararat.

⁵ And the water went on diminishing
  until the tenth month.
  In the tenth month, on the first of the month,
  were the mountaintops seen.

⁶ And it was at the end of forty days
  that Noah opened
  the window of the ark that he had made.

⁷ And he sent out the raven,
  which kept going out and returning
  until the water had dried from the earth.

⁸ And he sent the dove from him
  to see if the water had gone down
  from off the face of the ground.

⁹ And the dove found no resting-place for the sole of her foot, and she went back to him, to the ark,
  for water was on the face of all the earth,
  and he put out his hand and took her,
  and brought her to himself, into the ark.

¹⁰ And still he waited another seven days,
  and again sent the dove from the ark.

¹¹ And the dove came to him at evening time
  and, behold, fresh olive leaves in her mouth,
  and Noah knew:
  for the water had subsided from off the earth.

¹² And still he waited another seven days,
  and he sent out the dove,
  and she returned to him no more.

¹³ And it was in the six-hundred-and-first year, in the first month, on the first of the month,
  that the waters dried from off the earth;
  and Noah turned back the roofing of the ark,
  and he looked and, behold, the face of the ground had dried.

¹⁴ And in the second month,
  on the twenty-seventh day of the month,
  the earth was dry.

(viii) God's command to leave the ark

¹⁵ And God spoke to Noah, saying,

¹⁶ 'Go out from the ark,
  you, and your wife and your sons and your daughters-in-law with you.

¹⁷ Every animal that is with you, of all flesh, bird, beast, and every creeping thing that creeps upon the earth, bring out with you,
  and they shall teem in the earth,
  and shall be fruitful and increase on the earth.'

(ix) Leaving the ark

¹⁸ And Noah went out, and his sons, and his wife, and his daughters-in-law with him.

¹⁹ Every animal, everything running, and everything flying,
everything creeping on the earth,
according to their families
they went out from the ark.

²⁰ And Noah built an altar to the LORD,
and he took of every clean beast and every clean bird,
and he offered up burnt offerings on the altar.

²¹ And the LORD smelt the scent of tranquillity, and the LORD said to
himself, 'I shall no more curse the ground (*ha-adamah*) because
of humankind (*ha-adam*),
because the devising of the human heart is evil from youth up,
and I shall never again smite all life as I have done.

²² While the earth remains
seedtime and harvest, cold and heat, summer and winter, day and
night, shall not cease.'

In commenting on this third section of the Flood story it will be convenient to
run through some textual points, in order, and then return to discussions of
major topics.

In the first verse it is said that God remembered Noah. As already noted on
p. 110-11, in scriptural Hebrew a verb of perceiving or of activity in the mind is
not purely mental; it implies consequent action. What is said here is that God
acted as one remembering. It does not necessarily imply that God had forgotten. Also, all scriptural language about God uses metaphors drawn from
human life, since we have no words for the unspeakable. There is a necessary
imprecision in talking about God.

When, in verse 2, it is told that God stopped up the windows of the sky,
the word for 'window' is not that which means 'lattice' as was used when it
was said that the windows of the sky were opened. The word used now,
chalon, is the general word for 'window' and can represent windows of
various sorts. The wind which, in the first verse, passes over the water-
covered earth, is in Hebrew *ruach,* the word for 'spirit' when the story of the
seven days of the Creation tells that the spirit of God was moving on the
waters. Thus wind over water is common to the first day of the Creation and
the beginning of the earth's restoration after the Flood. In verse 14 is
another echo of the seven days. The word translated 'dry' (*yevashah*) is that
already used for the dry land exposed the gathering of water on the third of
the days of the Creation.

In verse 11 the fresh olive leaves were obviously the product of sprouting
within the previous seven days. Therefore 'Noah knew'. It is possible here to
translate the second part of the verse as 'and Noah knew that the water had
subsided from off the earth'. However, the musical notation disjoins 'Noah
knew' from what follows, so that the translation becomes that already given,

'and Noah knew: for the water...': the musical tropes make Noah's knowing more than an appreciation of the fact that the water had subsided. On pages 75 and 76 comment has already been made about the use of 'know' (*yada'*) in the Hebrew scriptures, and how it is more than knowing that this or that is so, more than knowing some fact, more than acquaintance.

The wording of God's command to leave the ark, in verses 15-17, has several subtleties. 'God spoke to Noah, saying...' is rather more formal than 'God (*or* the Lord) said to Noah...' The latter formula was used when God saw Noah as the one who was righteous and to be saved. From bad news and an offer of protection we have now gone to good news and the wider implications of responsibility for life. The responsibility put on Noah for people and animals alike is emphasised by the repetition of 'with you' (*ittakh*) at the end of each of the two commands to take living things out of the ark. Since each command is thus rounded off, to be a unit, the next words, 'and they shall teem in the earth', can be heard to apply to people and animals alike. Noah is told to 'go out...you, and' the other human beings 'with you' and to 'bring out' the animals,—two modes of exercising his responsibility.

Verse 19 is a little difficult to translate. Where I have put 'everything running' and 'everything creeping' it would have been possible to say 'moving' in both. The same verb, and its related noun, can mean simply moving, or creeping, or gliding through the water. I have tried, by writing 'running' to indicate movement on dry land, with 'creeping' where the movement is on the earth, in the sense of being along the ground.

The reference to a curse on the ground, with the coupling of ground (*adamah*) and humankind (*adam*), echo the story of the Garden of Eden.

***

Now that some details of the text have been dealt with, the decks are cleared for dealing with some of the text's features which have more general importance for our understanding of this section of the Flood story.

When the text said (7:20) that the mountains were covered with water, it was commented on page 133 that the only mountains in the Flood story are of considerable height. Now that the waters are subsiding, the ark comes to rest on the mountains of Ararat (verse 4): Ararat is the ancient country also called Urartu, and shown as such in Figure 4. Ararat corresponds approximately to the modern Armenia, principally within the Armenian Republic and Turkey. The 'mountains of Ararat' the highest in all the Near East, are steep and rugged, reaching 17,000 feet, and we cannot suppose the story to be about small hills.

Therefore the 'mountains of Ararat' are one of the text's guides to how it is to be read. The covering of such mountains by water does not indicate an inundation like others, only bigger. We are taken beyond simply magnifying known experience to something at the limits of imagination

The raven and the dove are the only animal life which appears as individuals. It would seem that the story is written for those who expect these birds to appear in it, since at their first mention they are called 'the raven' and 'the dove'. Clearly, by the time that the story was written down, as we have it, it was already known in some form. Since the Mesopotamian versions of the Flood story also tell of birds sent out by a floating survivor, it seems that versions of the Flood story circulated in the Near East at the time when this was written. It is likely that neither the Hebrew Flood story nor the versions known from Sumerian, Babylonian, and Assyrian clay tablets are the first versions known to speakers of their respective languages. (There are about 250 Flood stories, at least, in circulation among the peoples of this globe.) The incident of the birds has, in the Hebrew scriptures, however, a characteristic which is unique. Comparison with other Flood stories shows up this characteristic, but cannot explain it.

Let us make the comparison. In the Gilgamesh Epic (Babylonian, but known in an Assyrian version) we find this said: 'Forth went the dove, but came back to me'. The Israelite Flood story does not say 'Forth went the dove, but returned to Noah'. This would have sufficed to carry on the story line, but verses 8 to 11 of our text say much more.

We have a picture, as vivid as economical, of the relationship between man and bird. 'And he put out his hand, and he took her, and he brought her to himself, into the ark.' There are three intimate actions, leading to the words 'to himself', so that the final, otherwise dry, 'into the ark' becomes a culmination of tenderness. Read it aloud to yourself, taking each word as it comes, without haste. Again, the dove does not simply return to shelter and safety: 'and the dove came to him at evening time'. The personal bond between them here has a place in time, the time of homecoming and contentment.

The raven is different. It goes out and it returns, just that. He and Noah have some use of each other. What each does toward the other need be no more than enlightened self-interest. It could be said that the domestication of animals, if needing neither fear nor a confidence trick, derives from one or more of three sources: mutual advantage, innate nature, and the understanding by which 'the righteous knows the life of his beast' (Proverbs 12:10) and by which the beast may know us. The raven speaks to us of the first two, the dove of all three. The dove's innate nature, in the end, takes her from Noah. As in the well-known saying:

> If you love something let it go;
> If it returns you still have it;
> If it does not it was never yours.

The dove was never Noah's. He serves her, by divine command. Of God's word, God's command, comes the loving tenderness between Noah and the dove.

***

Noah's offerings, in verse 20, are given freely. He does not sacrifice by way of atonement, for there is nothing in what we are told that needs to be atoned for. He does not sacrifice to placate God, for God's destructiveness has passed, and there has been no anger against Noah. He does not sacrifice to appeal to God, for God has been close to him and protected him even when his need was more urgent. Noah makes offerings only after being saved. If they are taken within the context of the story within which they are an event, they must be expressing gratitude, relief, joy, perhaps, but not obligation. Noah fulfilled his great obligation when he obeyed God and saved life on earth. It is rather that Noah reaches out to God, just as he reached out to the dove.

Sacrifices in the Hebrew scriptures are often meals, and therefore the victims are fit to eat. Now, therefore, we see why only clean animals were taken in the extra numbers needed if animals were to be sacrificed while their species survived.

The Lord's smelling the sacrifices is a very powerful metaphor, since scents, far more than sights or sounds, are unanalysable wholes, tending to arouse entire states of being. The 'scent of tranquillity' is an attempt to render more literally what other translations give as 'a pleasing odour' or 'sweet savour'. The Hebrew term, *réach hannichoach,* is a quite formal expression which sometimes can have none of its literal meaning, even if one supposes that there can be any meaning for 'scent of tranquillity' that would qualify as literal. It is what goes from an offering towards God, who may (e.g. Leviticus 26:31) or may not (e.g. Numbers 28:2) accept it, or towards idols (e.g. Ezekiel 20:28) which, of course, have no sense of smell (e.g. Psalm 115:6). Thus any eagerness to take the 'scent of tranquillity' literally must be blunted by the formal cliché itself. What is left unblunted is the power of smelling as a metaphor for what the Lord was doing.

At the sacrifices the Lord says that he will no more curse the ground 'because the devising of the human heart is evil from youth up'. This is ambiguous. It may mean that the Lord will no longer exercise the curse which has the evil devising of the heart as its reason. Alternatively, it may mean that this tendency to devise evil is one reason the Lord will *no more* curse the ground; that is, the Lord is making an allowance for human nature. The ambiguity is clear and, in so intricately worked a text, with such evident exactness of wording, can hardly be due to sloppy writing. The two meanings can exist side by side and need not contradict each other. The ambiguity is not for self-contradiction but for enrichment.

At the end of this section is God's promise that 'seedtime and harvest, cold and heat, summer and winter, day and night, shall not cease'. These pairs represent the cycles of time established on Creation's fourth day, although seedtime and harvest are an aspect of these realised only through humankind. Here again is an instance of how the story turns the mind away from a bigger than usual catastrophe to something of another kind, something which these pairs, with their reference to the world's cycles, and the creation of those cycles, put into a cosmic context.

This point is made particularly by the promise that day and night should not cease. Some have taken this to mean that the story intends to say that day and night ceased during the Flood (e.g. Rashi* on Genesis 8:22), but this cannot be so. The dove returned at eventide, and there is no suggestion that this means other than what it says. The point is that day and night had not ceased. Therefore the promise that they should not do so puts the Lord's words to Noah in a wider setting than is offered by the Flood story in itself. The affirmation of day and night is part of the negation of the Flood, because the Flood is a partial reversal of Creation, and Noah's intercourse with the Lord after the Flood has much to do with the created world and its relation to humankind, as will be seen when the next section of the Flood story is considered.

***

The Flood story puts it firmly within the cycles of years, months, and days. The dating and lengths of time that occur in the text certainly seem to suppose the world's more obvious astronomical cycles, not a cessation of day and night. These indications of time can be put together, to give a calendar of events. In reconstructing this calendar, I follow the argument of Cassuto*, using his calculations throughout. Before this reconstruction is begun, however, the naming of months may be noted. In fact the months are numbered, not named. The names of months can vary widely even between very closely related languages, and it is likely that this was known to the ancient Israelites. It may be for this reason that the months are known in the Flood story by numbers, since the Hebrew Creation narrative is explicitly universal in intention, not ethnic. The reconstruction of the Flood calendar can be taken step by step; chapter and verse references are given in brackets, for reference to the translation already presented. The months are those of the 600th and 601st years of Noah's life.

Month 1 —day 1:   God's first communication to Noah (6:13). This is given no date. It would be on the 1st day of the 1st month if one takes the interval to the 2nd of God's communications to be the common scriptural period of 40 days. Since this puts the 1st communication on the 1st day of the year, it seems not to be an unreasonable assumption.

Month 2 —day 10:   God's 2nd communication to Noah (7:1), which is 7 days before...

Month 2—day 17:   ...the waters begin to come (7:11), for which the date is given.

Month 3 —day 27:   The 40 days of increase of the water (7:17) brings us to this date.

Month 7—day 17:   Date given for the grounding of the ark (8:4). The water prevailed for 150 days (7:24). This day is 5 months, that is 147 days, after the waters begin. Is 150 a round number of days, used as an expression for 5 months? (A lunar month has 29½ days, 29 or 30 on the calendar, with short and long months necessarily mixed, to keep the average to 29½.)

Month 10—day 1:   The mountain tops are seen (8:5); the date is given.

Month 11—day 10:   Noah opens the window and sends out the raven 40 days later (8:6,7).

Month 11—day 17:   The dove is sent out for the first time (8:8). This must be 7 days after the raven is sent out first, because the second sending out of the dove is said to be after *another* 7 days (8:10).

Month 11—day 24:   The dove is sent out a second time, 7 days later; the water has subsided (8:11)

Month 12-day 1 or 2:   The dove is sent out, 7 days later, for the third time (8:12).

Month 1—day 1:   The waters have dried off the earth (8:13), the date being given. If the calculation of the date of God's 1st communication to Noah is taken as correct, then the disappearance of the water covering the ground follows after exactly 12 months, that is, one lunar year.

Month 2—day 27:   This date is given for the earth's becoming dry (8:14). The first day of the waters of the Flood, and this first day of the dry earth, are the first and last days of a period of 12 lunar months and 11 days, which is one solar year of 365 days.

Since it is unlikely that the days of disappearance of water and dry earth end these two exact periods by coincidence, there is surely some calendrical plan in the story. (Incidentally, received source criticism, which breaks down the Flood story into the presumed 'documents' from which it is constructed, does not explain why there are two drying dates but has them in the same document, namely 'P', together with the other exactly stated dates of the story.) So the disappearance of covering water, and the subsequent dryness of the exposed earth, are used respectively to define two periods, one a lunar and the other a solar year long. One may doubt the inferred date, given above, for God's first communication to Noah, and therefore doubt whether the story embodies an intention to use a lunar year. The solar year, on the other hand, is given not by inference but by two of the Flood story's explicitly stated dates.

IN THIS FOURTH and last division of the Flood story, the three sections are each something said by God. What is said relates God, human beings, and beasts to each other. God relates himself to the others by a covenant. In the translation, which lies entirely within chapter 9 of Genesis, the spelling of 'You' with the upper-case 'Y' indicates the plural, as before. The division into lines accords with the Hebrew music marks.

(x) God's blessing and command to protect life

¹ And God blessed Noah and his children,
and said to them 'Be fruitful and increase and fill the earth.

² And the awe and fear of You shall be
on every beast of the earth,
and on every flying thing of the sky,
in everything that moves on the ground and in every fish of
the sea; into your hand they are given.

³ Everything moving that lives
to You shall be for food;
as the green herbage,
so everything have I given You.

⁴ But flesh with its life, its blood, You shall not eat.

⁵ But, also for Your blood, of Your lives, I will seek answer, from every
animal will I seek answer for it,
and from the human being, each for his brother,
for the human life will I seek answer.

⁶ Who pours out the blood of humankind,
by humankind shall his blood be poured out,
for in the image of God
he created humankind.

⁷ And You, be fruitful and increase;
teem in the earth and increase in it.'

(xi) God's covenant with the many

8 And God spoke to Noah
and to his sons with him, saying

9 'And I, here am I establishing my covenant with You,
and with Your seed after You,

10 and with all the animal life that is with You,
the flying things, the cattle, and every animal of the earth with You,
from all that come out of the ark to every animal on earth.

11 And I shall establish my covenant with You,
never again to cut off all flesh by means of the Flood's water,
and there shall never again be a Flood to destroy the earth.'

(xii) God and humanity to see the bow

12 And God said 'This is the sign of the covenant which I am putting
between me and You,
and all animal life that is with You,
for all generations.

13 My bow I put in the cloud,
and it shall become the sign of a covenant
between me and the earth.

14 And it shall be that, when I cloud over the earth with a cloud,
and the bow will be seen in the cloud,

15 then shall I remember my covenant which is between me and You,
and all animal life and all flesh,
and never again will water become a Flood
to destroy all flesh.

16 And the bow will be in the cloud,
and I shall see it, to remember the eternal covenant
between God
and all animal life,
all flesh that is on the earth.'

17 And God said to Noah,
'This is the sign of the covenant which I have established
between me and all flesh that is upon the earth'.

The original command, given to humanity and animal life in the sixth day's work of the Creation (1:29,30), to have a plant diet is here contradicted in verse 3. The words 'as the green herbage' must surely be a reminder about what is already permitted, so that there is a definite change. On the change, two comments are to the point. It is first to be noted that appointing of a green diet was for all human and animal life, not excepting those beasts which the writer must certainly have known to be naturally flesh-eating. It is therefore probable that the appointing of a green diet is meant to represent an unexperienced ideal state of the world, as foretold by Isaiah (11:7,65:25), looking forward to a time when the lion will eat straw like the ox. Secondly, the permission to eat flesh is given to Noah, whom the story will soon show to be the forebear of nations spreading over the earth. Although human beings can sustain themselves with a vegetable diet in much of the earth, there are regions where human life is possible in an enduring relation with the earth only if flesh is eaten. The concession that flesh can be eaten is made known when the story is about to take us to a humankind of many nations, widespread over the earth's surface.

The conceding of flesh-eating is immediately hedged by a restriction, not to eat blood. It is made clear that this is because the blood of anything is its life. That is to say, the permission to eat an animal did not absolve the eater from respect for the beast eaten. Unwillingness to kill beasts is not to be confused with respect for animal life, although the two are often found together, and the respect may be the basis for the unwillingness.

The distinction is important if one is to understand what is said of animals in the Creation narrative and elsewhere in the Hebrew scriptures. For example, one may meet a vegetarian who would not kill a beast, but who shows little respect for living animals. On the other hand, those who respect the life of the beast may kill animals, often but not invariably for the protection of human beings or the satisfaction of their essential bodily needs. The following incident in India is to the point here. The quotation is from Nancy Banks-Smith's review, in the Guardian, 23/11/1987, of *Man-Eating Tiger,* a Channel 4 television programme broadcast on the previous day.

> Toona Bai was gathering firewood in the forest when the tiger jumped on her back. 'I prayed with folded hands, "Please leave me. I'm the only bread-winner". The tiger did leave me and sat some distance away. When it came charging towards me, I caught his feet and bowed my head respectfully...'
> ...Toona Bai's tigress had killed twice before and was shot... When the tigress was driven into Jabalpur, strapped to the bonnet of a truck, the road was lined with people. They stood on roofs and followed running. They put garlands of yellow flowers on the tigress's neck as if she were a bride. They filed past and stroked her paws as if she were a saint. Even Toona Bai came. to touch the tiger and ask a blessing.

This is obviously respect, not terror. Danger from the tigress was no doubt felt during her life, but the respect shown her, recalling that paid to a bride or a saint, is clearly different from the fear of danger.

Following Noah's responsibility for animal life in the ark, and the trust and intimacy between him and the dove, God reaffirms human dominion over animals. With such dominion, licence to eat flesh still leaves a need to respect the life of the victim. The life, which is seen in the pulsing blood, may not be eaten. It is where responsible dominion meets human use of a non-human being that righteousness towards the non-human creation can be exemplified and tested. This is the meaning of eating flesh but not eating the pulsing life, which is the blood. The word used here for 'life' is *nefesh,* which is what the Adam became (not got) when the Lord breathed breath into him. This 'life' is not just undead existence, but is the individual in its entirety, life in its fulness.

The command not to eat blood is, in its wording, particular, rather than inclusive of matters over a wide field. However, the context makes it clear that what is spoken of is respect for non-human life, a matter of great generality. The setting of the prohibition of eating blood within the Flood narrative shows it to be particular in its wording not in order to be restrictive, but because it is a characteristic example of respect for non-human life and the precepts that this respect may imply. The wording makes clear that the prohibition of eating blood is about more than is literally in the prohibition. It is connected directly to life, and to the shedding of human blood and the inviolability of human life. This complex statement about blood, life, respect for animal life, and respect for human life, is preceded by God's statement of human dominion over animals, and followed by the command to be fruitful and replenish the earth. The particular represents the general, exemplifying, not restricting.

The force of the example depends upon the understanding of blood as being the life. If there is this understanding, then the prohibition bears upon the meeting between the use of non-human life and respect for it, as well as on the respect in itself. Not only Israelites, but other peoples, have eschewed and still eschew the eating of blood. Nevertheless others permit it, and for these, if they do not perceive an identity between blood and life, or the presence of life especially in the blood, the prohibition of eating blood may have no general implication. Therefore Jews, when identifying the rules by which all the righteous of humankind live, supplemented the prohibition of eating blood by that of eating a part taken from the living animal, which the Israelite scriptures, however, explicitly forbid only to Israelites and not to humankind in general. (Exodus 22:30 includes it.) In expressing these universal rules, the Jewish formulation nevertheless uses the prohibition of a part taken from the living, not that of eating blood (e.g. in Talmud Bavli*). As an example of respect for animal life, and of a rule bearing upon the meeting of this respect with use of the animal, it is likely to be more widely understood among the peoples of the world than is the prohibition of eating blood.

Therefore the command not to eat blood, given to Noah, whom the story makes the forebear of all later humankind, exemplifies the requirement to respect animal life, even when using it. This requirement can be exemplified also by the prohibition of eating a part taken from a living animal.

At various places in the Creation story, there have been words of God stating or implying precepts to govern the conduct of humankind. If these are formulated as precepts and put with their sources, the following list summarises those so far encountered.

The creation and blessing of the seventh day: 'You shall honour, not belittle, the name that cannot be spoken' (pages 31-38)

God sees that the wickedness of humankind is great in the earth and says that he will wipe them out: 'You shall have judgments among yourselves' (pages 119-121).

God's second saying that he will destroy humankind: 'You shall not rob or do violence' (pages 125-127).

God's prohibition of the eating of blood: This, being an example, can be stated as it stands ('Flesh with its life, its blood, you shall not eat'), or comparably ('You shall not eat a part taken from the living beast'), or generally ('You shall respect the life of the beast, even in your use of it').

The intention inherent in the Creation story must be that its instruction about human conduct applies to all humankind, since the Creation story is what has been called 'universal history' and 'primal history', not the story of a people or a part of humanity. Later in the Creation story nations form, and the Hebrew scriptures then show an origin for one particular nation—Israel, and a revelation to that nation of the rules for its own living. These cannot contradict the rules for all humankind, which includes Israel, and those which are applicable to Israel therefore show one way in which the universal rules can be manifested with less generality. In the Israelite view, the affirmation of the universal coupled with a revealed manifestation of what God requires for a particular people, is a pioneering event in human history. One people sees itself as the vehicle for showing how the Torah ('teaching') for all mankind is worked out as the Torah for a people, and Israel, as the means of exemplification, sees itself therefore as chosen. (Being chosen has its disadvantages, of course, and Jewish tradition makes the Israelites unwilling recipients of the Torah.)

This perspective may perhaps be useful in elucidating the implications of the prohibition of eating blood. Since the prohibition is an example, narrow in wording but wide in meaning, the wider meaning may be intended if respect for the non-human creation is sought in rules of life compatible with the universally applicable precept. If we see how the Torah for Israel deals with the matter, within the same Israelite scriptures which have the universally applicable rule, the general meaning of the prohibition of eating blood (or of eating a part from a living beast) will become more accessible. Examples can be taken not only from 'Torah' in the narrow sense of the first five books of scripture, but from the Hebrew scriptures generally.

After a series of sentences shouting happily in praise of the Lord, Psalm 115:16 bursts into exultation at enjoyment of the home of humankind.

> The heavens are the heavens of the Lord—but the
> earth has he given to the children of Adam!

As for the beasts in particular, it is said

> The righteous one knows the life (*nefesh,* 'person',
> 'soul') of his beast. (Proverbs 12:10)

> You shall not muzzle the ox when he treads out (i.e. threshes) the corn.
> (Deuteronomy 25:4)

Good behaviour towards an enemy includes good behaviour towards his beast (Exodus 23:5). Whatever we truly respect we are willing to learn from—

> Ask now the beasts, and they will teach you. (Job 12:7)

It is not surprising that animals will teach, in a body of scriptures which tell of a donkey as agent of God's word (Numbers, chapter 22), and which tell that God's salvation is for beast and humankind alike (Psalm 36:7; v.6 in English versions). As for the non-animal creation, the prohibition of felling fruit trees while besieging a city ends with the rhetorical question

> Is the tree of the field human, that you should come to besiege it?
> (Deuteronomy 20:19)

On this scriptural basis further rules of conduct were developed in post-biblical Jewry. The verse just quoted, about the tree, has become the basis for prohibiting wanton destruction generally, while Deuteronomy 11:15

> And I will give grass in your fields for your cattle, and you shall eat and be
> satisfied,

has become the basis for the rule that animals are to be fed before the human household eats. Thus we can get some idea of the underlying universal principle which the prohibition of eating blood, which is the life, exemplifies.

In what God says after the Flood animals are held responsible if they shed human blood. As it says in verse 5, 'But, also for your blood, of your lives, I will seek answer, from every animal will I seek answer for it.' This means that the animal and the human being are members of one community. The specification of this rule in the precepts for Israelites (Exodus 21:28-32) applies to domestic animals. This may suggest that making an animal answerable for shedding human blood presumed, within the Israelite framework of thought, that domestication is an ideal, so that the primal condition matches that prophesied by Isaiah (11: 6): 'the wolf also shall dwell with the lamb...and a little child shall lead them'.

***

The warning against shedding human blood is in three stages. First, there is the responsibility which the shedder of blood has for his brother's life, his brother's shed blood. The reference to the brother reminds the reader of Cain's repudiation of responsibility: 'Am I my brother's keeper?'

147

The second stage of the warning—is, in form at least, a proverb. 'Who pours out the blood of humankind, by humankind shall his blood be poured out.' There is a chiasma: the first half has the order outpouring-blood-humankind, the second has humankind-blood-outpouring. The original is more tight-knit, more proverbial in style, because of the similarity of *dam* and *adam*, 'blood' and 'humankind' respectively. There is a couplet which, with accents to mark the stress, can be transcribed like this.

> *Shofékh dám ha-adám*
> *Ba-adám damó yishafékh.*

It is a statement of the way the Creation is; bloodshed leads to bloodshed. Because of this Cain feared what would become of him, a killer, when he met other people. It is not a command to kill shedders of blood. The verb to 'pour out (*shafakh*) blood' never means to 'execute capital punishment' in biblical Hebrew. The proverbial form can remind the modern reader of the saying of Jesus in the Christian scriptures (Matthew 26:52): 'All they that take the sword shall perish with the sword'. This, of course, does not include all bloodshed, and is in any case about taking the sword, not necessarily using it; nevertheless it has a form very like that of God's saying to Noah, and is like that saying in that it is not a command to kill with the sword those who take the sword, but a statement of how things are.

The third stage of the warning against bloodshed is the reason: 'for in the image of God he created humankind'. The compactness of the couplet just before this permits the reason to be attached either to the declaration of the blood-shedder's responsibility, which comes before the couplet, or to the couplet itself. That is to say, it is ambiguous whether creation in the divine image is a reason why the shedder of blood is responsible for the blood shed, or whether it is a reason why those who shed blood will suffer bloodshed. In fact the ambiguity cannot be accidental. Our being created in God's image is a reason why bloodshed must be laid at the door of the shedder of blood, and also why people react to bloodshed by the extreme action of further bloodshed.

The statement that humankind is created in the divine image is, of course, a reference back to the work of the sixth of the seven Creation days: (1:26,27). Since the warning against bloodshed is obviously intended to be applicable in the past, the present, and the future, without distinction of time, our being in the image of God must also be always true. It therefore cannot be that the Creation story describes humankind as in the divine image only with respect to some unachieved future, as I have heard taught. Either what is meant is that we are now and always in the divine image, or else that the words of God to Noah, clearly echoing what has been said about the creation of humankind, nevertheless disagree with what is echoed, which is nonsense.

The difference between bloodshed in this passage and in the story of Cain is important for the meaning. Cain was faced with the natural consequence of his deed, and God protected him from this consequence. In the story of Cain, however, God gives no general instruction about killing, but makes a specific intervention to break the chain of bloodshed. In the words of God to Noah, the natural consequence is put in proverbial form in the couplet, but also God makes explicit the general proposition that the shedder of blood bears the responsibility for the act, and that the bloodshed is against God's image and therefore, by implication, that it touches directly on the Creator. Therefore the words to Noah go beyond those passing between God and Cain. There is what now amounts to an explicit warning or instruction by God against bloodshed, and this is general, not simply the identification of one particular act as a sin.

Here the Creation story, therefore, gives another precept attributed to God: you shall not shed blood. The way in which the precept is given shows its roots in three matters: responsibility of each for each, the working of the created order (here, more specifically, human nature), and human conduct as touching upon God. The third explains the others, and modifies nature's course, as God did in the particular instance of the sign given to Cain.

***

God has made a covenant with Noah. He now makes a covenant with all life (verses 8-11). The expression 'From all that come out of the ark to every animal on earth' is a literal translation. If 'every animal on earth' is distinct from 'all that come out of the ark', then there is a pointer here to the world repopulated after the Flood. This would be parallel with the words 'and with your seed after you' in the corresponding position at the end of the human part of the covenant.

The word 'covenant' (*b'rit*) presents some difficulty here. There is nothing about Noah's part in the making of the covenant or its fulfilment, although a covenant is by nature something between two parties. One way out of the difficulty would be to take this covenant as in some way continuous with that already made and established between God and Noah, before the waters come. This covenant however is not between God and Noah alone, since God says that it is between him and Noah, together with all the animals in the ark, and with all Noah's descendents; indeed the plural 'you' is pretty inclusive. How does God make a covenant with those not yet born. Clearly God is made by the story to accept animals and those unborn as making and fulfilling a covenant. Their responsibility within the terms of such a covenant can be only to be themselves. This is the point. They are themselves and God, for his part, will never again prevent them being themselves by sending a Flood.

The sign of the covenant is the rainbow. The sign of a covenant is no doubt a reminder to both parties. Nevertheless God's words about it refer only to the rainbow as a reminder to God. This image of the Creator and Destroyer reminding himself of an obligation puts humility and equity at the highest and most central place of the universal order.

This last section, about the rainbow, is rich in repetition, even to the point at which verse 16 may seem redundant at first glance. This is however the Flood story's coda, and the repetitions, with their differences, resemble the chords at the end of a symphony. The majesty becomes apparent when the section is read aloud, and is emphasised by God's reference to himself in the third person, in verse 16. The chords having piled up, the last verse, plain and serene, provides a contrasting closing cadence.

LIKE ALL THE CREATION narrative, the Flood story is densely written, language by art conveying much within a compass small for what is said. Thus far the richness of the detail and of the story's parts has been examined. It is now appropriate to see the Flood story as a whole. This will be done in three ways. First, attention is paid to the internal pattern of the Flood story, then to its relation to earlier parts of the Creation narrative, and last to its use of time, which points towards scriptural writings after those about the Creation.

First then, as to the internal pattern, this becomes obvious if the twelve sections of the story are set out in order, but with the series 'folded' in the middle. In this way the sixth episode comes opposite the seventh, the fifth opposite the eighth, and so on. The effect on the attentive listener or reader (who need not, of course, be able to articulate what is experienced) is a sense of being led up to a climax, and back down by a similar path. The pattern as shown in Figure 13 overleaf follows Cassuto*, who calls the pattern 'concentric parallelism'. Gordon Wenham*, who calls it 'palistrophe' demonstrates a similar 'folded back' structure of the Flood story, but does so with division of the narrative into portions smaller and more numerous than these twelve.

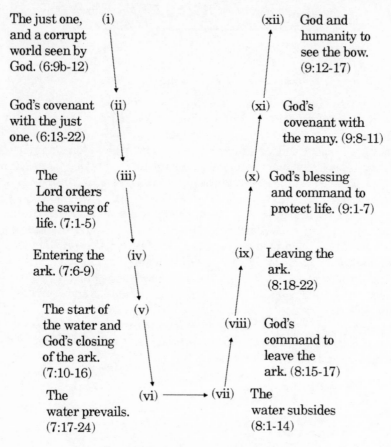

The just one, (i) — and a corrupt world seen by God. (6:9b-12)

(xii) God and humanity to see the bow. (9:12-17)

God's covenant (ii) — with the just one. (6:13-22)

(xi) God's covenant with the many. (9:8-11)

The (iii) — Lord orders the saving of life. (7:1-5)

(x) God's blessing and command to protect life. (9:1-7)

Entering the (iv) — ark. (7:6-9)

(ix) Leaving the ark. (8:18-22)

The start of (v) — the water and God's closing of the ark. (7:10-16)

(viii) God's command to leave the ark. (8:15-17)

The (vi) ———→ (vii) The water prevails. (7:17-24)

water subsides (8:1-14)

Fig. 13. *The Pattern of the Flood Story*

If an episode is taken with that opposite in the figure, it can be seen that each pair has a theme which its two members have in common. The match is, however, not evident between the first and twelfth episodes. The story starts with the corruption on earth. It does not finish with any prospect that corruption will not recur. Under the rainbow, at the sacrifices of Noah, God warns that the life of beast and human being is to be respected, and then enters into a covenant, with no undertaking from the other party, never to send the Flood again, while the source of the power of creation and destruction, in great humility, reminds himself of his obligation. As there is no return to the Garden of Eden, but only a gift of garments, so there is no return to the world before the Flood, only the giving of a new beginning under divine protection.

Thus, although the Flood story has an inner pattern, the failure of this pattern for the first and last episodes, gives a forward thrust, so that the story is not turned in on itself. The beginning of the tale is what God sees; the end, the rainbow, is what God and God's creation see together. In that God is one who is reminded, the rainbow is made by God to be an instrument bringing Creator and Created very close indeed, in fellowship.

The classical symmetry of the Flood story is disturbed by the baroque movement of its thrust. As Francis Bacon* wrote, 'There is no excellent beauty that hath not some strangeness in the proportion'.

***

The Flood story not only has an integrating structure within itself, but also is integral with the rest of the Creation story. This is shown by its echoes of earlier passages, particularly some in the telling of the seven days and of the Garden of Eden. During discussion of the Flood story, these echoes have been noted from time to time. It may be easier to sense the strength of the connection, if all these echoes are now reviewed together.

The Flood waters come from 'the springs of the great deep' and 'the windows of the sky' are opened. This confluence of upper and lower water is in opposition to the separation of water from water at the making of the expanse in the work of the second day. Creation is partly reversed by the Flood, and restored by the abatement of the water. The Creator does not set in motion the world of created things, to exist withdrawn from it. On the contrary, the power to do implies the power to undo.

It is therefore apt that the restoration of the world after the Flood is told in a way that recalls features of the seven days of the Creation and the Garden. Since these echoes of earlier narrative have already been noted in discussion of the Flood story, it is sufficient to. bring them together here as a bare list.

1. 'Every animal...shall be fruitful and increase on the earth' (8:17; episode viii). 'And God...said..."Be fruitful and increase and fill the earth"' (9:1; episode x). 'Be fruitful and increase' (1:22, 1:28; days 5 and 6).

2. 'I shall no more curse the ground because of humankind (the *adam*)' (8:21; episode ix). 'And to Adam he said "...cursed is the ground because of you" ' (1:17).

3. 'And the awe and fear of you shall be on every beast ...' etc. (9:2; episode x). 'Have dominion over every animal.' (1:28; day 6). Awe and dominion need not be the same for the reference back to the earlier story to be clear.

4. 'Everything that lives to you shall be for food; as the green herbage, so everything have I given you' (9:3; episode x). 'There is all green herbage for food' (1:29,30; day 6). There is a change here but, once again, the reference is obvious.

5. 'In the image of God he created humankind' (9:6; episode x). 'And God created humankind in his image' (1:27; day 6). Something said in the account of the sixth day becomes a reason for warning against bloodshed after the Flood.

153

These references between two stories within the Creation narrative act as cross links, reminding the reader of the unity of the whole. The power to create is thus reaffirmed even with changes. The unity of the Flood story with the story of the seven days and of the Garden of Eden therefore becomes an assertion that Creation is not once and for all, but is an aspect of the world's continuing existence, with God as eternal Creator.

***

The account of the Flood is given with reference to time, but the meanings of the way time is dealt with will be easier to examine after some note of time in the earlier parts of the Creation story. As already explained on pages 18-21, the work of the fourth of Creation's seven days includes the creation of time. This is time marked by heavenly bodies, even if the wording indicates that their movements are spoken of in relation to their being observable by other beings. This may be called cosmic time, and can give rise to calendar time, which is in the Hebrew scriptures based on the sun and moon, but has in addition the seven-day Sabbath cycle. When a calendar period does not depend upon some current natural period, and is thus like the Sabbath cycle, being also publicly recognized in a community, it may be called social time. Social time is not explicitly mentioned in the Creation narrative, in spite of the connection between the seven days of Creation and the Sabbath cycle of the week.

Distinct from cosmic time, and from social time, is inner time. When we are children a calendar year is longer for us than when we are adult. Markers of cosmic time, such as heavenly bodies, pendulums, and quartz crystals, may agree well enough with each other, but the agreement need not extend from their outer time to our inner time,—as I declare when I speak of moments that seem an age, or say that time just flew and that I had no idea how late it was. The same distinction holds good whether the outer time is cosmic or social. The story of Creation's seven days tell of the making of cosmic time, the measures of which are later supplemented by a further unit, the generation, which has a basis in a current natural rhythm and is therefore also cosmic. In the stories of Adam, Eve, and Cain, human experience may be related to an outer event, as when 'they heard the Lord God's voice moving in the breeze time of the day', and the experience has its own before and after. Nevertheless no connection is made between outer and inner time, since there is no outer duration or succession of events against which inner duration and succession are matched. After Cain's murder of his brother the Lord speaks to him, but Cain's inner time is not shown to meet a time scale set by the successive doings and presences of Abel and the Lord, since it is irrelevant whether anybody but Cain heard the Lord. Further similar considerations lead to the conclusion that, before the Flood story, the narrative never forces a confrontation between outer and inner time.

154

In the Flood story it is otherwise. Noah's own biography is fitted to the calendar of sun and moon. When still he waited another seven days, Noah's inner time and the cosmic outer time given by the sun meet to give the experience denoted by 'waited'. The Flood story brings outer and inner time together. This conjunction has three consequences. First, it puts the Flood into the sequence of human development. The confrontation between inner and outer time is an event in early childhood. Of course, we never make permanent peace between the two and, when inner duration concerns us, the markers of outer duration can be interruptions, nuisances, 'houres, dayes, moneths, yeares, which are the rags of time', irrelevant to John Donne's* lovemaking. The Flood story, presenting an inevitable developmental experience of each one of us, contributes by its treatment of time, as well as in other ways, to the telling of the creation of humankind.

A second consequence of the conjunction of inner and outer time arises from their different shapes. Outer time, insofar as it is cosmic, runs in cycles, giving repeating periods. Inner-time is not only cyclical but also markedly linear, running from infancy to death with open ends. In some ancient philosophies cyclical time strongly affects the view held of history, and the world is said to run through great ages which, more or less, repeat themselves. The Hebrew scripture make history linear, perhaps with a climax, but not repeating itself, although cyclical time is assured while the earth remains (8:22). It is described in terms of an emergence and succession, on to a consummation. Whether one's way of looking at history makes large its cyclical or linear aspects seems to depend on the way in which inner time and outer time are brought together. If there is an emphasis on human worth (for example, on our being made in the divine image) and on human responsibility, the importance of inner time, human time, will impose on history a linear emphasis, since inner time has a strong linear component. Conversely, if there is emphasis on the littleness of humankind in the cosmos, there could be a more marked contribution of outer time to its conjunction with inner time and, since cosmic time is strongly cyclical, a cyclical view of history might not be unexpected.

This leads to a consideration of history. The third consequence of the Flood story's conjunction of inner and outer time is that it prepares for history. That is, time is treated in a way that prepares the reader or listener for a transition from a non-historical manner of conveying, or trying to convey, truth, to an historiographical mode of narration, which needs both outer and inner time. Without outer time there is no history, only stream-of-consciousness writing. Without inner time, which is implied by waiting, by consideration and decision, by the study of motivation, and by other historical relevancies, we have no history, but only archive and chronology. This is not to say that the Hebrew scriptures pass into a new mode of narration immediately after the Flood story; they do not. Nevertheless, as we move from the Creation story to the story of the patriarchs and matriarchs just after it, we find a shift in the manner of telling, towards the historical. There is, however, more of the Creation story yet.

155

***

To speak of historiography and history while studying the Creation story will naturally lead to the question: what is the relation of this story to history? This will be a matter for consideration after the whole Creation story has been examined, when the truth of the story is discussed.

AFTER THE ACCOUNT of the Flood, the Creation story goes on to tell of one more incident of Noah's life. This incident centres on Noah's drunkenness but its ramifications, as will be seen, touch on several matters raised in the Creation story. The scriptural passage, of which the translation now follows, is entirely within Chapter 9 of Genesis.

18 And the sons of Noah that went out from the ark were Shem and
 Ham and Japhet (and Ham is the father of Canaan).

19 Three are these, the sons of Noah, and from these were dispersed
 all [the people of] the earth.

20 And Noah, the man of the ground, was the first to plant a vineyard.

21 And he drank of the wine and got drunk, and uncovered himself
 inside his tent.

22 And Ham, father of Canaan, saw the nakedness of his father, and
 he told his two brothers outside.

23 And Shem and Japhet took the garment and put it on the shoulders
 of the two of them, and went backwards, and covered their
 father's nakedness, and their faces were backwards, and
 their father's nakedness they did not see.

24 And Noah awoke from his wine, and he knew what his youngest
 son had done to him.

25 And he said, 'Cursed is Canaan; a servant of servants shall he be
 to his brothers',

26 And he said, 'Blessed is the LORD God of Shem; and let Canaan be
 a servant to him.

27 May God enlarge (*yaft*) Japhet (*Yefet*), and may he dwell in the
 tents of Shem; and let Canaan be a servant to him.'

28 And Noah lived after the Flood three hundred and fifty years.

29 And all the days of Noah were nine hundred and fifty years,
 and he died.

In this story various themes' are interwoven, but the passage nevertheless reads as a whole, so that the themes are like the voices of musical counterpoint. The first verse refers back to the Flood story which, with the passage before it (6:1-8) on the earth's corruption, has interrupted the item on Noah in the genealogy of the line through Seth.

This verse (18), however, by referring to Ham's fathering Canaan, looks forward to the presentation of the nations by the scriptural narrative, a presentation which will immediately follow the passage now before us. Nevertheless, the sentence 'Ham is the father of Canaan' can be taken primarily as about Ham, rather than as a statement about Canaan's origin. To speak of a man as 'father of...' is, in the Hebrew scriptures, to name with more precision, or to link the less known with the better known. To Israelite listeners or readers, neighbours to Canaan with whom their own history was entangled, it would have introduced Ham and would have given him a suitable handle to his name to have referred to him as Canaan's father.

After the Flood the Lord ceases to have a curse on the ground, and before this Noah's father prophesies that the son will 'comfort us from our works and from our hands' toil, which is from the ground the Lord cursed' (5:28). Now we find Noah, 'the man of the ground', planting the vine, an innovation in care of the earth, one yielding pleasure. This reference back leads to the new story, that of Noah's drunkenness. The new story, in turn, reintroduces Noah's sons, which provide a further mention of Canaan, to be considered in more detail in the next passage of scripture, when nations are named.

Finally, the complication of themes ends when the broken genealogical entry for Noah is completed. This is evident if verses 28 and 29 in this tale of drunkenness are joined to Genesis 5:32, immediately before the Flood story. The form of the genealogical item about Noah can then be seen to differ somewhat from that of the standard entry for his forebears. The death of Noah ends all reference to the Flood within the Creation story.

***

The description 'man of the ground' reminds the reader of the curse on the ground, and of the Lord's saying that he would no more curse it. The actual word for 'curse' when the Lord says he will curse the ground no more is not the same as the word used when the Lord first curses the ground, but there is an echo of sense if not of words. The two words are synonymous, that used in the Garden of Eden being favoured in scripture when a descriptive past participle (*arur*, 'cursèd', 'accursed') is written, while the word used after the Flood (*qalal*) is commoner for the active sense ('to curse', 'cursing', etc.).

From the vine comes, through drunkenness, Noah's uncovering himself in his tent, where he is unconscious, as the telling lets us know when we read that 'Noah awoke from his wine'. Brandon* has suggested that drunkenness is the fulfilment of the prophecy that Noah would bring comfort. There are two objections to this interpretation. The first is that the Hebrew scriptures, although commending wine which, with corn and oil, is one of earth's great gifts (Psalm 104: 15(14)), generally present drunkenness as an undesirable condition (e g. Isaiah 63:6), unless of course, one is to get drunk with love! (See Song of Songs 5:1, end of verse, where the New English Bible correctly points to the original Hebrew's injunction to do this.) The first objection, then, to making drunkenness the prophesied comfort is cultural; it supposes an Israelite attitude to drunkenness that the Hebrew scriptures do not support. The second objection is that the prophecy by Lamech, Noah's father, refers to the curse on the ground (5:28), which is the subject of the Lord's saying that the ground will be no more cursed (8:21). Can the ability to get drunk really be all there is to the ground's being no more cursed? Rather, Noah is 'the man of the ground' with whom the ground will no more be cursed, in token of which he is the initiator of our obtaining new riches, namely wine, from the earth.

Here the story presents an irony. Noah, intoxicated, is naked and unashamed. So were the man and woman in the garden, before eating of the forbidden tree (2:25). They, however, were unashamed 'before each other' but drunkenness dulls awareness of others in a way that leads from the possibility of shame to the actuality of shamelessness. Dehumanisation is not prehumanisation. That the Lord no more curses the ground opens up a way forward, not a return to the Garden of Eden. The way must be onward; there is no retracing of steps. The irony of Noah's lying naked and unashamed brings the lesson home. That Noah, presented as commendable, takes wine beyond gladness to folly need not surprise us. In the Hebrew scriptures even the most highly commended characters are commonly depicted with their defects, warts and all.

***

If our circle of attention is now expanded, to include Ham as well as his father, we come to the heart of the matter, which is not Noah's drunkenness but Ham's behaviour in the face of that drunkenness. Ham sees his father naked, leaves him so, and goes to talk about it. His brothers cover their father without looking at him, and their care in this is emphasised by the relentless particularity of verse 23, the cumulative detail of which stands out against the shorter sentences and terser style of the rest of the passage.

> And Shem and Japhet took the garment
> and put it on the shoulders of the two of them,
> and went backwards,
> and covered their father's nakedness,
> and their faces were backwards,
> and their father's nakedness they did not see.

The telling leaves no doubt that Ham is to be seen as wrong and his brothers as right. We can infer that Ham's attitude to Noah's nakedness shows lack of a son's due respect for his father, and that the disrespect lies in that it is unbecoming for a father's nakedness to be seen by his son. Further, since it may be presumed that Ham would not have shown disrespect to his father had the latter been awake and alert, the misdeed is compounded by taking advantage of the victim's disability.

Before going on to examine Noah's reaction to Ham's deed, it may be helpful to look at Noah's knowledge of it. We are not told how Noah 'knew what his youngest son had done to him'. For the purpose of the writing there need be no reason why we should be told how Noah knew. It is not relevant, and scriptural narrative tends to be economical. There is scope for the reader to imagine. Did Noah overhear, as he awoke, two sons chiding the third? Was he able to piece together what happened after asking why his cover was spread differently from usual? There is no given answer. The Hebrew literature of scripture engages the reader in active response. It is not a logarithm table or telephone directory, compact with explicit right answers. Sometimes critics argue that things have been lost from our text, because the oldest translations supply these unsaid details. Such translations need not, however, be witnesses to lost writing. They may simply be filling in, boringly, what the art of the original Hebrew has left unsaid. (The reader who is interested in gaps as a feature of the literary technique of the Hebrew scriptures may profitably consult Sternberg*.)

The expression 'what his youngest son had done to him' does not necessarily indicate physical interference with Noah. The verb 'had done' ('asah) is very general, and 'to him' (lo) can be understood as 'towards him', also very general. What verse 24 says that Noah knew is quite compatible with what verse 22 says of Ham's deed.

Nevertheless there are stories that Ham castrated his father or abused him sexually. Our oldest source for these is third-century rabbis reported in Talmud Bavli*, but they were probably already old stories when those rabbis lived. In the story as we have it, however, neither castration nor physical abuse is a possible interpretation. Verse 23 makes it clear that Ham's fault is in gazing on his father's nakedness and then gossiping about it, instead of discreetly covering it. If the more brutal stories were current when our version was first set down, their avoidance here can be seen only as firm and deliberate. A version of a text does not 'really' mean what is in another version and (to stress the obvious) any writing must be taken to mean what it says.

In verses 25-27 the name 'Canaan' is used. It makes sense only if Ham is meant, the plot requiring no change of person. Ham-Shem-Japhet in verses 22 and 23 becomes Canaan-Shem-Japhet in verses 25-27. However, the story says that Canaan is Ham's son. Can a man be the same person as his son? Yes, he can be, according to the literary style of the Hebrew scriptures, especially if the 'son' is a people or group of peoples. Thus in Chapter 36 of Genesis the reader is reminded that Esau is 'the father of Edom', a nation (36:43), and also that 'Esau is Edom' (36:8). If the Israelites had Canaan for their best-known representative of Ham's peoples, as they almost certainly must have done, 'Canaan' could have been used by them to stand for 'Ham' where this would not have caused confusion.

***

The content of Noah's curse is critical for an understanding of the story. Ham is to be a servant to his brothers. The word 'servant' (*'eved*), although also translated 'slave', is not the same in meaning as when one speaks of slaves in Greece, Rome, Arabia, the British West Indies, or the United States, for example. For example, in Israel a 'slave' was not inheritable property. What Israelite service had in common with at least some other forms was that there was a peculiar relation of master and servant which would have made it nonsense to speak of someone as servant to his brothers. That is to say, Noah was saying that Canaan—or Ham—was now outside the family.

Now we can see the connection between the offence and the curse. The family, in its more restricted sense as the 'nuclear' family rather than the clan, is defined in the Hebrew scriptures by the relatives who cannot marry each other by reason of consanguinity. This is expressed as a listing of those relatives whose nakedness one may not see (e.g. Leviticus 18). In fact the word for 'nakedness' (*'ervah*) in this story of Noah and Ham is the same as that used in prohibiting consanguineous unions; it is a word with marked sexual connotations.

Noah, in cursing Ham, is saying that Ham has put himself outside the family by his not observing the prohibition by which a family defines itself and is socially defined. The creation story has already had families. Here, for the first time however, the rightness of the family as part of the created order is asserted.

***

The family within the Creation will be taken up again, but there are matters arising from the story to be dealt with first. In particular, Shem, Ham, Japhet, and Canaan are, as will be seen, names within the Creation story's presentation of the nations. Do these names stand for nations in the story of Noah's drunkenness? Is this an Israelite story expressing disapproval of Canaanites and their fitness only to be the servants of other nations? Such an interpretation makes little sense. There is no historical situation which has ever fulfilled the condition that Canaan should be a servant to Shem and Japhet. When Israel, a descendant of Shem according to scripture, conquered Canaan, Canaanites were killed, or assimilated, or continued to live alongside the Israelites. Servitude was not a characteristic relationship, even

161

if some Canaanites became slaves of Israelites. As for the servitude of Canaan to Japhet, the historical case for it is even more tenuous, if any case at all can be made out.

The story is, moreover, quite unsuitable for expressing Israelite disapproval of Canaanites. Later, these Israelite scriptures express strong disapproval of Canaanite idolatry, but idolatry is not mentioned in connection with Noah and Canaan. It is true that Canaanite sexual practices meet with disapproval, but the disapproved sexual relations are connected with idolatry. Nowhere is it suggested that Canaanites, or any children of Ham, are lacking in filial piety, and it is this which is at the centre of the story of Ham and his drunken father.

There is therefore no reason to read into Noah's curse some ethnic meaning. There is every reason to see it as an assertion of the family as a part of the order of created things.

Noah's curse on Ham is followed by its being treated as part of the allotment of fate to all three brothers. Of Shem, Noah says 'Blessed is the Lord (*YHWH*) God of Shem'. The four-lettered name of God has already been used freely in parts of the Creation story with a bearing on humankind generally, and has occurred in telling of God in relation to Noah. It was in the sight of the Lord (YHWH) that Noah found grace (6:8), and the Lord was later to speak freely to Noah. So why is the Lord Shem's God? Surely the God of Noah and Shem is also the God of Ham and Japhet? In fact the Hebrew scriptures have a series of references to coming to know the Lord. Neither Cain nor his parents have anything less than a direct conversational relation with the Lord. Nevertheless it is at the birth of Cain's nephew Enosh that humankind began (or began again?) to call on the Lord's name (4:26). Now we have the Lord called the God of one of Noah's three sons. Although the Lord is said later to appear to Abraham, for example, Moses is told that the name was not known (i.e. totally apprehended in its wholeness) by Abraham (Exodus 6:3), and later Jeremiah, in whose time the name of the Lord (YHWH) was certainly known, said 'I will cause them to know my hand and my might, and they shall know that my name is the Lord (YHWH)' (Jeremiah 16:21). It is clear that all this is not about knowing God, nor about knowing that *YHWH* is a name of God, but appreciating and understanding what the name conveys. Given the scriptural treatment, taken as a whole, of this matter, and given what has been said of the Lord in the Creation story, it is difficult to see what other interpretation makes sense. It is noteworthy that this repeated extension of discovery, or recurrent rediscovery in, for example, Jeremiah, is typical of 'Lord' (*YHWH*) but not of 'God' (*Elohim*) The word *elohim* is, as already noted (page 128), a common noun, but the four-lettered name goes beyond words of explanation.

Shem then is capable of carrying, and therefore transmitting, an understanding of that of God which is conveyed by the name *YHWH*. Japhet is to dwell in the tents of Shem. This has no possible reference to anything that is known to have happened to the nations which, as will be seen, stemmed from Noah's sons. The meaning must be personal, and refer to the brothers themselves and, since 'tents' is plural, their households perhaps. The implication of the sayings about Shem and Japhet, coming together, is that Japhet will come to Shem on what concerns the divine name; there seems to be here a suggestion of instruction, of the transmission of an understanding. The reference to Ham as servant, in connection with what is said about each of his brothers, does not exclude his benefiting from what Shem has to offer, but he is in the tents of Shem and Japhet with an inferior personal status that excludes his being present as one of the family.

***

The force of Noah's declarations about his sons, including the curse which dissociates Ham from the family, is not simply prediction, nor is it simply an expression of Noah's wishes; indeed, it need not be expression of those wishes at all. In the Hebrew scripture, when a father or grandfather blesses the children and assigns them characteristics or destinies, he acts as God's agent. God acts through him. Of the brothers Manasseh and Epraim one must have the grandfather's (not father's in this case) right-handed blessing, and it matters to the extent that the grandfather, Jacob, has to override the right of the first-born, against the wish of the father, Joseph (Genesis 48:13). More striking perhaps is the blessing given by Isaac, who is deceived by Jacob, who is thus able to get the paternal blessing intended for Esau. Subsequent events in the story indicate that Jacob's cheating may be against God's ordering of things, but the blessing, we are given clearly to understand, has been destined for Jacob, even if the actual means of his getting it are to be considered wrong. The blessing by Isaac is also God's blessing on Jacob. The father is a channel for God's allocation of destinies.

Noah's curse, which makes Ham a servant to Shem and Japhet, is therefore God's curse. Consequently, Noah's assertion of the family against one who infringes the prohibition by which the family is defined, is God's assertion. Implicit, then, in this story of Noah's drunkenness is a precept given by God: there are nakednesses that you may not uncover. These precepts within the Creation story are given when God (or in this one case a father as agent of God) speaks or acts so as to state or imply a rule of conduct. The rule can be shown in each case to have a bearing on what it is to be human, that is, on the creation of humankind. This is the sixth of the precepts. The first four were summarised on page 146. The fifth, against bloodshed, was discussed on pages 147-149. There will be a seventh at the end of the Creation story, after which it will be convenient to review what the whole story has to say about human conduct.

'NOAH WAS A WHOLLY righteous man in his generations' (6:9). This can be translated also in this way: 'Noah was a man, righteous, perfect, in his generations'. This second way of translation reminds us that Noah is here called 'perfect'. The difference between the two translations is only this: in one, Noah is perfectly righteous, and in the other perfect and righteous. If the shade of meaning is in doubt, what is certain is that Noah is represented as perfect, either simply perfect or perfect in his righteousness. The Creation story has no other character of whom this, or anything like it, is said. Also of Noah, alone in the Creation story, is it said that he found grace in the eyes of the Lord.

There appears to be an invitation here to look at someone commendable. But what is being commended in Noah? To answer this we can proceed in two stages, seeking first to understand what is meant by saying that Noah is perfect, and then looking at the story to see what it tells about Noah that might explain his being called perfect.

In English to-day we often use the word 'perfect' to mean that the person so described has never done anything wrong, anything that we would call a sin. The Hebrew word (*tam, tamim*) appearing as 'perfect' in English translations. of the Hebrew scriptures does not mean this. It means 'finished', 'perfected', 'whole', 'complete'. There is also an implication of whole-heartedness in relation to the Creator, as shown by abstaining from idolatry (Deuteronomy 18:13, *tamim*) or total devotion to righteousness and the Lord (Job 1:1, *tam*). Similarly, in the Christian scriptures, perfection is not something out of human reach, made impossible by having done wrong. Jesus teaches the multitude, not the select few, in the Sermon on the Mount 'Be therefore perfect (Greek, *teleioi,* "entire") even as your Father in heaven is perfect' (Matthew 5:48). Jesus's saying follows the older Israelite notion of perfection (as well as Jewish doctrine of the imitation of God). The notion that perfection is attainable continues among some Christians (Benson*).

If Noah's drunkenness was a fault, it seems not to preclude his being perfect. It need not do so, for perfection does not mean faultlessness at every moment of life. However, it may also be helpful to understanding to appreciate that drunkenness is undesirable only according to its social setting. According to this setting it will affect other people to a greater or lesser degree, and affect the drunken one's development to a greater or lesser degree. There can be cultures in which drunkenness is caused only under exactly defined circumstances and without ill effects. In the Hebrew scriptures drunkenness is mentioned as clearly undesirable, but we now have too little information to know what might have been the weightiness or lightness of the fault among the ancient Israelites. For this reason we should not attach much importance to the fact that Noah got drunk, but see it simply as necessary to the plot of the story of Noah and his sons.

What can be meant by saying that Noah was 'perfect in his generations'? The older Jewish commentators took this to mean that Noah was righteous relative to others in his generation, but that he would have not appeared so in a generation of greater righteousness, such as Abraham's. This is contrary to the actual words which say that Noah was 'perfect', 'perfectly righteous', or 'wholly righteous'. The meaning must be that an absolute quality is meant, not something relative to the qualities of Noah's contemporaries. Either one is perfect or whole, or one is not; there are no degrees of perfection or wholeness. (A statement without reference to perfection, that said that somebody was righteous in his generation, might however mean that he was righteous relative to others of that generation.) There is another difficulty with the old Jewish interpretation, that it takes no account of the fact that 'in his generations' (*bedorotayv*) is plural. When the Hebrew scriptures speak of generations, in the plural, of such-and-such people, the reference is to the generations to come, those people's descendants. Therefore it does not seem that Noah is being commended in relation to his own generation but in relation to his righteous descendants. Nevertheless, there is a curious feature of the expression 'in his generations'. When the reference is to descendants the expression is 'for your (or their) generations'. The sense which I get on reading this statement about Noah is that he is said to be perfect inside the series of generations before and after him; that is, his perfection is seen within the context of the series of generations within which he stands.

The point may seem laboured, but it serves to turn attention from looking at a character in isolation, towards seeing him as part of the Creation story. If we are to understand Noah, we need to look at him within his generations, and range widely in the story. In this way we may find the reason for his being called righteous and perfect, or perfectly, wholly, righteous—have it as you will.

***

The telling of the Flood isolates Noah, leaves him standing clear of other people. This is not just because he is a survivor of massive destruction. There are eight human beings in the ark. Four of them, the women, are unnamed and take no part in the action. Three of the four men, Noah's three sons, are named on embarcation and disembarcation, but not during the Flood, when they are mentioned six times merely as his 'sons' and, like the women, take no part in the action of the Flood story. By bringing the three sons up to the Flood itself, before and after, but not within the space in which the telling is of the waters, their function in genealogical continuity is maintained without their intruding on the presentation of the solitary Noah. (It has been explained on page 86 why a genealogy in the Hebrew scriptures gives a series of male names.)

In order to explore further the way in which the narrative isolates Noah, I will turn to his maleness. Within the story there are three reasons why Noah is a male character. In the first place, he stands within a formal genealogy, running from Adam to Abraham, and on. Secondly, he builds the ark (6:14-16) and among the Israelites joinery was a male occupation, as it usually is to-day in modern Europe. Thirdly, Noah planted the vine (9:20) and, for those whose book this first was, viticulture was a male occupation, even if a lady might have a vineyard planted (Proverbs 31:16). (The reader curious to know what occupations might have been appropriate to an ancient Israelite woman can find spinning, weaving, trading in land, estate management, and selling cloth that she has made, all in Proverbs 31:10-31, as well as milling in Job 31:10, and any other examples that browsing through the Bible may yield.) That is to say, Noah is a male because of the social requirements of the story. On the other hand the references to his actual masculinity are only that he had a wife and fathered his sons, which are minimum requirements of the shape of the story. Interaction with a woman, by which a story can present a man's masculinity, is not there, and Noah, as far as we are told, neither takes part in tender exchanges, as between Adam and Eve, nor reacts crudely to the opposite sex as when his father's namesake Lamech boasts to his wives of his aggressive intentions.

In this way also the isolation of Noah in the telling of the story is developed. If Noah's wife is a cipher, Noah's masculinity is made of no concern. Thus Noah becomes capable of representing what is universal in humanity, what is common to us, irrespective of our sex. Whether the story takes advantage of this capability, whether Noah is in fact shown to us as a universal character will depend upon what converges on this solitary figure, and what diverges from it.

**

Before Noah are two human lines from Adam and Eve, one through Cain and the other through Seth. As far as the scriptural account goes, Noah is in Seth's line and the fate of Cain's is unknown. According to legend, Noah is the husband of Naamah, who is in the last generation of Cain's line, and the last-named of her generation. Whichever way one thinks about it, the literary structure presents a double line which is replaced by those in the ark, and of these Noah is the only human character with an active part in the story.

In the behaviour of Noah there is a convergence of the two lines, so that the literary structure is given a meaning. In Cain's line we have women, men in relation to women, human urges, and the earth. In Seth's line are men whose womenfolk are represented by silence, in a story without earth, but with a certain other-worldliness. Noah combines the characteristics of the two lines.

Noah is as pious as his father, Lamech, or his great-grandfather, Enoch, but he is also an artificer and cultivator, building the ark and being the first to plant the vine.

Thus the two lines of humanity converge on Noah, who is presented as somebody solitary even when accompanied. From Noah come two human developments, the family and the nations. The story has already told of natural families, and this is hardly surprising, since family life is a feature we share with the beasts. With Noah, however, the family is given a human and social colouring. Ham's behaviour towards his father's nakedness is contrasted with his brothers' behaviour. Noah's disapproval of Ham is expressed by the curse that Ham shall be his brothers' servant, therefore outside the family. In the Hebrew scriptures those who are considered members of the family (in its narrow sense, not the clan or 'extended family') are those who may not see each others' nakedness (compare Leviticus 18). (A wife and husband, therefore, who do of course see each other's nakedness, become of one family not in their capacity as 'each other' but as something undivided, 'one flesh', Genesis 2:24.) When Noah reacts to Ham's disrespect by excluding Ham from the family, the coupling of Ham's offence with that particular consequence implies that Noah sees the family not simply as a biological phenomenon, but as a human institution.

As will be seen, from Noah comes also another human grouping, the nation, since nations are first introduced into the story when Noah's descendants are presented. Noah then can be seen within the Creation story as a node, a spot on which the lines of humanity converge, and from which the family and the nation arise.

***

Since the story starts what it has to say of human nature by telling of Adam and Eve, and centres what follows on Noah, it may be fruitful to see how Noah relates to the couple in the garden. Therefore, to this end, we may look at the human condition as it is shown by Adam and Eve, comparing each point with what the character of Noah presents.

The couple fail to fulfil their humanity, in the image of God, when the man blames the woman and she blames the snake. They fail to take responsibility. As a result there is disturbance on each side of the triangular relation between the man, the woman, and the non-human creation, the triangle in Figure 5 on page 69. The man who had acknowledged his wife as 'bone of my bone', detachedly puts the blame for his own action on to 'the woman whom you gave to be with me' (3:12) vitiating the affectionate relationship which had been on the side of the triangle between man and woman. Between the woman and the non-human creation comes the curse on the snake, with which she had had converse, but which is now to be at loggerheads with her, its descendants with her descendants. (3:14,15). Correspondingly, between the man and the non-human creation comes the curse on the ground, which will now yield to the

167

man only with frustration and distressful labour (3:17-19).

Noah provides a contrast. First of all, he takes responsibility, not just in one particular but for all human life and the life of beast and bird. On the side of the triangle between the male and the non-human creation there is first the prophecy by Lamech, Noah's father, that the child will 'comfort us from…our…toil, which is from the ground the Lord cursed' (5:29). After the Flood the Lord addresses Noah in terms which recall the curse on the ground, spoken to the man in the garden (3:17). To Noah the Lord says 'I shall no more curse the ground (*adamah*) because of humankind' (literally, 'the Adam', 8:21). One possible meaning of this is that the curse put upon the ground because of the Adam is removed on Noah's account. This is the most obvious meaning. After the Flood we find Noah as 'the man of the ground' who is the first to plant the vine (9:20). The ground, no longer cursed, yields a new treasure to the husbandman. The primal man's failure to take responsibility leads to the vitiation of his relation with the ground. Noah's taking of responsibility is integral with his being the one for whom the vitiating curse is to be no more.

There is also the contrast between Noah and the woman. Her passing the blame leads to her, the mother of all living, finding herself in conflict with the now cursed snake. Noah, in taking responsibility for beasts and birds, enters into a tender relation with the dove when 'he put out his hand, and he took her, and he brought her to himself, into the ark' (8:9), as already discussed on page 138. It is in addressing Noah that God sanctions meat-eating (9:3), despite the earlier allocation of a green diet (1:29,30), but with the requirement for respect for the beast's life, which is the blood. The primal woman's failure to take responsibility leads to the vitiation of her relation with God's beast, the snake. Noah has fellowship with another of God's creatures, the dove, and is the recipient of God's word on respect for animal life.

Thus Noah repairs the sides of the triangle between the male and the non-human creation, and between the female and the non-human creation. Since he takes on the restored functions of the man and of the woman, the male and female meet in him. The sexes in the created world are obvious when the male and female are individuals and come together as a couple. Nevertheless, the polarity is present in the individual, in the social unit, and in the nation also, as will be discussed when the variety of nations is considered. (The full union of the male with the female within the individual was held by the alchemists to be an aspect of the completion of the alchemical spiritual work.) Since Noah is presented in his singleness and singularity, the reconciliation of male and female is effected by him at the level of the inner state of the individual. Were the form of the story to incorporate a couple rather than an individual, we may speculate, this reconciliation would be between two people.

So Noah, at the central human flaw, takes responsibility. From this centre comes out his amending of the spoilt triangle of relations between male, female, and the non-human. Beyond this triangle, however, and associated with the cursing of the ground and the snake, are the four sufferings decreed for the woman (1:16) and the man (1:18, 19) in the garden. These sufferings have been taken together on pages 68-69; although two are decreed to each of the couple, the nature of the sufferings is such that none can be confined to individuals of one sex. Although there is happiness in being fruitful and increasing, children are a source of sorrow also. Although being male and female is a delight, marriage can be imperilled by power. Although the vine-yielding earth is bountiful, its bounty is a response to painful toil. Although there is strength from glimpses of eternity, the cycle of death and birth is tragic to the percipient mind. These are the sufferings inseparable from human life, when the fruit of the forbidden tree has been eaten and we know things on a scale of better and worse. They remain with and after Noah. If his male side receives vintage from the earth, the vine is planted and dressed by labour and the tragedy of the human life cycle is around him in the destruction of a generation. As for the sufferings decreed to the woman, Noah had tragically to act against his own offspring as Ham brought sorrow.

The ending of the curses is not the ending of the sufferings. The removal of a curse need not stop that which the curse has set in train, but it frees human beings to face the sufferings, even to transform them and their meanings, rather than be passive victims. Noah offers wholeness, and within this one can enter into tragedy and, by interaction with it, come to wisdom. The sweat running off the face can meet with the contentment of unalienated creation, possible because we are in the Creator's image. The awareness of death and birth can meet with our apprehension of eternity. The tragedy which issues out of bearing children can meet with our joy in them and with the meaning that the succession of the generations has for us. The vitiation of marriage by sexual power can be confronted by being one flesh. The sufferings remain. There is no return to the Garden of Eden, except past the terrible cherubim and the turning, flaming sword to a tree untasted before the expulsion. But that would be a differently experienced garden. Noah's wholeness points the way forward; there is no way back.

***

In the latter of the works of the sixth day of the Creation (1:26-29) humankind is made in the divine image, male and female, to have dominion on earth. The fulfilment of this work is set in train when the Lord God forms the Adam out of the dust of the ground and breathes into the Adam's nostrils the breath (*neshamah*) of life (*chayyim*), so that the Adam becomes a living soul (*nephesh*) (2:7). Now in the language of scripture (although not necessarily in later Hebrew) neither *neshamah,* nor *chayyim,* nor *nephesh*, is peculiarly human. All these may be used, in the Hebrew scriptures, in speaking of beasts. Therefore this first breathing into the Adam's nostrils does not in itself constitute the making of humankind; it is the first step. Eventually, however, the story takes us to one who is called 'perfect', that is, perfected, complete. This is Noah. Thus it is that the making of humankind is presented in a way that requires the reader or listener to attend not simply to one episode, but to the whole succession of the narrative. Indeed, the making of humankind continues after the death of Noah, with the formation of the nations, but the story from the Adam to Noah comprehends what is being said with special attention to the individual.

As doors into some initial understanding of what is being said about humanity, three themes will be brought successively to the centre of attention: growth, completeness, and the fulfilment of the image of God. Concerning *growth,* it has already been noted how an initial concordance between sexes, and between the human and the non-human, become disturbed by failure to take responsibility, and how the concordance is restored at the taking of responsibility. This can be interpreted as a process in three stages. First there is the harmony of innocence. Then comes the disturbance when the forbidden fruit is eaten but the consequence of the act not faced. Third is the restoration of harmony, not in childish innocence but as a strength for the work of fulfilling the divine image.

The narrative indicates not only process, but also the *completed state* of being human, so that the span of the story is about the human condition at one moment. In this way we are offered a picture of human completeness. To start in the Garden of Eden at one side is the female, intimate with God's creature of the earth. In the presence of the female, and because of it, the male can realise itself, but not with full differentiation. This is the aspect of humanity which is towards the earth and towards our roots in it. Its love is the love which nurtures.

Away from this side the masculine develops and the feminine is correspondingly different. Here is the love that respects, that recognizes 'bone of my bone' and shares precious fruit, the love that is imperilled by shirking responsibility and sealed by accepting it. Feminine and masculine are here a pair, face to face.

Still further, and opposite our feminine side, is our masculine aspect, where there is the love that aspires, of which St. Augustine* of Hippo wrote 'Thou hast made us for thyself, and restless is our heart until it finds its rest in thee'. This upward and outward aspiration is expressed by Noah in sacrifice that is neither petitioning nor atoning (8:18-21, and see p. 139). It is an aspiring towards the Creator, and that is its purpose, even if other purposes such as thanksgiving, are one with that primary purpose.

Beside growth and completeness, there is in the story the *fulfilment of the image of God.* First there is the stage of perfecting, of healing, when the relation between masculine and feminine, and between human and non-human, is made whole, when responsibility is accepted. Next comes the accession of wisdom when wholeness meets the suffering decreed when the couple are expelled from the garden. Third is the stage of ascent, in which the cherubim and the turning, flaming sword are faced and passed in order to reach and eat of the tree of life, of the fruit offered by the creative Word. (This is not a return to the state before the forbidden fruit was eaten. See pages 71 and 72.) These three stages need not succeed each other, but can overlap or even run together.

To say that the Creation story speaks of our growth, of our completeness, and of our fulfilling the image of God, is not to say that it presents a neatly worked out, self-contained, philosophy of the human condition. The Hebrew scriptures are not there to provide a sterile dogmatic pattern to which we may or may not conform. They are an invitation to us to interact with them, making them and ourselves as we do so. A similar point has been made by R.J. Stewart* about Geoffrey of Monmouth's *Life of Merlin,* and what I have just said uses phrases of his. If I write 'making them and ourselves', what can this mean, for is not the written word constant? Indeed yes, and it is for this reason that I take always as my starting point some consideration of what may be the plain meaning of the words. Nevertheless, it is in the struggle to be honest and clear about the meaning that the words become alive and speak beyond their detail and in their wholeness. This wholeness can be viewed from an infinity of aspects, so that there is a new aspect for every new witnessing. This is not the same as free or dogmatic interpretation without meticulous respect for the meaning of the words. That way lies madness. As for making ourselves, if we read the Hebrew scriptures, perhaps most especially the story of Creation, without doing this, we are missing the point, even if not every point. Writings can be like people; when we really know them, as one living being knowing another, we are changed by our knowing. This is not the same as using a writing as a builder's drawing or instruction manual, although such guidance also has its value.

Our growth, our completeness, and our fulfilling the image of God, are not, then, unavoidable elements of the structure of the story, but rather matters which come into the foreground of my own visual field when I look at the Creation story's presentation of the human condition. They are not, of course, wholly distinct from each other. Their working out is a matter not just for the Creation story but for the Hebrew scriptures as a whole, and for human encounter with those scriptures down to this day. The Creation story in Genesis, however, has yet to be completed, for it goes on until it has told of humanity not only as individuals, as couples, and as families, but also as nations.

CHAPTER 30: *NATIONS*

THE STORY AND HUMANITY have converged on Noah. Noah has, in the matter of his sons and his nakedness, made the family a conscious social construct. Now another social grouping arises, the nation. The translation which follows is of the whole of Chapter 10 of Genesis.

[1] And these are the generations of the sons of Noah. Shem, Ham, and Japhet: and to them were children born after the Flood.

---

[2] The sons of Japhet are Gomer, and Magog, and Madai, and Javan, and Tubal, and Meshech, and Tiras.
[3] And the sons of Gomer are Ashkenaz, and Riphat, and Togarmah.
[4] And the sons of Javan are Elishah, and Tarshish,
Kittim and Dodanim.
[5] From these the coastal nations spread in their lands, each according to its language, according to their clans and in their nations.

---

[6] And the sons of Ham are Cush, and Misrayim, and Put, and Canaan.
[7] And the sons of Cush are Seba, and Havilah, and Sabtah, and Raamah, and Sabtecah,
and the sons of Raamah are Sheba and Dedan.
[8] And Cush fathered Nimrod and he began to be a mighty man on earth. [9] He was a mighty hunter before the LORD. [10] Whence it is said: 'Like Nimrod, a mighty hunter before the LORD'. [11] And the beginning of his kingship is Babylon, and Erech, and Akkad, and Calneh; in the land of Shinar. [12] From that land went out Asshur, and he built Nineveh, and Rehobot-Ir, and Calah, and Resen between Nineveh and Calah; that is a great city.
[13] And Misrayim fathered Ludim, and Anamim, and Lehabim, and Naphtuhim, [14] and Patrusim, and Casluhim (whence come Pelishtim [Philistines]), and Caphtorim.

[15] And Canaan fathered Sidon his firstborn, and Het, and the Jebusite, and the Amorite, and the Girgashite, [17] and the Hivite, and the Arkite, and the Sinite, [18] and the Arvadite, and the Zemarite, and the Hamatite, and afterwards the clans of the Canaanite spread.

> [19] And the border of the Canaanite was from Sidon, until you come towards Gerar as far as Gaza, [and then] until you come towards Sodom and Gomorrah and Admah and Zeboyim, as far as Lasha.

[20] These are the sons of Ham according to their clans, according to their languages, in their lands, in their nations.

---

[21] To Shem also offspring were born, to him also, the father of all the children of Eber, the elder of Japhet's brothers.

[22] The sons of Shem are Elam, and Asshur, and Arpachshad, and Lud and Aram.

> [23] And the sons of Aram are Uz, and Hul, and Gether, and Mash.

[24] And Arpachshad fathered Shelah,
and Shelah fathered Eber.

> [25] And to Eber were born two sons; the name of the one is Peleg, for in his days the earth was divided (*niphlegah*), and his brother's name is Joktan.

>> [26] And Joktan fathered Almodad, and Shelef, and Hazarmavet, and Jerah, [27] and Hadoram, and Uzal, and Diklah, [28] and Obal, and Abimael, and Sheba, [29] and Ophir, and Havilah, and Jobab.

>> [30] All these are the sons of Joktan. And their dwelling was from Mesha, until you come to Sephar, the mountain of the east.

[31] These are the sons of Shem according to their clans, according to their languages, in their lands, according to their nations.

---

[32] These are the clans of the sons of Noah according to their generations, in their nations, and from these the nations spread in the earth after the Flood.

***

173

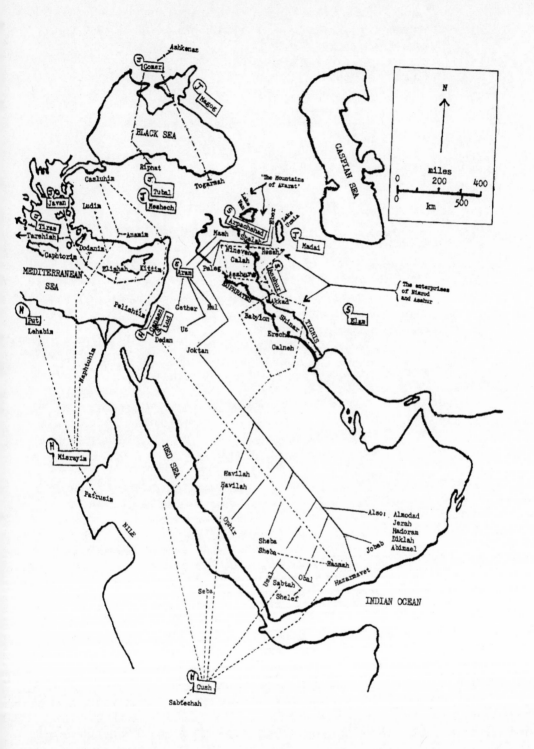

N

miles
0   200   400
0   km   500

Ashkenaz
Gomer
Magog
BLACK SEA
Riphat
Togarmah
Tubal
Meshech
'The Mountains of Ararat'
CASPIAN SEA
Casluhim
Javan
Ludim
Anamim
Arpachshad
Mash
Shelah
Hesah
Tiras
Tarshiah
Dodanim
Caphtorim
Elishah
Kittim
Nineveh
Calah
Madai
MEDITERRANEAN
SEA
Aram
Paleg
Asshur
Asshur
The enterprises of Nimrod and Asshur
EUPHRATES
Akkad
Felishtia
Gether
Hul
Babylon
Shinar
TIGRIS
Elam
Put
Canaan
Lud
Uz
Erech
Lehabim
Dedan
Joktan
Calneh
Naphtuhim
Misrayim
Havilah
Havilah
Patrusim
RED SEA
NILE
Ophir
Also: Almodad
Jerah
Hadoram
Jobab
Diklah
Abimael
Sheba
Sheba
Hazarmaveth
Usal
Sabtah
Obal
Hazarmaveth
Seba
Shelef
INDIAN OCEAN
Cush
Sabtechah

174

Although this is part of the Creation story, the names in it are of nations which, or many of which, must have been known to the first readers or hearers. In this way the account of the nations descended from Noah points towards the next part of the Hebrew scriptures, the tales of the patriarchs and matriarchs, tales which have the literary form of biography. Not only do known nations help this transition from the Creation narrative to a style in which concrete particulars matter, but concrete examples are necessary within the Creation story itself. In myth, proverb, fiction, and other non-historical forms, words must still have concrete referents, so that the words 'cow' or 'stone', for example, can be used only because it is known what a cow or stone is. Similarly, although the chapter about the nations has a general bearing on the human condition, as will be discussed, it needs real nations in its make-up. Therefore the names will now be examined in turn, in order to identify, if possible, each nation, and give it a location. This will enable the names to be put on a map, as in Figure 14. In what follows there will be given the reasons for the locations of names, and the figure can be used as the reasons are explained.

Fig. 14. *The nations according to Genesis , Chapter 10, verses 1-32. Sketch map of Near and Middle East. J, H, S = Children of Japhet, Ham, and Shem respectively. Explanation in text. (The nations of Canaan are omitted here and shown in Figure 15.)*

The sketch map of the Near and Middle East in Figure 14 has the names of the nations in Chapter 10 of Genesis, except the children of Canaan, which will more conveniently be set out in another map. The names of the children of Shem, Ham and Japhet are enclosed in boxes, with the father's initial in a bubble at the corner of each box. Further generations are linked by lines. Among Japhet's descendants the lines are of alternate dots and dashes, with broken lines between the descendants of Ham and solid between Shem's. The lines show affiliations given in the text; not movements of peoples. It will become evident that the certainty of locations is very uneven, varying from great assurance in the placing of some, to guessing in ignorance for others, and grades of certainty between. Later in the book of Genesis, but not in the Creation story, Northern Arabia and the adjacent lands become populated by descendants of Peleg; the Israelites will be among these.

***

Before turning to the nations themselves, comment may be made on the names of Noah's three sons. *Shem* is the Hebrew for 'name' or 'renown', but it is not possible to say whether this explains the origin of the name or whether we have a coincidence. 'Ham' suggests the Hebrew word for 'hot', but it may be the Egyptian *Khem* a name of Egypt itself. (In the text itself 'Misrayim' is simply the Hebrew for 'Egypt'.) Japhet has a name which appears to be a form of that of the Titan, Iapetos. Iapetos, according to the Greek mythographers, fathered Prometheus, who fashioned mortal human beings in the likeness of the gods (Apollodorus*, and see Graves*). Thus the Greeks make Iapetos to be, in a sense, a forebear of humankind, while the Hebrew scriptures make Japhet a forebear of the Greeks, as will be explained.

The birth order of the three brothers is given by two statements. In the story of Noah's drunkenness, Ham is referred to as Noah's youngest son. Here, in verse 21, Shem is called the elder of Japhet's brothers: The Hebrew could mean either that Shem is Japhet's elder brother, or that he is the elder of Japhet's brothers, as I have written here. Here, in speaking of Shem, use is made, in identification, of his descendant Eber and his brother Japhet. To extend someone's name by saying who is that person's eldest brother is, like naming the father, a convention, as when we read of 'Miriam the prophetess, the sister of Aaron' in Exodus (15:20). Using Japhet to extend the naming of Shem must mean that Japhet is the eldest brother. So the birth order is Japhet-Shem-Ham.

***

As I have turned fairly frequently to Westermann* and Cassuto* for help in identifying nations, for the rest of this chapter I will merely refer to them

176

together as 'W & C' whenever they are being relied on.

In general, the seven children of Japhet have names that correspond well with known nations. GOMER appears in cuneiform writings as Gimmirai, who were known to the Greeks as Kimmeroi, that is, Cimmerians: At first they lived north of the Black Sea, between the Don and the Danube. After a defeat by the Scythians, they moved, in the late Eighth Century B.C.E., around the eastern end of the Black Sea into Urartu, the biblical Ararat, now Armenia, and in the Seventh Century went further south, to settle in Cappadocia, in Asia Minor north of Syria. They are not heard of after the Sixth Century. (See W & C.)

MAGOG is not certainly identifiable, and in this is more problematic than his six brothers. Ezekiel (38:2) makes Magog the land of the prince Gog, who is chief of Meshech and Tubal (considered below), and he associates it (39:6) with the coastlands.

MADAI is the biblical name for the country of the Medes, in the north-west of what is now Iran. Outside the Hebrew scriptures, Assyrian references to the Medes go back to the Ninth Century B.C.E., but the much older designation, Manda, found in Mesopotamian writings, may refer to them. (See W & C.)

JAVAN is the Ionians. (The correspondence is between the Hebrew *Yawan* —here represented as 'Javan'—and the Greek *Iwon-*, the archaic form of *Ion-*.) Eventually Javan came to be a name for all Greeks, although here it may refer simply to Ionian settlements in Asia Minor and the coasts and islands of the Aegean Sea.

TUBAL and MESHECH are named together not only elsewhere in the. Hebrew scriptures, but also in Mesopotamian inscriptions and by Herodotus*, who writes of Tibarenoi and Moschoi. They lived in Asia Minor, at first in the centre and south-westwards to the Mediterranean Sea, but later further north, by the south-eastern shores of the Black Sea. (See W & C).

TIRAS may be the Turusa, which the Egyptian writings describe as attacking Egypt from the sea in the Thirteenth Century B.C.E. (See W & C.) Names possibly related to Turusa and Tiras are found among Aegean and Italian peoples.

Of the children of Gomer, ASHKENAZ is a northern people (Jeremiah 51:27), and the Assyrians associate a people called Ashkuza with the Gimmirai, already noted as corresponding to Gomer (See W & C.) The Assyrian and Hebrew forms may be considered as equivalent, since the sound of *n* inside a word is readily lost, especially in Semitic languages, which both of these are. It is also a sound that can intrude, in some languages, because a vowel has become nasalised. Now the Greeks wrote abundantly of the *Skuthoi*, Scythians, and the Greek *Skuth-* may correspond to the Assyrian *-shkuz-*. The Scythians lived north of the Black Sea, from which region, as already noted, they drove the Cimmerians (Kimmeroi, i.e. Gomer). RIPHAT cannot be identified, but Josephus*, 1700 years ago, put it in Paphlagonia, on the southern shore of the Black Sea. TOGARMAH is certainly in Asia Minor, being attested as a city and district of the Hittite empire in the late Fourteenth Century B.C.E.. Later the Assyrians show knowledge of a city Tilgarimmu on the border of Tubal. Togarmah is therefore probably in the eastern part of Asia Minor. (See W & C.) According to the tradition of the Georgians, many of the peoples living south of the Caucasus range (i.e. in 'Transcaucasia') are descended from Thargamos, a great-grandson of Japhet (Bealby*). Togarmah is, of course, Japhet's grandson in the biblical story, but there seems to be some common tradition underlying Togarmah and Thargamos and a child can be named after a parent, although it is perhaps unlikely in this sort of tale. Here is a field for investigation.

Among the children of Javan, ELISHAH looks like Alashya, the Hittite and Mesopotamian name of Cyprus, or of some part of that island. TARSHISH is in scripture a distant destination for ships. It may be Tartessos, the region, facing the Atlantic in south-west Spain, around the part of Cadiz, known anciently as Gadeira, then Gades. An objection to this identification might be that Tartessos was a colony of Phoenicia, that is, in biblical language, of Sidonians, and Sidon is here a child of Canaan, not of Javan. However, Herodotus* relates that Tartessos was Ionian Greek before it was Phoenician. KITTIM are the people of Kition, in Cyprus, near the modern Larnaca. DODANIM is written as 'Rodanim' in the First Book of Chronicles (1:7), which would correspond to 'Rhodians', making ' Kittim and Rodanim' the peoples of two large islands. The difference in shape between *dalet,* the first 'letter of 'Dodanim', and *resh,* which begins 'Rodanim', is slight in the Hebrew script of the last two-and-a-half millennia, and a scribal error might have become perpetuated if and when Rodanim became unknown to the copyists. This amendment seems legitimate, since it elucidates the name without affecting the meaning of the passage as a whole, and is supported by a version of the passage elsewhere in the Hebrew scriptures. (There is here no contradiction of the general rule that one does not amend a passage solely because the amended version is easier to understand or fits better with one's hypotheses or prejudices). It has been suggested also that *Dodanim* and *Rodanim* are forms of *Dordanim,* the Dardanians, who lived in north-west Asia Minor, around Troy.

In the sentence 'From these the coastal nations spread' (verse 5), does the word 'these' refer to the children of Javan, just mentioned, or to all Japhet's children? Some have said that the 'coastal nations' (*iyye-haggoyim,* 'the coastlands of the nations), are only the children of Javan because it is only to them, of all the Japhet nations, to whom the description applies. Ezekiel (39:6), however, links *ha-iyyim,* 'the isles' or 'the coastlands', with Magog, in a passage which refers to Meshech and Tubal. There is no reason to think that only the children of Javan are littoral among Japhet's nations, and the statement in verse 5 can be taken as about what is typical of Japhet's children, rather than what is precisely applicable in every possible example. Also, verse 5 corresponds in its position at the end of the Japhet section, with verse 20 and 31, which are explicitly about the children of Ham and Shem respectively, and concludetheirsections.

Another aspect of the sentence 'From these the coastal nations spread' is noteworthy. There is here a reference to an event or a series of events in which 'these' give rise to 'coastal nations', but the coastal nations referred to cannot be exclusively, if at all, those already named. That is to say, there is no claim in this passage that an exhaustive list of nations is provided.

***

Ham's children are all identifiable. CUSH is the biblical name for Ethiopia, the land south of Egypt, Cush extending farther north than modern Ethiopia. MISRAYIM is, as already noted, simply the Hebrew name for Egypt. Although PUT could be the ancient Punt, the Somali coast of the Red Sea, the Egyptians called the Lybians 'Put', and this is consonant with the use of the name elsewhere in the Hebrew scriptures. CANAAN is well-known from scripture, and will be looked at again when Canaan's children are discussed.

The children of Cush are not easily placed. The Hebrew scriptures, taken together with Greek writers, indicate that SEBA adjoins Cush, but more than that is unclear. It could be on the East African coast, or between Cush and Egypt, or even one of Cush's cities. HAVILAH, to follow other biblical references to it, must be in Arabia. In the telling of humanity in the garden, Havilah has been mentioned, with the river Pishon going round it (Genesis 2:11), but the knowledge that Havilah is in Arabia helps but little to clarify the position of the garden and makes little difference to the conclusion already drawn on pages 54 and 55, that the writing implies that to ask where the Garden of Eden is, is an inappropriate question. SABTAH may also be in Arabia, the name being that of an old commercial city of the Hadramaut, the southern coastal region of the peninsula. RAAMAH could be Ragmat, an old southern Arabian city; the *g* and *t* sounds would be present or absent according to quite ordinary regularities of the differences among Semitic languages. SABTECA remains a puzzle; there was an Ethiopian Pharaoh of Egypt called Shabataka, and it has been suggested that Sabteca is this name, given to a city founded by him. Raamah's child SHEBA was a rich nation of south-west Arabia. The Queen of Sheba's visit to Solomon (1 Kings 10) has become famous. The other child of Raamah, DEDAN, is mentioned in southern Arabian inscriptions, although the location of this or another Dedan appears to have been in the north of Arabia, in Edom (Jeremiah 49:8; Ezekiel 25:13), and Dedan has been archaeologically identified with the modern Al-'Ula, a north Arabian oasis (Naveh*). (See W & C on all the children of Cush. Cassuto, for his part, would have 'Cush' here refer to a people of Transjordan. However, on why 'Cush' must mean Ethiopia, see page 54.)

In the interlude (verses 8-12) about NIMROD, he appears to be not an individual standing for a nation but, rather, the builder of an empire out of materials to hand. The land of Shinar is the lower, south-eastern part of

Mesopotamia, that is, the land of Babylon and of Sumer and Akkad. BABYLON, ERECH, and AKKAD are all known to history, the first two having been located and excavated. CALNEH, on the other hand, is unknown. There was a Babylonian city Kul-unu, but it has not been located. Calno, in Syria, sounds a possibility, but is not likely to have been grouped with Babylon and Erech. ASSHUR is also a city, but the name is also of the whole land of Assyria, which is here Asshur the son of Shem (verse 22). In that land the greatest city was NINEVEH, while CALAH, about twenty-five miles to the south, was the royal residence. RESEN is not known, but the text itself gives the location. REHOBOT-IR is simply the Hebrew for 'the streets (*or* squares) of the city'. The expression 'That is a great city' must refer to the whole of what has gone before in verse 12, that is, to Nineveh with its associated towns and its open concourses.

The children of Egypt (MISRAYIM) vary considerably in the certainty with which they can be identified. The LUDIM are, it seems likely, the Ludioi, the Lydians, of Greek writings. The Lydians were a powerful nation in the west of Asia Minor, allied with Egypt (Ezekiel 30:5), which they supplied with bowmen (Jeremiah 46:9). Ezekiel and Jeremiah were both alive in 600 B.C.E. but their remarks about the Lydians may reflect a long-standing close relationship; the Lydians first appear in written records, those of Assyria, in the Seventh Century B.C.E. but their true antiquity depends on whether they are identical with the Maeones, who were living in Lydia at an earlier time. The ANAMIM have not been satisfactorily explained. One suggestion puts them in Cyrenaica, but I wonder whether their names is that of the city Anemurium (now Anamur) in Asia Minor north of Cyprus and opposite Egypt. The LEHABIM may be Lybians and, if so, are to be associated with Put if, as already suggested, this name also indicates Lybians, although not necessarily the same ones. The expected Hebrew form corresponding to 'Lybians' would be *Lubim,* which does in fact occur in scripture, so that the question may be whether Lehabim and Lubim are the same people. The NAPHTUHIM, it has been proposed, are the people of Lower Egypt, the name being seen as related to an Egyptian expression meaning 'north land'. The PATRUSIM are more certainly the people of Upper Egypt, the name being related to the Egyptian for 'south land'; their country appears as Patros elsewhere in the Hebrew scriptures (Isaiah 11:1; Jeremiah 44:1,15; Ezekiel 29:14, 30:14). *Misrayim* is, in form, a dual plural and may perhaps represent the union of Upper and Lower Egypt, a union attributed to Menes, the founder of the First Dynasty of Egypt. CAPHTORIM are the people of Crete, for which the biblical name is Caphtor. The PELISHTIM (Philistines) are well-known, living to the south and southwest of the Canaanites and, later, the Israelites. Who then are the CASLUHIM 'whence come Pelishtim'?

The problem here is not simply about the Casluhim, but also about the Philistines. In the Hebrew scriptures (Deuteronomy 2:23; Jeremiah 47:4; Amos 9:7) the Philistines are said to have come from Caphtor (Crete), not from Casluhim, as here. One explanation is that there has been a copyist's error, and that the remark 'whence come Pelishtim' should be attached to Caphtorim, not Casluhim, in the text. Since the Philistines were well-known to Israelites through most of the scriptural period, and since we may presume that a people's origin was taken to be what that people said it was, it is unlikely that Israelite scribes could have been so unaware of the Cretan origin that, the mistake could have been standardised, uncorrected. In copying after the scriptural period, copyists would have been just as strongly influenced, not now by direct knowledge of Philistines but by Jeremiah and Amos. In any case, the textual explanation is unnecessary. The earlier biblical references to Philistines (Genesis 21 and 26) are about a people ruled by a king in Gerar. After the Israelite entry into Canaan the Philistines have no single king but are based on five independent cities, none of them Gerar. The arrival of these 'second' Philistines, a little later than the first entry of the Israelites into Canaan, is archaeologically attested, according to Albright*. It would appear that the Israelites used the name 'Philistine' for two successive dominant peoples in different but adjacent areas. Thus we can have Philistines originating from the Casluhim, and then those from Caphtor, Crete. Now, to return, who were the Casluhim? Cassuto* has suggested that their name is that of the Pelasgian city of Skulake in north-western Asia Minor. The *h* of Casluhim represents a guttural sound, nearer to *k* than the spelling may suggest, while the alternation between *Cas-* and *Sk-* is like that heard when people say 'ax' instead of 'ask' (as some certainly used to do), or when 'Exe' replaces the older 'Isca'. The uncertainty that the Casluhim came from Skulake (usually spelled Skylake) is very great, but it is the best guess I know of. (Incidentally, Cassuto, citing Gintz, offers *three* waves of Philistines!)

After which it is a relief to turn to the children of Canaan, which present rather less of a problem. They could not be packed into the sketch map of Figure 14, so Figure 15 has another map, to help with Canaan's peoples, as in verses 15-19.

181

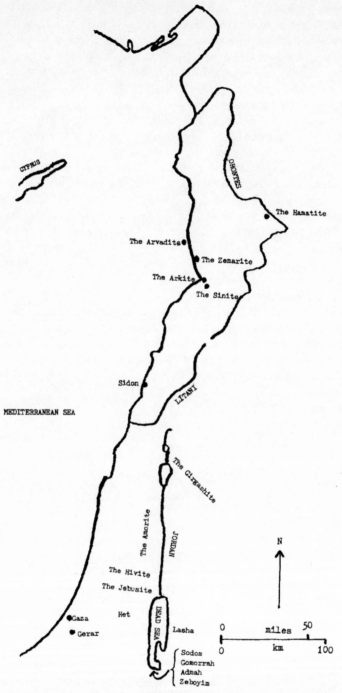

Fig. 15. *Map of Canaanite peoples in Genesis, chapter 10, verses 15-19.*

SIDON was the principal city of Phoenicia, that northern part of Canaan which was known to the Assyrians and in the Hebrew scriptures simply as 'Sidon' or 'the Sidonians'. (The port of Tyre became a leading city only in the time of David and Solomon, about 1000 B.C.E..) We use the name Phoenicia following Greek usage, but the people of the region about Sidon called themselves Canaanite. HET is the Hittites of Canaan. They are frequently mentioned in scripture, and the Assyrians called Canaan as a whole 'the land of the Hittites', but the exact historical reason for a sharing of the name with the great Hittite empire of Asia Minor is not clear. The southern limit of the expansion of the Hittite empire was the valley, now called El Beqa'a, between the Lebanon and the Anti-Lebanon mountains. The JEBUSITES lived in and around Jerusalem. The AMORITES were a numerous and powerful people of the region. Here the reference is to those of them in the land of Canaan only. Elsewhere in the Hebrew scriptures 'Amorite' can be used as a term for the non-Israelite Canaanite peoples as a whole. As the GIRGASHITES are otherwise known only from Phoenician inscriptions, they would seem to be of the north of Canaan, and may be the same as the Gergesenes of the Christian scriptures (Luke 8:26), who lived by Kinneret, the Sea of Galilee. The HIVITES are mentioned in scripture as an inland people of Canaan, at Gibeon, Shechem, and the foot of Mount Hermon. On the map Het, the Amorite, and the Hivite are shown as less widespread than they were, while for the Girgashite and Jebusite, on the other hand, the lettering probably spreads too far for the actual locations. The ARKITE, SINITE, ARVADITE, ZEMARITE, and HAMATITE belong to five identifiable Phoenician cities, as shown on the map.

The 'border of the Canaanite' (verse 19) can refer to the territory itself, rather than just its edge. The description is of length and breadth. The length is from Sidon in the north to GERAR in the south, and from GAZA (that is, the territory of Gaza, which may reach the sea) in the west to SODOM, GOMORRAH, ADMAH, and ZEBOIM in the east. These last four were in the plain of the Dead sea, and were later destroyed, according to Genesis 19; therefore the sketch map shows them together, with only a general indication of their location. The only clue we have to the location of LASHA ('as far as Lasha') is a Jewish tradition that it is near Callirhoe, which was on the eastern side of the Dead Sea. Some would identify it with Laish, about 150 miles further north, on the other side of the Jordan, but I find it difficult to make sense of this within the text itself. Gerar is later mentioned as a Philistine city (Genesis 26:1), as Gaza became after the time of the Israelite (and 'second' Philistine?) invasion, when it was one of the five Philistine city states. Sidon is here described. as Canaan's northern limit, and this must refer to Phoenicia in general, not the city of Sidon in particular, since the children of Canaan include cities north of Sidon, as the map shows.

***

The children of Shem are adjacent nations, ranged in a horseshoe. (See Figure 14.) ELAM, to the east of Babylonia and in the south-west of what is now Iran, is known from the Third Millennium B.C.E., its independence ending by Assyrian conquest in the Seventh Century B.C.E.. ASSHUR is the name of a city and of the whole of Assyria. Here it probably has its wider meaning, since the other identifiable sons of Shem are peoples or countries, while Asshur in verse 12 appears with other cities and must be the city of that name. Thus Nimrod, Ham's grandson, has attributed to him a group of cities, from which goes Asshur to build more cities, which are in the country of Asshur, Shem's son. In the name ARPACHSHAD, Arpach- corresponds with Ptolemy's* Arrhapachitis (*itis* being an adjectival ending), a land just north of Assyria, adjacent to Armenia (as Urartu, or Ararat, later became), and immediately south of the Niphates Mountains, themselves close to the southern shore of Lake Van. In the Akkadian language of Assyria the component -*shad* would mean 'mountain', and Arrhapachitis is indeed mountainous. ARAM is the usual biblical name of Syria. The order of the names suggests that LUD may lie between Arpachshad and Syria. But who, or what, is Lud? The town of Lud (now Lod, in the Land of Israel, and Lydda in Greek) is at least two thousand years old and may perhaps take its name from the Ludai, who are known, in the Third Century C.E., as brigands in the Land (Talmud Bavli*). Could these have been the remnant of an older people called Lud? Much of the territory of Canaan and Transjordan was called Ruten by the Egyptians, but Egyptian writing did not distinguish r from l, and Lud may perhaps represent a name which also had a form such as Luten or Lotan.

The children of Aram, in the order of their naming, make a series from south to north. The biblical UZ is to the east of Edom, in the modern state of Jordan, south-east of the Dead Sea. Since an Aramaic *t* can be represented by a Hebrew *sh*, GETHER appears to be the biblical Geshur, which is in Bashan, to the east of Kinneret, the Sea of Galilee, and also in modern Jordan. HUL may correspond to the Aramaic *chol,* meaning 'sand' and may be the name of a sand region, perhaps in the desert where Syria meets Arabia. (The *H* of Hul is a guttural *ch,* as in *chol* and in 'loch'.) The word *hol* in Aramaic means not only 'sand' but also 'phoenix', and Herodotus* tells a story of this bird's regular visits to Arabia. MASH may have a name which is a form of Masius, a mountain now called in Turkish Mazi Dagh, near the northern limit of Syria.

The name Masius, like others already mentioned, is from Greek and Latin authors. We may therefore be comparing a biblical name with a Greek or Latin name of quite different age. Migration, however, was much freer anciently than now. Thus, for example, we find in the Roman period a name such as Veneti turning up in regions hundreds of miles apart. If we use Greek or Latin authors to identify nations named in Genesis we must be cautious about the locations of those nations, although such help is undoubtedly valuable if used critically. Cities are less mobile, of course, but two cities may have the same name.

To return to the names of Shem's descendants, those issuing from Arpach-shad can be considered personal, in view of what is to follow in Genesis 11. However, in the present context these names must be taken also as national. It is possible that SHELAH (*shelach*) corresponds to the Silices, whom Pliny* places near the upper waters of the Great Zab, just south of the territory already proposed, on page 184, as that of Arpachshad. If this location is correct, there is in Shelah's land a mountain now having the Turkish name Altindagh Silsilesi, 'the Gold Mountain of Silsiles'. If EBER's name is in that of Mount Imbarus (now Ispiriz Daghlar), a range to the southeast of Lake Van, then Arpachshad, Shelah, and Eber are all within 'the mountains of Ararat'.

Eber requires some attention, if only because Shem is given the title 'father of all the children of Eber', drawing alertness in advance to the line of this descendant. The word 'Hebrew' (*'Ivri*) *is* simply 'Eberite' according to its form and literal meaning. Similar names appear in the Caucasus. The Iberes were a nation in the heart of what is now Georgia. Westward, but still in Georgia, is the country of the Imereti. The forms *Iber-* and *Imer-* may be related, if both are related to the name of Mount Imbarus, as a mountain in Armenia was called in classical times. There is an old tradition that Eber and 'Ivri ('Hebrew') are from the verb *'avar* ('go across'), so that a Hebrew is someone from across the river (*'ever han-nahar*), that is, east of the Euphrates. It is a matter of point of view. The Akkadian 'Ebir-nari must mean 'west of the Euphates', the view being Assyrian, and this view can be taken even in the Hebrew scriptures (1 Kings 5:4, 4:24 in English versions). It is in any case difficult to bring a derivation from the verb *'avar*, or from its related noun *'ever* ('region beyond'), into agreement with the primary use of the name 'Eber' (*ever*) in Genesis. There is no suggestion that Eber crossed the Euphrates, and the traditional explanation of 'Ivri, ('Hebrew', but also 'Eberite') looks forward to a crossing of the Euphrates by Abraham, six generations later.

Who are 'all the children of Eber', by whose ancestry Shem is titled? According to the writing under consideration, these include, as will be seen shortly, a number of Arabian peoples. Later portions of the Hebrew scriptures would add to these the Ammonites, Moabites, Ishmaelites, Edomites, and Israelites, as well as peoples stemming from the children and grandchildren of Keturah (Genesis 25:1-4). In scripture the term 'Hebrew' (that is, Eberite) is used of Israelites when an Egyptian, Philistine, or other non-Israelite, is speaking or being spoken to, or when a distinction is being made between an Israelite and one of another nation. In all these cases 'Hebrew' may mean no more than 'Israelite', although the scope of the word is not always so restricted by context. If 'Hebrew' means 'of a group which contains Israelites at least', it will always make sense. (Whether it refers to Israel only will be important in, for example, the precepts distinguishing Hebrew servants, where the restricted meaning seems more likely.) A people called Habiri are said in the Tell-el-Amarna letters, an Egyptian correspondence of 1400 B.C.E., to be making incursions into Canaan from the direction of the Arabian Desert. If the dating is reliable, the

185

Habiri can scarcely be Israelites, who became a threat to Canaan only after another century, but the reference may nevertheless be to other Eberites.

The name PELEG, that of one of Eber's sons, will, when consideration is given to the peculiarities of Hebrew, Aramaic, and Greek, be seen to correspond exactly with Phalga, the name in Greek for a city in the eastern part of what is now Syria, near where the Chaboras flows into the Euphrates, about thirty miles south-east of the present-day Deir-es-Zor. The explanation of Peleg's name, 'for in his days was the earth divided', is a pun on the verb *palag* ('divide'), evidently referring to the dispersal of the nations. (In the Hebrew of scripture *peleg* means 'water channel'.)

Peleg's brother JOKTAN, since at least two of his children are fairly obviously Arabian nations, is surely the Qaḥtan of the Arabians. The peoples of Arabia are, according to their history of themselves, either Bā'idah (extinct) or Bāqiyah (existing), the latter being either 'Āribah (Arabian) or Musta'ribah (Arabicised). The 'Āribah are of the south of the peninsula, and are descended from Qaḥtan. As will be seen, this agrees with what Genesis says of the children of Joktan. The Musta'ribah come late into Arabia, from the north, and are descendants of Ishmael, whom the Hebrew scriptures make a sixth-generation descendant of Joktan's brother Peleg, and whose language became that of all Arabia and much later, with the spread of Islam in the Seventh and Eighth Centuries C.E., of countries from Iraq to the Atlantic. This note on Arabian tradition is based on Hitti*. The names Joktan (*Yoqtan*) and Qahtan may perhaps find another form in Chaulctaei, the name by which the Greeks knew a people of north-west Arabia.

The thirteen children of Joktan are not all identifiable. The name AL-MODAD is Arabic for 'the friend'. This is not obviously gentilic. Was Almodad held, perhaps, to be not only the founder of a nation but also the friend of God, as in the expression 'Abraham thy beloved' (2 Chronicles 20:7)? The name SHELEF would be a regular Hebrew equivalent either of Shilf, a district of the Yemen, or Shalf, a Yemenite people. The Hadramaut, still a great region of southern Arabia, and an ancient kingdom known to archaeologists, appears among Joktan's children as HAZARMAVET. Perhaps an ancient deity is represented by JERAH, which means 'moon', and might be a people known by the name of its god. Since HADORAM can mean 'the exaltation of Hadh', who is a god, there may be here also a national name with reference to a divinity. A personal name similar to Hadoram is said to have been found in a south Arabian inscription. According to Arabian tradition, UZAL is the pre-Islamic name of San'a, to-day a major city of North Yemen. In Arabic DIKLAH means 'date-palm', and so could be a place name, perhaps then becoming the name of those who live there and nearby. One well known example of a city named after the date-palm is that called Palmyra or Tadmor, both referring to the palm, between Damascus and the Euphrates. Given the importance of the date-palm, not only for its usefulness, but as a marker of sites with water and otherwise good to live at, such a name seems normal for a town. There need not be only one example; to-day there is a village of Diqla in Egypt, near the Mediterranean Sea and the Gaza area of Palestine. OBAL corresponds with 'Abil, in the Yemen. If the south Arabian dialect is presumed, ABIMAEL means 'God is indeed my father', and must be a personal name, perhaps of one held to be progenitor of a nation. The nation called SHEBA is at first north Arabian, then spreading south, and is the Saba known through archaeology as one of the Arabian kingdoms. Sabaean royal inscriptions, however, have not yet thrown light on the Queen of Sheba who, according to 1 Kings 10, visited Solomon, king of Israel. (Sheba, as has been seen, is also a grandchild of Cush, a matter which will be discussed when these nations are reviewed as a whole.) In the Hebrew scriptures OPHIR is known as a source of gold, and some mentions of it seem to indicate a position on or near the Red Sea. HAVILAH, like Sheba, has also an origin from Cush, and this double origin will be considered with that of Sheba. If the name Havilah (*chawilah*) is derived from *chowl*, 'sand', it may name more than one country. Havilah in the description of the location of the Garden of Eden (Genesis 2:11) is 'where there is gold' and, if this Havilah is the same it would lie naturally in the list of Joktan's children next to Ophir, also renowned for gold. Whether the inclusion of Havilah in this passage about the nations can help to locate the Garden of Eden has already been considered on page 179. While JOBAB cannot be identified with any reasonable assurance, one suggestion connects it with the Yuhaybit, a south Arabian people.

Neither MESHA nor SEPHAR, the mountain of the east, have been identified (verse 30). The intention seems to be simply to indicate the extent of the territory of Joktan's children.

The conclusion (verse 31) of the account of the descendants of Shem is like that for Ham (verse 20), though there is some difference from the conclusion of the passage on Japhet's nations (verse 5).

***

The conclusion (verse 32) of the entire passage about the nations tells us that 'from these the nations spread'. Clearly, we must infer from these words that there is no intention to name all the nations that were to be, and indeed the Hebrew scriptures tell of the birth of a number of nations. Also, in 'from these the nations spread', the word 'these' can refer to any nation or person already named, so that there is no explicit intention to exclude descendants of Shem, Ham, and Japhet collateral with those actually mentioned. The expression 'So-and-so fathered...' need not introduce a complete list of offspring or even of sons. The naming of generations depends on the purpose. (Only one of Adam's sons is given by 1 Chronicles 1:1, for example.) It is therefore appropriate now, having given some concrete meaning to these national names, to consider the more general matter, the meaning of this account of the nations.

CHAPTER 31: **THE MEANING OF
NATIONALITY**

THE ACCOUNT of the nations in the Creation story says of itself that it is not an exhaustive list (page 187). If it is not a gazeteer, what is it? To be more exact, what meaning can it convey to the reader? To answer this, it is necessary to go beyond the examination of detail and, using the appreciation of detail already attempted, to look at the list of nations in its entirety and scope.

The structure of the list is genealogical. The nations are presented as fathers, sons, grandsons, cousins, and so on. To-day's reader, influenced perhaps by modern thought habits, may take the list of nations as a family tree, in the literal sense, of the male ancestors from each of which a nation is descended. The evidence of the text itself is, however, not favourable to such simplistically biological interpretation.

In the first place, some names are frankly not of individuals. Even if we think the writer means to tell us that all Canaanites are descendants of a man called Canaan, even if we suppose the text to mean that all Ionians have family lines going back to an ancestor called Javan, we cannot thus interpret names such as Caphtorim (10:14), which means 'Caphtorites', 'Cretans'. We can imagine that Caphtor (Crete) or Caphtori (Cretan) could have a singular personal reference, but surely not the plural Caphtorim. Noah's grandson Misrayim (Egypt), with a name that is already a dual plural, begets seven children, every one of which has a plural name. The list of nations can hardly be understood as a family tree of individuals.

Evidence from elsewhere in the Hebrew scriptures shows that someone can be given as the child of another although there is not simple biological parentage. After all, if all the 'Children of Israel' have the man called Israel as their immediate father, he must be living to a much greater age than scripture claims for him. In fact a 'child' of Israel need have no biological relation at all to Israel the individual. 'The children of the third generation that are born unto them (that is, to Edomites and Egyptians) may enter into the assembly of the Lord' (Deuteronomy 23:9). Those in the 'assembly of the Lord' are all the Children of Israel, and are all in one or other of the twelve tribes, each descended from one of Israel's sons. One does not, in scripture, need to be born into a nation; one can join it.

Another complication for any attempt to read the list of nations as a family tree is that some nations have a double origin. Havilah's father is Cush (10:7), a child of Ham, and is also Joktan (10:29), Shem's great-great-grandson. Similarly Sheba is Cush's grandchild (10:7) in Ham's family, and Joktan's child (10:28) in Shem's. Going beyond the list of nations, Ham's great-grandson Dedan (10:7) later turns up as a grandson of Abraham (Genesis 25:3), a descendant of Shem. While it is conceivable that someone combining two sources into the nation list was so incompetent as to leave an apparent double origin where he did not intend it, it seems more likely that some peoples recognized a double origin in themselves.

To-day we use of languages the terms Hamitic and Semitic, but it is most unlikely that the listing of Ham's and Shem's nations is invariably arranged so as to show linguistic affinities, even if some nations closely related in the list have also related languages. Consider, for example, Canaan. The language of the Israelites varied from the languages of their Canaanite neighbours only by differences such as might distinguish dialects. The similarities must have been obvious at the time, and Canaanite peoples, including Israel, were surely able to understand each other. Nevertheless the Israelites, in their own scriptures, have Canaan as a child of Ham (10:6), while Israel is descended from Shem's great-grandson Eber.

If the city-builders, or state-organisers, Nimrod (10:8) and Asshur (10:12) are regarded as individuals only, and not as nations (Nimrod being obviously an individual in 10:8-10: and Asshur the nation appearing later in 10:22), then there are just seventy national names, two of them, Havilah and Sheba, being repeated and each counted on both appearances. This number may not be accidental. Seventy is a recurring number in Hebrew scriptures, as when Lamech used it, added to a previously stated seven, in his boasting (4:23). We do not know how old is the Jewish tradition that explicitly gives the number of nations as seventy but, if it goes back to ancient Israelite times, we would have an example of fitting a pattern to a number. (We have no evidence from scripture independent of the nation list, but the seventy bulls sacrificed, according to Numbers 29:12-34, in the Temple on the Feast of Tabernacles, have been held, at least since a time soon after the sacrifices ceased, to be on behalf of the seventy nations.) Fitting the pattern to the number is certainly a proven practice, since it is seen in keeping Israel's tribes to an exact twelve. If Levi is put into a distinct category or is not mentioned, Ephraim and Manasseh are given as two tribes of Joseph (as in Numbers 34:19-28) but, if Levi is included, Ephraim and Manasseh are unnamed and the tribe of Joseph named as if single (as in Deuteronomy 27:12,13). In either case the total is twelve. The appearance and disappearance of nations does not change the total of seventy in Jewish legend, which ignores actual variation.

***

189

Thus it is to be seen that the genealogical form of the list of nations necessarily implies degrees neither of biological kinship, whether through single ancestors or not, nor of linguistic kinship. There is no claim to completeness, and the number of nations suggests that the text should be read as purposefully formalised. Within the structure there is no explicit indication of what is meant by a nation, but the characteristics of nationality are given when we read, 'These are the sons of Ham according to their clans, according to their languages, in their lands, in their nations' (10:20). 'Clans' here represents the Hebrew *mishpechot*, 'families', but extended families are usually meant by the term. This leaves unsaid what are the criteria by which a group of clans is held to constitute, say, one nation or two. Again, did the Israelite writer setting out Shem's children 'according to their languages' (10:31) mean us to understand that Joktan's thirteen named nations spoke exactly thirteen languages, no more, no less? (The archaeological evidence is in favour of somewhat less variety of language in Arabia, and the writer of so detailed a list is unlikely to have been unaware of the general conditions known to traders there.) As for 'their lands', a nation's land was often poorly demarcated by physical geography; rather, it was the presence of a people that defined its land. We must conclude that clans, languages, and lands provide differences between nations, but that none of them can define what a nation is.

It probably makes best sense to see the biblical idea of a nation as a unit of the God-given but not unchanging ordering of humankind, manifested in a people's awareness of itself. This internally bonding sense of belonging causes a people to be seen by others as a nation. Thus a nation has two aspects, that towards those whom it comprises, and that towards other nations. For the first of these aspects the Hebrew scriptures use the word 'people' (*'am*), while for the second the word is nation (*goy*). In general the Children of Israel are called a people in relation to themselves, and a nation in matters concerning their standing among other nations. Hence Israelite writers in scripture, when speaking of the 'nations' (*goyim*) often mean non-Israelite nations; in this way *goy* has come in later Jewish usage to mean not only a nation but also a non-Jew. (The word 'Gentile' for a non-Jew comes correspondingly from the Latin word, *gens* 'nation'.)

Although 'nation' in biblical usage is the word corresponding to the external view, on one occasion the Children of Israel are called a 'people', not 'nation', by a non-Israelite taking a decidedly external view of them. The king of Egypt speaks to his people (*'am*) about 'the people (*'am*) of the Children of Israel' (Exodus 1:9). This has a double effect. First, it is a reminder to the Egyptians that the two peoples are distinct, which prepares for their being treated by two legal standards, although within one state. Secondly, while putting the Israelites outside, as it were, it does not allow them the status of nation (*goy*). A nation can be conquered, put under tribute, or even exiled, but it cannot deliberately be made to exist no longer, which is the king of Egypt's intention for Israel (Exodus 1:16). The word 'nation' implies a status incompatible with the intention.

What we have here is not a contradiction of the common biblical use of 'people' and 'nation', but a story which gains strength if the reader knows the common usage.

When a people, felt as such by its members, is seen by others to exist, it is to these others a nation. According to the Israelite view, expressed in the Creation story, nations are part of the divinely created ordering of humankind, because it is part of the God-given nature of human beings to be not only in human society generally, and in couples, and in families and households, but also in peoples.

***

The arrangement of the nations in a family tree has meanings which may now receive consideration. One implication of the family tree is that no nation can claim to be autochthonous, sprung from its own soil. All are of one ancestry, which is of the earth and of not-earth, of the dust and of divine breath. Where a nation lives is due not to natural law but to the particulars of history, with the Creator and the created continually working in and though history.

Not only are all nations of one origin, of a single humanity, but their rulers also are of this origin. Nimrod, who has kingship (10:11), is of Ham's family. There is no place in this scheme of things for kings of divine ancestry ruling mere humanity. Within this pattern of common ancestry there is little point in a nation's claiming superiority through antiquity. Nations arise from nations, and all go back to Noah. The Israelites by this, their own, account were latecomers on the world's stage, but rooted themselves through Jacob, Abraham, Eber, and Shem in Noah, and hence in the Adam, whose name is 'humankind'.

To relate nations to each other in a single family, and to present one's own nation as of late existence among much older neighbours, seems to imply that a nation is not an end in itself but has a place in some wider scheme, and therefore serves some more inclusive purpose. Such a view of one's national origins was not universally held in the ancient world. The Greeks, although recognizing that many of themselves succeeded the Pelasgians in their land, nevertheless believed that the Athenians and Arcadians were autochthonous, sprung from their own soil. The Romans, although believing themselves to be descended from bandits, gave their rulers divine ancestry, with descent from a son of Venus. To the Israelites nations, including their own, are matters not of divine descent but of, divine ordering, within which human actions have their effects for good or ill. This may be compared with the initiation of arts by Cain's human descendants, not by gods or demi-gods, as in Saturn's gift of agriculture or Asklepios's gift of medicine. By the exaltation of the indivisible Creator above human works, and by the responsibility of human beings who are in the Creator's likeness, the Hebrew scriptures combine an extreme awe of the divine with a radical humanism, while making all humankind kindred. What is said of nationality is an aspect of the humanism. (It may be mentioned that the humanism is expressed also by the accessibility of the divine, awesome as it is.)

Since the nations are a necessary manifestation of the creation of humanity, the Creator who is later in the Hebrew scriptures called Lord God of Israel is shown also as Lord God of the nations of the earth. Before looking into this matter, however, there is still to be considered a conspicuous feature of the list of nations, that it is organised in three branches, of Japhet, of Ham, and of Shem.

For each of the three branches there is a concluding remark (10:5,20,31). The conclusion concerning Japhet's nations has the peculiarity that they are said to be coastal. If these nations are considered one by one this is indeed seen to be so (pages 177-179); even Tubal and Meshech, perhaps inland at one time, are coastal at another (page 177). The expression 'From these the coastal peoples spread' (10:5) is, more literally, 'From these (the peoples of) the coastal regions of the nations were divided'. The sense is of dividing and spreading. There is a similar remark about the nations generally (10:32), but this dividing or spreading is not mentioned in connection with Ham (10:20) or Shem (10:31). The families of Ham and Shem are of course shown to be dividing and spreading. The implication is that it is appropriate to state explicitly of Japhet's family, but not of either of the others, that it divided and spread.

Ham's family is strongly biassed towards empire-building. Egypt (Misrayim) is his child (10: 6), and Nimrod his grandson (10:8). Nimrod founds Babylon (10:11), a metropolis of empire, whose land of Shinar gives rise to Asshur (10:12), the founder of Nineveh, the capital city of the Assyrian empire. This concentration of empire-building in Ham's family gains point when it is observed that Asshur, presumably as the city Asshur and the Assyrian people, is a son of Shem, and not of Ham's family at all (10:22). Another of Ham's family, his son Cush (Ethiopia), is less of an imperial power than Egypt, Babylon, or Assyria, its but its rulers were at one time strong enough to conquer Egypt and place an Ethiopian dynasty on the Egyptian throne. (Ham's son Canaan was also an empire-builder in that Carthage, near the modern Tunis, was a Phoenician, that is, Canaanite, foundation, but the making of the Carthaginian empire, in the Fifth Century B.C.E., is almost certainly later than the writing of this list of nations.)

Just as the account of Japhet's family has the reference to coastlands, and that of Ham's the ventures of Nimrod and Asshur, so Shem has the peculiarity of the designation 'the father of all the children of Eber'. Logically, this is redundant, since Eber is Shem's great-grandson, and Shem must therefore be the forefather of Eber's offspring. The implication seems to be that the Eberite line is in some way typical of Shem's family, or that the characteristics of the Eberite line are what distinguish the family as a whole. The line from Eber reaches to Abraham, and one of the lines from Abraham goes on to the covenantal people Israel, to which the Israelite scriptures, not surprisingly, pay more attention than to other nations stemming from Abraham. To say that Shem is 'the father of all the children of Eber', and especially to say it in the context of the Hebrew scriptures, links Shem to the covenanted people and to their relation to the Lord God and the Lord's requirement for righteousness. The implication is surely that Shem is to be associated especially with knowledge of the Lord God, who has earlier been referred to as 'the Lord God of Shem' (9:26).

The three emphases made by the text about the three sets of nations can be seen to correspond to three essential features of nationality. The spreading Japhet nations, the empire-building Ham nations, and the concern of Shem's descendants with the Lord represent these functions: the occupation of a dwelling place, and organisation, and the transmission of understanding.

There is another way in which the three may be seen. The Japhet nations spread to their settlements and are by the lower, female, waters of the Creation (page 15). Contrasting with this suggestion of femininity are Ham's organisation and military might of empire, somewhat more male characteristics. Shem's nations could be said to be concerned with the inclusively sacred which holds feminine and masculine together in wholeness. This notion of the feminine, the masculine, and the third which comprehends them, is not offered as a conclusion, but is a fumbling towards something that may prove fruitfully suggestive.

It is interesting to compare how the three families of nations are related to the mountains of Ararat, where Japhet, Ham, and Shem are said to have disembarked with their parents and wives from the ark. As the map on page 174 shows, Japhet's nations are spread out from Asia Minor and the Black Sea coast, as though they might indeed have first come down from Armenia and the Caucasus. One of Shem's lines, that through Eber, stays in this region for three generations, and the others can be imagined as having spread from it. No such centre in or near these mountains is related to the countries which must be assigned to the children of Ham. What is curious however is that, through the enterprises of Nimrod and Asshur (10:8-12), Ham's peoples are brought to the upper Tigris, on the plain at the foot of the mountain mass which includes the mountains of Ararat. The reader may see a meaning in this late pointing of Ham's family towards Ararat; I will suggest none.

***

In order to see how the Israelite philosophy relates the Creator to the nations, it is helpful to look also in the Hebrew scriptures outside the Creation story. It is presumable that, if the Lord God makes humankind in nations, then the relations between nations and the way they fit together in time and space are matters of concern to the Creator. The point can be made more clearly with examples.

When the Lord promises Abram, of the line of Eber and Peleg, that his descendants will come into the promised land after being long in another country, the delay is 'because the iniquity of the Amorite is not yet complete' (Genesis

15:16); the name 'Amorite' is sometimes used for Canaanites generally. So the Lord God sees the inhabitants of the land pointed along a course of deterioration, the consequence of which will be that the Israelites will come against them to overcome them. The Lord God is concerned not only with the people to whom the land will be given, but also with the victims of that nation's coming. Israel's taking Canaan will be just only because, as things are, the Amorites' losing it, and suffering in the losing, will also be just. The God who will, later than the Creation story, be called in scripture the Lord God of Israel is the Creator of all nations.

A consequence of the Lord God's being the God of all nations is that righteousness includes the requirement that there is law and justice in the relations between nations. This is seen when the Israelites are east of the Jordan, before crossing that river into Canaan. Edom stands in Israel's way, but Israel may not hurt Edom (Deuteronomy 2:2-8). When the Edomites refuse to give the Israelites passage, the latter are bound by law to go round Edom (Numbers 20:14-21). Similarly, the Israelites go round Moab (Numbers 21:13, Deuteronomy 2:18) whom, with Ammon, they are forbidden to attack (Deuteronomy 2:9,19). The Israelites then meet the Amorites under Sihon, and ask them for free passage (Numbers 21:21,22, Deuteronomy 2:26-29), but Sihon replies by attacking Israel and is defeated, so that the Israelites take his territory (Numbers 21:23-25, Deuteronomy 2:32-36). This introduces two legal complications. The first is that Israel comes to occupy land not within Canaan as promised, but this is said to be brought about, foreseen, and justified by the Lord (Deuteronomy 2:30-31). The second complication is that the Amorites had taken territory from Ammon and Moab, territory which had become occupied by the Israelites, who were forbidden to attack Ammon or Moab and who had not done so. Much later the Ammonites made this an occasion of attacking Israel, whose leader in those parts, Jephthah, used the argument that the Ammonites had made no formal protest in the three hundred years since the land was taken by the Israelites from Sihon and the Amorites (Judges 11:12-27). Whether the God-given laws are, in any one case, the motivation of action, or whether they are not, those laws are assumed to provide a framework which has to be respected.

The sense that nations are part of a divine ordering of the world is expressed by the prophet Amos (Amos 9:7): 'To me, are you Children of Israel not like the Children of the Ethiopians?, says the Lord. Have I not brought up Israel from the land of Egypt, and the Philistines from Crete, and Syria from Qir?' (We do not know where Qir is.)

Prophecy sees nations not only in their origins under the Lord, but also in the world's still unfulfilled condition. When the diminished kingdom of Judah, the remnant of Israelite independence, was threatened by Assyrian ruthlessness and was neighbour to Egypt, the other great empire, the prophet Isaiah said (Isaiah 19:23-25): 'In that day there shall be a road from Egypt to Assyria, and Assyria shall come into Egypt, and Egypt into Assyria, and Egypt will worship with Assyria. In that day Israel will be a third for Egypt and for Assyria, a blessing in the midst of the earth. For the Lord of Hosts has blessed, saying, "Blessed be Egypt my people, and Assyria the work of my hands, and Israel my inheritance".'

Nations, then, according to Israelite philosophy, are an essential feature of humankind, not a mere accident of the way people come or stay together. They are within God's ordering of the world, held responsible before God for their deeds, and are instruments of God's purposes as far as prophecy can reach. The Hebrew scriptures therefore give the list of nations this meaning: being in nations is an essential part of being created human, and the nation list is a necessary part of the Creation story.

Although the nation list belongs to the Creation story, with its timeless quality, it makes sense only because actual nations are named. It is through some knowledge of them that any general patterns become accessible. Thus it is that the list of nations has two literary faces. One is formalised, and looks back to the style of the story in which time is created, Eden is unlocalisable, and the Flood has its own unique name. The other face is presented by named historical nations, and looks forward to the biographical, and then historical, styles to be found later in the Hebrew scriptures.

***

If every nation, like every individual, has a place in the created order, then every nation, like every individual, has its own particular contribution to make to the Creation. That is to say, every people is a chosen people, even if it does not always fulfil that for which it is chosen. The experience of the Children of Israel, of being chosen, came to them as an event unique in the world. Historically, this need not be considered as far-fetched, since they may well have been pioneers in the understanding of the meaning of nationality, with which understanding the Israelite sense of chosenness is integral. As pioneers they have, according to their own scriptures, to be bearers of Torah in a double sense, not only of standards and instruction applicable to all people (as in the Creation story itself) but also of standards and instruction peculiarly applicable to themselves, as an example or model, as it were, of the particularisation of universal instruction for a nation's uniqueness. It is not surprising that Jews have traditionally been aware of this chosenness not only as a source of joy, but also as a heavy burden.

Since each nation is in some unique way a chosen people, it is possible for various peoples at one and the same time to consider themselves chosen, and this as the result of true awareness, not false consciousness. The Jew thanks the Creator 'who has chosen us from all peoples to give us his Torah', while Christians at evening prayer, taking the Church as a people, ask God to 'make thy chosen people joyful'. Neither body objects to the other calling itself chosen, nor should it. (A Christian claim to 'supersede' Israel is another matter since, although peoples come and go, none can be a replacement for another, least of all for another that is still there.)

That members of the Christian Church can take it to be a people reminds us of another characteristic of being a nation or people: it is an imprecise concept. One's consciousness can accommodate being of one people in some respects and of another in some others. A sense that, for example, one belongs to the Scottish people does not preclude awareness that one belongs also to the people that is the Christian Church. This reminds us that being of more than one people need not make one of more than one nation. Nationality is peoplehood within the context of other peoples, and in that context a people will generally be seen as of one nation only. Thus one may be of a people, such as the Church, that few or none would call a nation. Nevertheless, it is possible that some people, certain Romanies or Jews for example, are seen to be of two nations. A further complication arises because statehood, although quite different from nationality, may affect one's sense of peoplehood and other people's awareness of one's nationality. Thus the person who is Welsh or Catalan by nationality and British or Spanish by statehood nay have some feelings of peoplehood attached also to Great Britain or Spain. Something like imprecision of this kind seems to be present within the nation list itself since its nations, conforming, already noted, to no definition, are some of them empires, some are smaller groups bound by custom and language, some are city-states.

To return to chosenness, the sense of being chosen does not necessarily entail seeing other peoples as in some way inferior. Two examples may help to make this clear. In the Seventeenth Century many of the English believed that the world's last age was upon them, and that England would have a uniquely important part to play in the events of the last days. These were people who, far from being hostile to foreigners, cultivated friendly overseas collaboration in the increase of knowledge and were among the most active in learning from those of other nations. A second example is from the Jews, whose notion of themselves as the chosen children of Israel is illustrated by the legend that each of seventy nations of the earth, the Israelites being one of them, has an angel to speak for it at the throne of God's glory.

One may perhaps take this matter further by saying that a nation which has no sense of chosenness, of its peculiar vocation, is sick, perhaps sick unto death. On the other hand, the nation that dissipates itself in hostility of spirit, betrays itself. History has, of course, abundant examples of national consciousness being manifested as exclusiveness, hatred, aggression, and destructiveness. The Creation story has something bearing upon this also. What it has to say will become apparent when consideration is given to its next episode, the story of the unfinished city. Meanwhile, if we blame nationality for international conflicts, do we condemn individual freedom because it makes possible personal fights, or would we abolish the family because vendettas exist?

DURING THE ACCOUNT of the nations it was said of Peleg, 'For in his days
the earth was divided' (10:25), which may refer to the dispersal of the nations
(page 186). Peleg is the first of his line with a name indicating a position outside
the mountain mass which includes Ararat; he appears to belong to the adjacent
plain where it is watered by the Euphrates. Later the line from Shem, through
Peleg, to Abraham will be continued, the names from Shem to Peleg being
repeated. Therefore, although the nation list and the genealogy of Abraham
are writings of two different kinds, as will be seen, the separation of one from
the other is a sort of interruption. The passage which interrupts is the story of
the unfinished city, which is thus placed within the telling of Shem's line so as
to relate it closely to the list of nations, as well as to the biography of Abraham.
The story has indeed a bearing on what the Hebrew scriptures have to say
about nationality. The story of the unfinished city, a translation of which now
follows, lies entirely in Chapter 11 of Genesis.

1 And everybody was of one way of speaking and of few words.

2 And it happened in their travelling from the east that they found a plain in the
land of Shinar, and they settled there.

3 And they said to each other, 'Come, let us make bricks and let us burn [fuel] for
burning [them] and they had brick for stone, and bitumen they had for
mortar.

4 And they said, 'Come, let us build ourselves a city, and a tower with its top in
heaven; and let us make a name for ourselves, lest we become dispersed all
over the earth'.

5 And the LORD came down to see the city, and the tower which children of
Adam [that is, human beings] had built.

6 And the LORD said, 'Indeed, one people and one manner of speaking for them
all, and this is their beginning of deeds! Nothing will be denied them of all
they purpose to do.

7 Let us go down and there mix up their way of speaking, so that they will not
understand each other's manner of speech.'

8 And the LORD dispersed them thence all over the earth, and they ceased
building the city.

[9] Therefore its name is called Babel [Babylon], because the LORD there mixed
(*balal*) everybody's way of speaking, and thence the LORD dispersed them
all over the earth.

The translation needs explanation on three points.

1) In verse 3 we have 'Let us make bricks and let us burn for burning'. It
is difficult to translate exactly the Hebrew:

> *Nilvnah levenim*
> *ve-nisrefah lisrefah.*

Word for word, this gives:

> *Let-us-make bricks*
> *and-let-us-burn for-burning.*

However, *nilvnah* alone means 'let us make bricks', so that *levenim*, 'bricks', is
redundant for the word-by-word meaning. The effect of saying *levenim* is give
a couplet with an internal pattern of rhythm and related words. The result
sounds like a Hebrew proverb, but Hebrew-speakers lived where stone, not
bricks, was used, and are unlikely to have had a proverb about bricks. Original
material must, then, have been given a form like that of an established
proverb, a literary technique that can remind us of composers who use
material in a folk idiom without quoting any actual folk music.

2) In verse 7 'way of speaking' and 'manner of speech' both translate the
Hebrew word *safah,* which will itself be discussed later. In verse 1 'way
of speaking' translates the same Hebrew word.

3) Babel is the usual Hebrew name of Babylon. The reader should not be
misled by translations that use 'Babel' here and 'Babylon' elsewhere.

***

The story comes to a climax of human activity in verse 4. Then the Lord intervenes and the telling comes to a second climax, this time of divine activity nul-
lifying human endeavour. As I write this I get a strong sense of the meaning of
the English proverb: 'Man proposes, God disposes'. If we take the story as
having two parts, one about human enterprise and one about divine intervention, we can fold it, so to speak, so as to bring the two halves opposite each other,
as was done with the Flood story on page 152. The pattern can then be as in
Figure 16, where the verses are indicated by number.

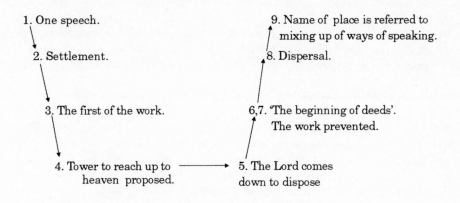

1. One speech.

2. Settlement.

3. The first of the work.

4. Tower to reach up to → 5. The Lord comes
   heaven proposed.   down to dispose

9. Name of place is referred to
   mixing up of ways of speaking.

8. Dispersal.

6,7. 'The beginning of deeds'.
     The work prevented.

Fig. 16. *Pattern of the story of the unfinished city.*

In Figure 16 episodes of the story face each other in pairs, each with a common theme, but with the members of each pair expressing the theme in opposition to each other.

***

The first thing that we are told in this story is that 'everybody was of one way of speaking'. Who is 'everybody'? The Hebrew has *kol-ha-aretz*, literally 'all the earth'. This need not mean every single human being on the earth's surface. For example 'everybody (all the earth, *kol-ha-aretz*) sought out Solomon to hear his wisdom' (1 Kings 10:24). There the meaning must be that Solomon was visited by numerous people coming from many countries, not by every human being alive. Similarly, this story is about a large population coming from many places. There is another reason why we cannot think that everybody on earth is meant. In verse 2 it is said that these people came to the land of Shinar when they were travelling from the east. This means that they were approaching the site of Babylon from the general direction of Elam (see the map on page 174). If all humankind were doing this, then there would be a difficulty in making the story agree with what has already been told about the Flood and the nations. People from the mountains of Ararat would have kept together while migrating east of the Tigris, and would then have crossed that river into the land of Shinar, finally dispersing from the site of Babylon. To fit this, Shem's line, for example, would have had to return to Ararat in order to follow the general path indicated by the names in the nation list. It seems simpler to suppose that the writer or writers intended to say that Shem's family belonged first to places near Shem's disembarcation, whence they spread. In that case, of course, they did not mean the reader to understand that every existing human being was engaged on the work in the story of the unfinished city. This point has to be stressed because the story is so often said to be intended as an explanation why humankind came to speak different languages, and that explanation requires that the whole of humankind was at the building of the unfinished city and its tower.

If 'everybody was of one way of speaking', did those present on the plain of Shinar have one language, even if they did not share it with those elsewhere? The text does not necessarily mean that those present spoke one language. To see why this is, it is necessary to look at the 'one way of speaking'. This 'way of speaking' translates the Hebrew word *safah,* 'lip'. This is a very frequent word in the Hebrew scriptures and, more often than not, it means not an anatomical lip or a physical edge, but a manner of speaking. Lips lie or praise, stammer or are righteous. The word for 'lip' could refer to a human language in only three places: Isaiah 19: 18, Isaiah 33:19, and Ezekiel 3:5 and 6. In the first of these it is best translated 'dialect', since it is the speech of non-Israelite Canaan in comparison with Hebrew. In the second and third examples the reference is to people whose speech is 'deep', and whose language is difficult to understand. It is not clear that 'lip' alone could mean language. There is no place in the Hebrew scriptures where *safah,* 'lip' necessarily means a language, in the sense that Chinese and Italian are different languages. In more than a hundred instances in which it refers to speech, it certainly does not mean that.

It is hardly surprising that 'the way of speaking' is not a natural language, since the story says as much directly. 'Everybody was of one way of speaking and of few words'. Whatever speech was being used, it was peculiar in having 'few words'. Now we know well how people may come to have common speech with few words; it happens with a technical jargon used among people of different native languages, and also with a form of speech used not as a complete language but for special contact only, as between sailors, or between fishermen of different countries habitually in the same waters. Seen in this way, the 'way of speaking' is of a piece with the technical enterprise of building a city and a tower if the builders are already of different native languages. When scripture speaks of a language, the word *lashon,* 'tongue', is regularly used, as already in the list of nations (10:5,20,31). This word does not occur in the story of the unfinished city.

This discussion has had to be detailed and somewhat wearisome, but the notion that the story of the Tower of Babel is about the origin of the diversity of languages is very often expressed in writings about scripture; indeed, it is the received wisdom. However, we are not free to see what the story is about until we have disencumbered ourselves of what it is not about.

***

'They found a plain in the land of Shinar' (verse 2). This is not simply cor-
roborative detail to lend verisimilitude to an otherwise bald and unconvinc-
ing narrative. Shinar is where Nimrod, child of Cush, was king in Babylon
(10:8-11). (From this arises the tradition that Nimrod was the leader in the
building of the city and tower.) The episode of Nimrod and Asshur, in 10:8-
12, is less about the origin of nations than about the organisation of states.
The size and complexity of Babylon obtained from ancient times, and this
may well have been well-known among Israelites at the time when the
Creation story was written, or when it received its present form. In Shinar,
of course, there is indeed not the rock from which to take building stone, and
there buildings are of bricks shaped from clay and burnt or sun-dried. The
reference to Shinar, and the location of the action at Babylon, give the
reader a sense of organisation, and the political and economic power that
large-scale organisation requires.

When a manner of speech, although of few words, is in use, there can be co-
operation in an enterprise such as building a city and a tower up to heaven. The
building might have been done by many people of one nation and one language.
That it was done in the way it was is related to the aim of the building: 'and let
us make a name for ourselves, lest we become dispersed all over the earth'. The
nations, in the ordering of created things, spread according to their languages
in their lands. Here, however, 'all the earth' is in one land, and has overcome
language barriers, in order to carry out an enterprise 'lest we be dispersed'.
There is clear opposition to the created order, to being in nations. To this end
the building is to 'make a name for ourselves'.

A name, a reputation, is in the Hebrew scriptures represented as desirable
(as in Ecclesiastes 7:1), but it crowns human worth and is not an end in itself,
nor is it coupled with action contrary to the created order. There is a difference
between a good name from righteous living, which itself has a purpose in accord with the created order, and a shallow repute based on concern about what
people will say of us. It may be relevant that the word used here for 'name' is the
same as that for 'renown' when we are told of the 'men of renown' worthy to be
wiped out by the Flood (Genesis 6:4).

The name which the builders want is to come from something limited, a
building. The building, the desired repute, and the avoidance of being in nations form a complex of purposes. These purposes point only to each other, so
that the builders are taken up with what is partial, not with being part of the
One Creator's world. The idiom 'with its top in heaven' may mean only 'very
high', but nevertheless suggests worship. Quite apart from this, the story itself
raises the question what the builders were worshipping, what was their god.

The builders defy the creation of humankind in nations and so turn away
from the Creator, their source. What god will help them not to spread as nations? 'Let us make a name for ourselves lest we become dispersed' (verse 4).
This name, this repute is somehow to prevent dispersal. The exact mechanism
of this is not set out, nor need it be. The reader can understand that getting and

maintaining reputation is a motive for coming and keeping together. Their repute substitutes for the Creator as the builders' direct activating force, and serves neither the Creator nor the Creator's image in humanity. Repute becomes a supposed entirety, a substitution of the partial and created for the whole and creating. The builders, that is, have made their repute an idol.

This idol has its ritual, and an exercise for its worship: 'Let us build ourselves a city, and a tower with its top in heaven; and let us make a name for ourselves...' Just as the reputation is the god which is to grant the builders that they will not be dispersed, so the buildings are to enable this god to be reached. Thus a city and a tower are made to function as the graven images by which the god is represented and approached Whether the images themselves are idols, their use is idolatrous since they serve an idol. Idol worship may have three elements: that which is isolated from the whole (here 'name', reputation), the object by which the isolated thing is approached (the city and the tower up to heaven), and thirdly a motive contrary to the created order, contrary to the Creator's ordering of the Creation ('lest we become dispersed'). The 'graven image', here the city and tower, may itself be what is isolated, or there may be idolatry without such a concrete object, although, for historical reasons, the graven image has been the typical idol.

All idolatry has material means (the 'graven image'), which serves that which is less than the whole, which in turn drives and leads contrary to the Creation and its Creator, and to the Creator's image. It is therefore contrary to humanity in its fulness. In history, therefore, idolatry is associated with oppression. Indeed, oppression always indicates idolatry, however words, even ostensibly about God, pretend otherwise.

Thus the three elements of idolatry depend upon each other in a series. 'Let us build ourselves a city and a tower with its top in heaven'—this is the material means. 'And let us make a name for ourselves'—this is what is less than the whole. 'Lest we become dispersed all over the earth'—this is the purpose contrary to the Creation, the purpose which prevents the name, the repute, for instance, from functioning as part of the universal whole, and confirms it as a fragment. As each of the three needs the other two to constitute idolatry, so the material means alone, the 'graven image', is not necessarily an idol. To build a city with a high tower in order to worship the one Creator, or in order to fulfil the human needs and aspirations that tend to make the divine image manifest in us, is not to make an idol. The Hindu whose 'seeing' (*darshan*) of an image as an aid towards a cosmic principle, is not using the image as an idol. Here there are differences among those of humankind who are not idolaters. While some use images in worship, others, such as Moslems, Jews, and most Protestant Christians, avoid images in order to prevent idolatry, and it is arguable that eschewing images in worship prevents the slide into idolatry that might take place when they are used.

Similarly, the second in the series need not be an idol. In our story 'to make a name for ourselves' is idolatrous. But making a name can be, in some circumstances, the expected by-product of action according to the created order, or be intended to facilitate such action. In such circumstances a good name is to be sought and valued. The name sought by the builders is explicitly to frustrate human creation by preventing dispersal into nations. An aim contrary to the created order is directed to a part, not the whole. This can, to take the matter further, be related to William Blake's* writing that 'If the doors of perception were cleansed everything would appear to man as it is, infinite'.

The pursuit of the partial cannot honour the God who is one, but only an imagined god of less than everything. This is an idol, and the repute which the builders seek is that idol. The city and tower which serve that idol are the graven image which is an idol. The two are aspects of the same idol. It is all one: the city and tower, the name, the avoidance of dispersion.

***

The first limb of the story (page 199, Figure 16) has been about how man proposes. In the second limb God disposes, bringing the tale from a climax of human drive to a climax of divine frustration of that drive. The second limb begins 'And the Lord came down'. This expression is used in the Hebrew scriptures only when there is an awesome intervention by the Lord in human affairs, as when Torah is given on Sinai (Exodus 19:11,18,20, 34:5), or when the Lord's spirit comes to the seventy elders (Numbers 11:25) or to judge between three prophets (Numbers 12:5), or when there is a fearful deliverance, personal (2 Samuel 22:10, Psalm 18:10) or public (Isaiah 31:4); Isaiah 64:1-4 conveys the terror. A reader familiar with the Hebrew of scripture meets the words 'And the Lord came down to see the city', and feels a shudder as though what has already been recounted is about to be stripped away, exposing reality.

In verse 7 the words 'Let us go down' introduce the Lord's deliberation. This deliberative way of expressing divine purpose has already been seen in the work of Creation's sixth day, where God says 'Let us make humankind in our image' (1:26). (The use of the plural when one person deliberates is, of course, heard also in English, as when one says 'Let's see now…') The deliberation by the Lord is an aspect of the telling's deliberateness, which is expressed by saying that the Lord sees, reflects, resolves, and acts, in each of verses 5-8 respectively. The succession gives insistence and crescendo, powering the thrust of the final action. It also emphases that the Lord acts here with reason. The Deity of the Hebrew scriptures is not some Homeric god of whim and pique. Indeed, it is because God usually acts reasonably in scripture that the Lord's apparent unreasonableness in, for example, the stories of Isaac's binding (Genesis 22:1-14) or of Job has such power to engage the reader's attention and to raise questions about the meaning of the stories.

If the builders were frustrated in what they wanted to do, does this mean that they lacked freedom of action? Certainly there can be no freedom without some degree of predictability of consequences. It is totally in accord with freedom of action that, if one spits into the wind, it blows back in one's face. Here, however, it must be asked whether such natural law operates when the Lord intervenes in the course of events. On this two comments may be made. First, in the Hebrew scriptures divine intervention often does not so much interrupt the expected natural sequence of events as express it. God's intervention is prompted by human action and direction of oneself, as when Cain's realisation that 'my iniquity is too great to forgive' (4:13) is followed by the Lord's intervening to protect him. Secondly, the way the story is told introduces what the Lord says about the work of the builders and so gives, as will be seen, a precept for conduct. The force of explicitly giving a rule as the Lord's words can be seen if one compares the natural consequence of Cain's sin ('anyone who finds me will kill me', 4:14) with the Lord's condemnation of bloodshed (9:5).

What the Lord condemns is the idolatry manifested in the attempt to frustrate the creation of humanity in nations. The frustration of nationality, in relation to idolatry, can be seen in two ways. Here the idolatry actuates and arises from the attempt to override national differences. On the other hand, when the nation itself is made into an idol, it accretes to itself functions contrary to the created order. There is a process which relates the two idolatrous perversions of nationality to each other. First, the sense of nation in people is diverted to the state, which is confused with the nation. Meanwhile corporate interests (to-day often more powerful than many states) develop. These are commonly dedicated to the idol of material acquisition. The state plays a double part. It is set up as superior to every other good and so, together with the nation with which it is falsely identified, becomes an idol, and at the same time facilitates the idolatrous corporations. The wholeness of things being thus fragmented between idols, the twisted remains of maimed nationality become occasions of conflict which, pretending to be about what might once have been real (and in the heart still is), deflect attention from the idols' priesthoods. In the obfuscation so useful to those officiants, words purporting to be about God can play a part. Rallying of people to the non-idolatrous worship of the divine Unity is met, however, with the objection that religion must be kept distinct from politics and economics. So something called 'religion' is separated from life, which is thus fragmented also, and the sacred name is belittled by making 'God' a title for what is reduced to partial relevance, an idol.

***

The Lord's intervention in the building of the city and tower, with the words spoken by the Lord in the story, make up a clear condemnation of what was being planned and done. This activity has two aspects, the particular, an attempt to frustrate the making of the nations, and the more general, the service of an idol. Since the work against the created order is, as has been seen already, an element of the idolatry, the condemnation is of both aspects of the activity is primarily of idolatry, the more inclusive. Here then the Lord's words and action imply the precept: *you are not to serve idols.* This is the seventh of the precepts, which, in this study, has been shown to arise from the story of the Creation, and is the last of the them emerging from the story. It is therefore now appropriate to review the seven.

CHAPTER 33: *CONCERNING RIGHT ACTION*

EVERY READER of the Hebrew scriptures must surely know that they are concerned throughout with right action. The story of the Creation, which is a key to much else in scripture, is unlikely to differ in this respect from the rest. It is therefore proper to ask of the Creation story what it offers concerning right action. The question can be made more precise. The opening is 'In the beginning God...', and the Creator is throughout given, unargued, known by unmediated experience and by that which comes forth, word and work. The deeds with which the story begins, the eight works of the seven days, are each introduced by 'And God said...'; the word is the work, it is the word of power. Therefore we may ask of the Creation story what the Creator says about right action, and what the saying may mean in the light of the circumstances in which the story sets it. To answer this question the words of the Creator can be reviewed in order, as the story presents them.

First, God speaks in the telling of Creation's seven days (1:1-2:3). Humankind is made in the image of the Creator, after the Creator's likeness. Thus we are creators, with our part in bringing the Creation to its culmination, the seventh day. On pages 31-38, especially pages 36f, it has been argued that this leads to the first precept: *you are not to belittle the name that cannot be spoken.*

Next, the Lord God speaks to the Adam and to the couple in the garden (2:4-3:24). God curses the ground and the snake, and bars the couple from the tree of life, sends them back to their native soil, and gives them garments. None of these implies a precept of action, although three precepts, to emerge later, are foreshadowed. The naming of the beasts anticipates the injunction to respect animal life, the marriage of the couple is background for the precept concerning nakedness, and the sanctioning of the possession of garments bears upon one aspect of the prohibition of robbery. The forbidding of the fruit that is eaten is not to be taken as a precept to the reader, since it is an essential of our humanity that we have eaten of the tree of the knowledge of good and evil. The disobedience is necessary to the Creation, not contrary to it (page 61).

When the Lord speaks to Cain (4:1-16) it is to warn, to call to responsibility, to open Cain's ear to the condemnation from blood and the ground, and to assure Cain of protection. Although the Lord's later prohibition of bloodshed is obliquely anticipated, there is here no exhibit prohibition; it is assumed that bloodshed is a sin, and that it leads to more bloodshed.

The generation of the Flood is explicitly condemned by the Lord's words (6:5-7). The condemnation implies a second precept: *you are to have judgments* (pages 119-121). That generation is again condemned by God (6:11-13), the condemnation implying a third precept: *you are neither to rob nor to do violence* (pages 125-127). After the Flood God gives Noah two explicit precepts (9:1-7). One is not to eat a beast's blood, which is its life, and this implies (pages 143-146) within its context a fourth precept: *you are to respect the life of the beast even in your use of it.* The other is the prohibition of bloodshed, discussed on pages 148-149, giving a fifth precept: *you are not to shed human blood.* When Noah curses Ham (9:25) he is making a statement about the nature of the family (pages 161-162), and his curse, within the conventions of the book of Genesis, represents God's word (page 163), giving a sixth precept: *there are nakednesses that you may not uncover.*

Now, in the story of the unfinished city, we have the Lord's condemnation of its builders. This is, as already discussed (pages 201-204) a condemnation of idolatry. Thus we have the seventh precept: *you are not to serve an idol.*

***

These precepts occur in Jewish teaching (Tosefta*, Seder Olam Rabba*, Talmud Bavli*) as injunctions given by God to all the Children of Noah, that is, to all humankind. In Hebrew literature (but not scripture, where they are not listed) the seven precepts are known by their short names: blessing the name ('blessing' being a euphemism for cursing), judgments, robbery, bloodshed, a limb from the living beast, the exposure of nakedness, idolatry. The sequence, derivation, and discussion of the seven, as presented here, are however unlike the sequence, derivation, and much of the discussion in Jewish sources, and I make no claim to reproducing them, but want only to acknowledge the priority of Jewish tradition in formulating the seven precepts of the Children of Noah. In fact both Seder Olam Rabba* and Talmud Bavli* derive all the precepts from the permission to eat of any tree of the garden (2:16, first part), by way of underpinning them after their truth had become evident for historical reasons that lie outside the scope of this work. (As far as the Jew is concerned, the non-Jew who lives by the seven precepts is as righteous as a Jew who lives by all the more extensively particular precepts given to the Children of Israel.)

This note on Jewish teaching about the seven precepts of the Children of Noah is by way of acknowledgment. However, although I take them from Jewish teaching, I put the emphasis somewhat differently from that in rabbinic writings, since I see them as emerging from the Creation story as a whole, and as integral with its philosophy. Obviously, if something is true to experience and reason, and if it is implied by a true philosophy (which at present I am assuming the philosophy of the Creation story to be), then it is reasonable that it can be derived from experience and held to be compatible with the philosophy, as with the ancient rabbis, or that it can be derived from the written presentation of the philosophy, as I have derived it in this work.

Returning to the present discussion of the seven precepts, it may be helpful to examine the relations of the precepts among themselves, and then relate them to the Creation story.

In looking at the relations between the precepts we may note that four of them are in two pairs. Those concerning judgments and robbery are both from the condemnation of humankind before the Flood. Those concerning bloodshed and respect for the life of the beast are closely coupled in God's speaking to Noah after the Flood. The precepts *you are to have judgments among you* and *you are not to rob or do violence* not only fall together in the story; they are complementary. If both are fulfilled, judgments control violence, and the avoidance of robbery and violence gives a character to the judgments, in that the law is then not only to be complied with but is itself socially equitable, not permitting the strong to do as they will with 'whomever they chose' (6:2).

The pairing of *you are to respect the life of the beast* with *you are not to shed human blood* is of another kind. The story couples them by the theme of blood (9:4,5). Then God's requirement of responsibility for bloodshed (9:5) is referred (9:6) to the making of humankind in the image of God (1:26,27). Thus the making of humankind in the divine image is linked to the prohibition of shedding human blood, and this is linked, through the theme of blood, to respect for the life of the beast. Since the making of humankind in the divine image is, in its place, coupled with dominion over animal life, the triangle is completed: respect for the beast's life, respect for human life, the making of humankind, each linked to the other two.

If each of the two pairs of precepts is taken as a unit, the seven become five. Respect for the divine name, which represents the absolute unity, and idolatry, which is the practice of dividedness, represent the poles between which our actions move. Between these poles the other five precepts, four in two pairs and one singly, form a triad: the just society (judgements, robbery and violence), respect for life (animal and human), and the ordering of nakedness (that is, of sexual relations). These are interdependent, since the negation of any of the three vitiates the other two. There is, of course, no reason on why the interdependence should be respected. One might, for example, claim to respect human life, although in fact threatening it by a failure of equity in judgment. The overall coherence of the triad requires an orientation towards a principle outside it. This principle is represented by the precepts concerning respect for the name which represents the ineffable Unity, and concerning its negation, idolatry. Thus the seven precepts form a coherent system. This is true not only for their fulfilment in publicly visible conduct, but also in their effect on, and their requirement within, the individual who practises them. This matter may, however, be conveniently deferred until after the entire text of the Creation story has been examined, and some of its implications explored.

Having looked at the seven precepts as a system, coherent within itself, we can also view them as part of the Creation story. That is to say, each precept can be related to the part of the story in which it occurs.

The Creation story has four stages: totality, disintegration, re-creation, and diversification. These have their precepts, one for the first and two for each of the three others. Totality is the comprehensive view of the Creation in the seven days. It has all time within it. From this representation of totality, and in particular from the telling's culmination in the seventh day (pages 31-38), comes the precept *you are not to belittle the name that cannot be spoken*. This is the precept corresponding to Creation's unspeakable mystery.

In the second stage human life, and other life with it, is corrupted by a disintegration which begins with a failure to take responsibility and ends with the generation of the Flood, which is characterized by violent oppression between sections of society. From the Lord's condemnation of this generation there are to be inferred the precepts bearing upon social relations: *you are to have judgments among you*, and *you are neither to rob nor to do violence*. The personal aspect however of the second points towards the next stage of the story, and the precepts in it.

Now comes the Flood, the partial dissolution of the Creation, when the separated upper and lower waters (1:6,7) meet (7:11). Through this lives the integral Noah (pages 164-169), in whose presence there is re-creation (8:22) by the Lord, at which God makes known the necessary conditions for human participation in Creation, that is, for humankind to fulfil its being made in the Creator's image, 'But flesh with its life, its blood, you shall not eat. But, also, your blood, of your lives, I will require...each for his brother' (9:4,5). This implies the precepts *to respect animal life* and *not to shed human blood*.

In the fourth stage of the Creation story the diversification of humankind into families is presented so as to imply that *there are nakednesses that you may not uncover* (page 163) In the diversification into nations, the condemnation of those who try to frustrate it implies that *you are not to serve an idol* (pages 201-204). Idolatry could, it may be presumed, be associated with other stages of the story or, more precisely, its prohibition could, but the story links it to the attempt to frustrate diversification into nations, and history shows that the association of idolatry with abuse of nationality, as well as with its suppression by forcible *Gleichschaltung,* has a basis in experience.

***

The seven precepts of the Children of Noah are not laws, although they constrain what the laws may be. For example, it rests with interpretation whether the prohibition of bloodshed protects the embryo or a person about to kill somebody else. The prohibition of robbery and violence may reasonably be held to include the prohibition of theft, but what constitutes theft must depend upon a society's laws of ownership. What nakedness is forbidden to be uncovered will depend upon family structure and the character of marriage; there is sexual intercourse which is, in a monogamous society, adultery but which might, in a polygamous society, be a valid marriage, by the sharing of a bed, between an already married man and a woman thus far single. Laws may differ between peoples and still fulfil the requirements of the seven precepts. This, of course, does not mean that all legal codes fulfil those requirements. For example, it was assumed nearly two thousand years ago, in the Tosefta*, that killing people for entertainment, as in Roman civilisation, must lie outside any valid limits set by the prohibition of bloodshed.

Because the seven precepts set limits, rather than enjoin exactly specified activities, some are expressible as prohibitions and some must be so expressed. Creation, insofar as it is given and to be accepted as it is, limits the possibilities of action that is not ultimately self-negating. Within the limits thus set it leaves freedom for the creative work of human beings. Negative rules tell where the boundaries are; positive injunctions leave less choice.

The seven precepts do not correspond to virtues or dispositions, but to fields and directions of action. A virtue is an inherent power, enabling or assisting right action. As examples we may take the four cardinal virtues: fortitude, temperance, prudence, and justice (in its older sense, which is near to 'righteousness'). Since the three mentioned first are strengths, the fourth may be taken to be of the same kind, so that it is to be understood as uprightness, a shade of meaning which the Latin *justitia* has. (The four cardinal virtues come to us through a Christian, Latin tradition, but go back at least to the Greek of Plato*.) As an example of a disposition and of the general quality of action to which it disposes, we could take honesty or kindness. Dispositions and virtues need not be distinct. The three Christian virtues, faith, hope, and charity (1 Corinthians 13:13), are inherent powers, and so dispositions. On the other hand, they do not point to the fields or limits of action. Faith in what? Hope for what? Love that activates the Inquisitor (as it does)? A virtue, however, bears upon more than one of the fields of the seven precepts. Already, in the Creation story, individuals have shown virtues, as when Noah acts so as to suggest all four now called cardinal and all three now making up the Christian set. In general, the seven precepts set social norms, being applicable to ascertainable activity. Virtues and dispositions, on the other hand, although socially affected and acting socially, are in the individual person, are known by their fruits, for which fruits the seven precepts provide criteria.

One sometimes meets with the notion that virtues and dispositions are first to be cultivated so that appropriate actions can then flow from them. In fact our actions help to form our virtues and dispositions. Doing does not depend upon the state of being without any dependence of being upon doing, but doing and being are of a piece. Virtues and dispositions are aspects of our being, but one hears it said that, for example, one must love, as though being a loving person could be achieved by muscular effort, like shifting a boulder. (Interestingly, Jewish comments on 'Thou shalt love thy neighbour as thyself', Leviticus 19:18, use it as a criterion of actions more than of dispositions.) Just as one cannot, by taking thought, add a cubit to one's stature (Matthew 6:27, Luke 12:25), one also cannot by such means increase the circumference of the arm; the arm may however develop with exercise. To require of somebody a virtue or disposition (as distinct from making them aware of what it is) is to demand the immediate enlargement of the biceps. One inculcates an unproductive sense of guilt and, since virtues are less accessible to the senses than muscles, encourages hypocrisy. To ask that the rules of the game be observed is a quite different requirement. The seven precepts are presented as rules of the game according to the created order (given their further specification). If they are such, then the exercise of them can be expected to develop the virtues and dispositions by which the creation of humankind in the divine image is furthered. According to the biblical Creation story our actions can be part of our being created. When they are, we may, to give them a name, call them right action.

***

The last passages of the Creation story to be considered have been about the nations. In what follows the emphasis is again personal, leading into what scripture presents next, after the Creation story.

CHAPTER 34: *THE MANY AND THE ONE*

NOW WE COME to the end of the Creation story.   Although it is an end, it is also a beginning, since it opens the next part of the book of Genesis. This will be seen after the passage itself has been read. It concludes chapter 11 of Genesis. The divisions between lines correspond with the punctuation indicated by the musical marks of the Hebrew text.

[10] These are the generations of Shem.
Shem was a hundred years old,
and fathered Arpachshad two years after the Flood.

[11] And Shem lived after he fathered Arpachshad five hundred years,
and he fathered sons and daughters.

[12] And Arpachshad lived thirty-five years
and fathered Shelah.

[13] And Arpachshad lived after he fathered Shelah three years and four hundred years
and he fathered sons and daughters.

[14] And Shelah lived thirty years
and fathered Eber.

[15] And Shelah lived after he fathered Eber three years and four hundred years,
and he fathered sons and daughters.

[16] And Eber lived thirty-four years
and fathered Peleg.

[17] And Eber lived after he fathered Peleg thirty years and four hundred years,
and he fathered sons and daughters.

[18] And Peleg lived thirty years and fathered Reu.

[19] And Peleg lived after he fathered Reu nine years and two hundred years,
and he fathered sons and daughters.

[20] And Reu lived thirty-two years and fathered Serug.

[21] And Reu lived after he fathered Serug seven years and two hundred years,
and he fathered sons and daughters.

²² And Serug lived thirty years and fathered Nahor.

²³ And Serug lived after he fathered Nahor two hundred years,
and he fathered sons and daughters.

²⁴ And Nahor lived twenty-nine years
and fathered Terah.

²⁵ And Nahor lived after he fathered Terah nineteen and a hundred years,
and he fathered sons and daughters.

²⁶ And Terah lived seventy years
and fathered Abram, Nahor, and Haran.

   ²⁷ And these are the generations of Terah. Terah fathered Abram, Nahor,
   and Haran, and Haran fathered Lot.

   ²⁸ And Haran died in the lifetime of Terah his father, in
   the land of his kindred, in Ur of the Chaldeans.

   ²⁹ And Abram and Nahor married wives. The name of Abram's wife
   is Sarai, and the name of Nahor's wife, Milcah, daughter of
   Haran, the father of Milcah and father of Iscah.

³⁰ And Sarai was barren: she had no child.

   ³¹ And Terah took his son Abram and his grandson Lot, Haran's son, and
   Sarai his daughter-in-law, wife of his son Abram, and they* went out with
   them* from Ur of the Chaldeans, to go to the land of Canaan; and they
   came to Charan** and stayed there.

³² And the days of Terah were five years and two hundred years,
and Terah died in Charan.

Notes: *—Either the first 'they' is impersonal: ('one went', 'people went' with them), or 'they 'refers
to two of the named people and 'them' to the other two.

   **—Some translators spell this name 'Haran' in English, but this makes it the same as that
of Milcah's father, which it is not; in the Hebrew 'Haran' begins with the sound of h in 'hat', while
' Charan' begins with the sound of ch in ' loch', that is, with the letters hé and chet, respectively.

This genealogy has the last item, that about Terah (verses 26 and 32), interrupted by particulars of his family. Otherwise the items have the same
general form as those in the geneaology from Adam to Noah (5:1-32,
9:28,29); however, only in the earlier passage is each generation concluded
with the total life-span. The lengths of the lives have already been discussed
on pages 96-101.

Verse 10 makes Shem a hundred years old two years after the Flood.
Genesis 5:32, however, has Noah 500 years old when Shem, Ham, and Japhet
are born, while 7:6 makes him 600 when the Flood began. Thus there appears
to be a discrepancy of two years. However, Genesis 10:21, for example, makes
it clear that the reader is not to take Noah's sons as triplets. Therefore Genesis

5:32 means that Noah began having his three sons when he was 500. Shem, the second son (page 176), must therefore have been 100 two years after Japhet reached that age, Japhet being 100 when the Flood began. Ham was the youngest (Genesis 9:24). The point of this analysis of an apparent discrepancy between 11:10, here, and 5:32, is to show that, even if the story has been put together from different sources, there is no evidence that the editing has been a botched job. On the contrary, whether the story is or is not compounded of more than one original text, it is, as we have it now, a single coherent work, and it is proper for us to read it such.

From Adam to Noah there are ten generations, and from Shem to Terah there are nine. There is a tenth generation in the verses (27-31) about Terah's family. Of this generation Haran dies, and in verse 31 Nahor has been slipped out of the story. Abram is the tenth-generation child to whom the genealogy points.

Verse 29 gives Haran two daughters, one of whom marries her uncle Nahor. The other daughter, Iscah, is not said to have married, while the two daughters' other uncle, Abram, marries Sarai. In Jewish tradition, Sarai and Iscah are two names for the same woman. This certainly tidies up verse 29, but is it reasonable on any other ground? Of the four matriarchs, Sarah, Rebecca, Leah, and Rachel, only Sarah (here called Sarai still) is given no family history. If she is Iscah, there is no longer this deficiency. The matriarchs and patriarchs (including Abram) attached importance to marriage into their own family. This requirement is also satisfied if Sarai is Iscah. If she is Iscah then Sarai (later to be called Sarah) is the niece of her husband Abram, just as Milcah is the niece of her husband Nahor, Abram's brother. If Sarai is Iscah, and therefore Abram's niece, another story becomes clearer. In Genesis 20:12 Abraham (as Abram comes to be called) says that his wife Sarah is his sister and his father's daughter. He wishes to conceal that she is his wife, but were his words in fact untrue? In Genesis 29:15 the word 'brother' means a nephew, so why should 'sister' not mean a niece? Similarly, in Genesis 31:28 the word 'sons' is used to represent grandsons, so that Iscah, the granddaughter of Abram's father might be called 'daughter' of that man. Therefore, if Iscah is Sarai, not only does verse 29 get a pleasing compactness of structure, but there is a resolution of other difficulties in the story of Abraham and Sarah. It is as well for the modern critic to keep in mind that traditions coming down from ancient or mediaeval rabbis, or from the Church Fathers, may actually be based on careful textual criticism.

***

The names from Shem to Peleg in this genealogy have already appeared as nations (10:22,24,25). Of the names that now appear, but were not given among the nations, Reu is not identifiable, but Serug, Nahor and Terah all have names identical with those places near Charan (Westermann*) which is in northern Mesopotamia, the region called in Hebrew Aram-Naharaim, that is, 'Syria of Two

Rivers', Tigris and Euphrates. What we have here, then, is a continuation of the account of the nations, and with five generations of overlap. The overlap is important. It is just because Shem, Arpachshad, Shelah, Eber, and Peleg are common to both lists that the differences between the lists are shown up. As already explained on page 188, the family tree of nations cannot always refer to individuals, as some of the names cannot be of persons, but only of populations. On the other hand, each generation from Shem to Terah has a clearly stated age at fathering the son, and an unambiguously calculable age at death. This is the genealogy of individuals, not a scheme of nations. With a series of five names common to the two lists, we are given, for the same names, a change of style and, with it, a change of aspect, from the social to the individual.

The Creation story has throughout kept in play the individual and social aspects of humanity. At first they are not to be distinguished: all humanity is the creature whose name is Adam, humankind. The tale of Cain is about personal sin leading to personal tragedy, but Cain's descendants are the authors of inventions of a social kind. The lines of Cain and Seth lead to the generation of the Flood, in which one social group oppresses another and all flesh is corrupt. In the cataclysm that follows the story keeps its continuity through the character of a single character, Noah. Again, however, there is a shift from the individual to the social and, beyond that, to the cosmic, as the covenant is made after the Flood. Then the narrative tells of Noah's family and the earth's nations. Now our attention is taken back to individuals, with the point made sharper by the changed treatment of the five generations from Shem to Peleg. (If the two accounts of these generations come from different sources, I have to admire the inspired art of the editor who combined them into the form we have now.)

With Abram and Sarai there is no double aspect: they are individuals. Their names are certainly not of nations, tribes, or cities. They open a new mode of telling: biography. The story of the Creation finishes. The story begins of the three patriarchs and four matriarchs, who present seven paths to perfection and embody the promise of re-enacting the Creation in the making of a people. Or to put it differently, the story of Creation does not end but is continued in other ways. Indeed, if the story is true, then, even as I write, the work of the Creation is not wholly fulfilled. Whether it is true is a matter now to be considered.

CHAPTER 35: *IS IT TRUE?*

NOW THAT THE BIBLICAL text of the Creation story has been followed through, it is possible to review it generally, to draw conclusions, and to apply it to human living. Before consideration of these general matters, however, it may be advisable to inspect their foundations by asking whether the Creation story is true. In this way some feeling may be gained about what kinds of generalisation and conclusion, if any, it might bear.

Throughout the work, thus far, the story has been taken without questioning whether it is true. This is a matter of method. The examination of a writing cannot begin with implied denigration. Reading is like opening a conversation: one listens first, and then proceeds as though giving the interlocutor the benefit of any doubt. In that way, when a more critical position is taken up, the critic knows what it is that he is criticising. One cannot fault or contradict what one reads unless one is prepared to go along with it and hear what it says. (This principle is usually observed in literary criticism and Christian New Testament scholarship, but less often in political polemic and Christian Old Testament criticism.) In this work the point has now been reached at which it is possible to ask whether it is true, although hitherto the general policy has been to meet the text actively in order to hear what it is saying, and to make sense of what is heard.

In the Invitation with which this book opens, some of the comments now to be made were foreshadowed in, for example, references to some kinds of biblical criticism and to differences between types of literature in their appropriate ways of being read. These matters were brought into the Invitation so that the reader should not expect of me what I was not going to offer. They are raised now, as topics of detailed discussion, in an attempt to answer the question whether the Creation story is true.

***

In order to examine whether a writing is true or false, we need to know what sort of writing it is.

Scientists reporting experiments are likely not to describe the work as it happened, but will draw out and rearrange the relevant material so as to make the scientific logic clear. A paper in a learned scientific journal, describing experiments, may be true to a scientist but false to an historian, since the paper's

215

reconstruction of the experiments can be untrue in sequence of events and misleading in its selection of them, although not from a scientist's point of view. Such a paper is true because it claims for itself to be scientific, not historical. Were it to be taken as historical, what would otherwise have been truth-displaying conventions would be methods of falsification.

If I wish to consider the truth of Shakespeare's statement that 'Lilies that fester smell far worse than weeds', I do not compare the odours of a clump of weeds with that of diseased or rotting lilies. The statement, in its context, has obviously nothing to do with anything that such an experiment could reveal; Sonnet 94 is about change of a certain kind in a person's character. This is plain to the reader who grasps that the writing is a poem and who reads it as poetry. As in a scientific paper, the truth or falsehood of words can be judged only when account is taken of the work of which they are a part.

It is open to discussion whether still waters run deep, but discussion is pointless if we forget that we are considering a proverb. As a matter of plain logic, still waters do not run. Even if the meaning is taken to be that deep waters are quiet at the surface, the proverb is not about water, but merely refers to an assumed property of water; it is about people, as we all know. We know not to waste our time testing the saying by considering water, and we know this because we can tell the difference between a proverb and a statement in hydrodynamics. The question whether the saying is true is a question about human nature and behaviour, a question which could have meaning even if the hydrodynamic image were untrue in our experience.

Science, history, poetry, proverbs, each has its criteria of truth and falsity. If we want to know whether a statement is true, we need to know to what class it belongs, and there are more classes of statement than the four mentioned. Of course, we classify statements more or less unconsciously before judging them, and it is only occasionally that we misunderstand something by misclassifying it. Drama and fiction provide further examples of the peculiarities that may occur according to the type of literature. The truth of *Dr. Faustus* does not depend on whether Helen of Troy can be made visible two or three millennia after her death, nor does the truth of *Hamlet* depend on the outcome of comparing it with sources for the history of Denmark. We ask of *Great Expectations* whether it is, for example, a true picture of human development, but not whether Pip corresponds with someone knowable from, say, letters or parish registers. Of course, in practice we know to what class a work belongs not only by what is said of it, but by what it says of itself, usually at least.

Now this may seem an awful lot of fuss as a mere preliminary to asking whether the Creation story is true. It would indeed be fortunate if the remarks just made were unnecessary. However, as may now become apparent, the biblical Creation story is so commonly said to be true or to be untrue according to inappropriate criteria, that it is expedient to go back to the bases of argument. What does the story itself have to say about the sort of story it is?

First of all, as already discussed (pages 18-21), the Creation includes the creation of time, and the text makes sense most readily if time is seen as a child of the fourth day's work. Time however cannot begin inside a history, for a history is filled with a continuity of time or of times, which already accompany the history or are manifested in it at the moment of its beginning. Therefore the Creation story has not the form of history, and cannot have been intended to be read as history. Its truth or falsehood is not to be sought by asking where it is historically true.

As the Creation story proceeds it necessarily becomes compatible with the biographical and historiographical forms of exposition which follow it. Thus the story moves eventually to historical nations, which are the setting for the biographies which emerge in continuity from the Creation story. (The criteria of truth and falsehood in biographies of various kinds are not relevant here.) The mountains of Ararat, and the nations also, provide a geographical setting. Nevertheless, just as the narrative moves from the non-historical to material with an historical reference, so also it comes to have a geographical reference only after moving from the non-geographical. The apparently geographical statements about Eden imply that it has no geographical location (pages 52-55). This point is made more explicitly by the narrative when it says that the Lord God planted a garden in Eden (2:8), and that a river goes out of Eden in order to water the garden (2:10). This contradiction is a clear warning to the reader against giving all the Creation story a geographical setting (page 54). The creation story, which has at its start no time, also has no place.

On the Flood, the text prevents the reader from slipping too soon into the historical and geographical mode of understanding. The Flood is spoken of in strange words (pages 127-128) water is held back by trellises (pages 132-133) and covers mountains higher than the Alps (page 133), wetting the earth for exactly one solar year, the story probably having a lunar year also (pages 140-141). Any one of these features of the Flood story, taken alone, need not mean that an historical mode of telling is not intended, but their cumulative effect, in a context already provided by the timelessness of the seven days and the placelessness of Eden, must be to warn the reader against supposing the Flood narrative to be intended as history.

There have been many studies relating parts of the Creation story to history. Hertz*, for example, points out that the evolutionary view of the history of life is in agreement with the story of the seven days. Ford* sees the story of the Garden of Eden as a version of the history to be inferred from current palaeontology, anthropology, climatology, and studies of folk-lore. Others have said that Cain's name (*Qayin*) must originally have been that of the eponymous ancestor of the Kenites (*Qeynim*). Warlow* argues for changes in the earth's axis, among the effects of which would be massive flooding. Berlitz* has gathered explorers' evidence that the remains of the ark are still among the mountains of Ararat. The catalogue of a county library (or even one of its branches) will show that such authors are in numerous company. The is no reason why the Creation story should not incorporate material from oral or written history, or

217

from other branches of learning. It may even be that such elements give force to the narrative, which would then be, in one of its aspects, an interpretation of things known. Whether such lore, scarcely known to the modern reader, might help appreciation of the Creation story to-day, is an open question. Any use of historical material to give meaning to the Creation story can however be made only with respect to the story itself, and in fact it disowns any historical intention except insofar as it introduces and has literary continuity with material in historical or biographical form.

The so-called fundamentalist, who claims to take literally the words of scripture, is not thoroughly fundamental. He takes the Creation story to be history when its own words say that it is not. On the other hand, the rationalist who says that the Creation story is untrue because it is incompatible with history, is not being rational, since he confuses categories; the Creation story says of itself that it is not historical. The fundamentalist and the rationalist are like people who have trouble with maps as representations of reality. They look at an Ordnance Survey 1:50,000 sheet, and at its blue motorways. The fundamentalist says that the map is true, that therefore motorways are blue, and that those who rely on their eyes, seeing black asphalt, are in error. The rationalist believes his eyes when he sees the black asphalt, and therefore puts aside the map, with its blue motorways, deeming it to be false, and useful only as a pretty picture that has come down to us from primitive and irrational surveyors. Those who want the truth about a map, and from it, are little troubled by either the fundamentalist or the rationalist.

***

If the Creation story is not, in great part at least, to be taken as history or geography, by what criteria is it to be judged? Let us look at the other side of whether a writing is true, starting not with the writing but with ourselves; how do we know that anything is true? In the end we cannot claim truth for that which is contrary to experience, whether the experience is of the observed world, of historical sources, of people in everyday life, of what we meet in ourselves, or any of many other things. Experience alone can be fallacious, however, as further experience may demonstrate, and we therefore use reason. As Hippocrates taught of the medical art, its twin pillars are experience and reason. Reason is more than mere rationality. Nevertheless experience can go beyond reason's reach, and reason beyond experience's; the mystic and the mathematician each has a path to truth. (To be beyond reason is not to be contrary to it; to be beyond experience is not to be contrary to it. Although one outreach the other, within the truth they are not in conflict, and they are inseparable except in the extreme case.) In the Hebrew scriptures the word *emet* ('truth') implies that which is worthy of absolute trust, and which is therefore at the core of experience.

The notion of a writing as a magic book, the truth of which is to be accepted, whatever experience and reason tell one, is just nonsense. It means that there are two standards of truth, one for statements in the magic book and another for history, science, poetry outside the magic book, or novels, for these can all be falsified by experience of the evidence. If we accept any of these on the word of somebody else, it is not only because we think them probable, but also because we know them to be open to checking by experience and reason, if not always our own (since checking in some fields may need the training of perception or of methods of reasoning). Some will argue for a magic book on account of its wonderful origin. That is, however, an historical hypothesis, open to historical examination. It is then not the magic book that has logical priority, but the historical explanation on which its proposed truth rests. Furthermore, when the historical underpinning of the book's authority is in the book itself, then the argument for the book's truthfulness is circular. If what is in scripture (anybody's) is true, it is true not because it is in scripture; rather, it is likely to be in scripture because it is true. To look at probability rather than certainty, if a writing or collection of writings has survived many generations and is held to be true, it is likely that confidence in it has been reinforced by experience. Thus it survives while much other writing becomes lost.

Now, if I take the Creation story and set it down alongside my experience, how am I to evaluate the story? If I walk about in a landscape, a piece of printed paper in hand, and compare the paper with the land to see whether it speaks truly of the latter, then I must not confuse a map with an aerial photograph and, if the paper is a map, I need to know the meanings of the map's colours and symbols. Thus I am back to asking what sort of discourse the Creation story is. It is not to be judged as history or natural science; that much has been explained. To be more positive, to note what the story is, as well as what it is not, we may first note its scope. It takes in the universe, calls its first human character 'Humankind' (that is, the Adam), and deals with choice and self-awareness, righteousness and unrighteousness, copulation and birth, destruction and salvation, individuals and nations, divine love with divine correction. I find that too much of this is already real life, for me to take it as allegory or parable. The story to me, coheres to present a rich but single picture of the human condition, including my own, if not of more also. All this I find within a compactness that confronts me with breathtaking craftsmanship.

I am doubtful whether it helps one to understand or criticise the story, to put it into any named category. Rather, I would say that what the Creation story says of the human condition, whether in solitude or communality, what it says of the God in us and in which we are, and what it says of us in relation to the non-human creation, are all in accord with my experience and do not go against reason. In view of the scope of the Creation story, to find it true is to find a rich mine of truth.

Others may or may not agree with me. I only show the way I have gone. You may not agree with me about what it is that we are seeing on the journey. I am however sure enough of my own experience and what the Creation story says of it, that you, even if you finally deem it not true, will not have expended effort in vain, in coming with me. Though we may differ about what it is to which the journey has taken us, and although someone else may not, at journey's end, see the treasure which I see, we may nevertheless agree that we are each the richer for the travelling.

I have deliberately refrained from giving a detailed argument why I find the Creation story true to my experience, and why I believe it to be true to the common experience of humanity. It is my purpose not to press the case that I am right, so much as to invite your interaction with the text, asking, listening, answering back, listening again, and so on, until the sense of the Creation story comes to you according to your own reading. The listening is not easy, for we are beset by centuries of interpretations, Christian, Jewish, or other, which are liable to interrupt or just drone on whenever we are listening for the story's own voice. If you feel that there is merit in a fresh approach, or if you have, in reading this work, become more familiar with the story, much of my purpose is fulfilled. D.H. Lawrence* has put the matter well.

> Now a book lives as long as it is unfathomed. Once it is fathomed it dies at once... The Bible is a book that has been temporarily killed for us, or for some of us, by having its meaning arbitrarily fixed.

***

In the invitation with which this work began I said that I would not use the term 'divinely inspired', because it can lead to misunderstanding. Nevertheless, at this point, when the question of the Creation story's truth is before us, the related matter of divine inspiration may usefully come within our view.

It happens to us that a work of art comes to life. A living work is inexhaustible. One does not expect there to be an end to the possible interpretations of, say, Elgar's Second Symphony, by performers and hearers, even among performances all true to a single score. One does not anticipate any inevitable exhaustion of the mine of meaning that is *Hamlet,* although players, audience, or readers use the one text. The work of art, coming from its maker like a baby from its mother, takes on a life of its own, just as does the baby. Thus the work can have true meanings not intended by its maker, and be truly perceived in ways in which its maker never knew it. The maker may be aware that the work goes out into the world with its own life. As Josef Hora* wrote,

> Both sad am I and glad as well;
> What once was mine is mine no more.

When a work speaks beyond anything intended or imagined by its maker, we may say that the work is inspired, that the maker's genius is in receiving inspiration (that is, what is in-breathed) and transmitting it alive, to grow in the soil which is the maker's fellow-humanity.

Thus there is a large measure of agreement that an Orthodox Christian icon, Wordsworth's *The Prelude, Don Giovanni, Great Expectations,* and the melody of *Greensleeves,* are all inspired. Nevertheless, there are degrees of inspiration, since some works yield more than others, though all be met with goodwill and receptivity. By 'more' here I mean that the fields of experience reached by the range of meanings is greater, and that in each field there is a greater depth of penetration, the meanings still being true. In this sense I would suggest that *Macbeth* is more inspired than *Timon of Athens,* and *Great Expectations* than *Pickwick Papers,* although some might not agree.

Sometimes meaning and relevance are indefinitely wide and deep. A work then touches on all experience and at the greatest depths, so that, however long people continue to encounter the work actively, it still offers them open perspectives in every direction. It is inexhaustible, and the convergence of all things on it brings them into a unity. For those who see in the universe that which is a unity and in which all things have their being, the unity of the work expresses this unity in and of the world, and in which the world is. The work may then be seen to be not only inspired, but divinely inspired. There is, of course, no limit to the number of possible divinely inspired works, since there is no limit to the number of places out of which the wholeness of things can be contemplated.

Not every look-out point, however, is accessible to every people, so that a work which is divinely inspired in the experience of those of a particular people or worshipping community is not necessarily divinely inspired for others. When a people generally come to find a work to be divinely inspired, they are likely to give it the status of a sacred writing, and it will indeed become numinous for them. The sacred status of a writing is therefore communal, and it may be acquired by the writing only after several generations have had time to reflect upon it. A sacred text will then be taught as divinely inspired, even when those receiving it (youngsters, for example) do not yet know it well enough to have experienced its divine inspiration in their own lives. The teacher must ask for such trust, since it is by assuming in the first place that the work is divinely inspired that some people will be able to know for themselves whether it is, by matching experience to hypothesis, so to speak. Without the initial assumption such people may remain cut off from the work, although others may be seized of a work's divinely inspired character through solitary access to it. These latter are few by comparison, and thus there is a functional circularity. People are brought into relationship with the work because it is a sacred text. This enables them to find in it the divine inspiration which makes the text's status reasonable for them. Some of these people bring others into relation with the text, and so on. The point at which those who do not themselves feel the text to be divinely inspired are nevertheless brought to meet it, is where transmission depends not on the text's inherent power, but on its being taught. If there are changes in the quality of teaching or of the willingness of the young to test for themselves what the elders recommend, then the sacred text will lose its status as such although, of course, it is still divinely inspired. Since one reason for such a breakdown is that the teachers themselves have, little by little, come to teach the text in such a way that the work itself is muffled, and only the teacher is heard clearly, a vicious circle is set up, with feebler transmission leading to feebler appreciation, which conditions yet feebler transmission. Under these circumstances the designation of the text as divinely inspired becomes arbitrary, instead of being a consequence of the inherent power of the writing, so that more and more people come to regard the sacred status of the writing as contrary to reason, which for them it is.

It is characteristic of divinely inspired writings that they are accompanied throughout their history by an oral tradition. Their very richness of meaning invites interpretation, and those who transmit an appreciation of a sacred text will inevitably interpret it. The tradition of interpretation has a twofold effect. When teaching is directed towards letting the voice of the text be heard, then interpretation illuminates the text, exemplifying how it yields riches and stimulating the learner to interaction with it. When teaching drowns the voice of the text, the oral and written traditions are brought into conflict. The teacher then, in asking the learner to accept the oral tradition, is likely also to be asking for the text to be read contrary to reason.

Under these circumstances, those of us who are moved to do so, return to the text and, finding it divinely inspired, wish to share the experience and make possible perhaps a revival of the line of transmission. Where we know oral tradition to run alongside the text, the two now complement each other. When I was at school I had the good fortune to be taught by a Peter Maclean (who died fighting in Tunisia). He would say to a boy who became muddled in giving an answer, 'Now moisten the lips and start afresh'. What I read and hear about the Creation story leads me to think that this is what we must now do. The muddled communication is not offered by any single person, but it is up to the individual who sees that there is a muddle, to moisten the lips and make a new start.

As I write, that seems as good a reason as any why I should now end this diversion, and return to more direct consideration of the Creation story itself.

IN THE CREATION story there are awakenings. The male who has been in a deep sleep recognizes the female. Noah awakes and knows what his youngest son has done to him. If we take awakening as arousal in general, there are more instances. Awakening can then be related to the act of creation itself.

The work of the Creation has three creative acts, each of which makes possible the making of things. It has already been explained why the notions of creating and making must be read as distinct in the Creation story (page 23). The opening sentence of the story opens up, by creation, the making of the works of the first four days. The creation of the tanninim in the work of the fifth day marks the introduction of animal life into the story. In the sixth day's work humankind is created, and the main features of its making are briefly stated. The making dependent on each creation is itself an awakening. It is of these awakenings, taken in order, that I would now write.

The prime creation is unformed and void. Over the dark deep the spirit of God is hovering, and the Word of power is spoken to awaken first light, and then the division of the waters, the separation of land and sea, the earth's plants, the heavenly bodies and the time they mark. All this is made with what the prime act of creation presents. The spirit on the waters, and the Word, awaken the Creation. The awakening of matter and energy is the *first awakening*.

Next, animal life is created. This is the fifth day's work, in which God's blessing arouses this life to fulfil itself in increase. Reproduction is, of course, a characteristic of life, but the Hebrew scriptures tend to distinguish between animal life and other things, including plants, rather than between non-living and living in the sense of those terms in modern biology. Here the new creation, that of the tanninim (1:21), marks the introduction of animal life into the story. This life is aroused to increase. The awakening of animal life is the *second awakening*.

In the sixth day's work humankind is created (1:27). The awakening of humanity now occurs throughout the subsequent story, fulfilling the power of the Word, 'Let us make humankind in our image, according to our likeness, and they shall have dominion...' (1:26). This creation and making of humankind, as in the telling of the sixth day, is retold in more detail, beginning early in the story of the garden. 'Then the Lord God formed the Adam (i.e. humankind) of the dust of the ground, and breathed into his nostrils the breath (*neshamah*) of life (*chayyim*) and the Adam became a living (*chayyah*) soul (*nephesh*)' (2:7). The dust of the ground brings matter into the making of humankind, and to this are added the characters of animal life, for scripture uses the terms *neshamah, chayyah* (*chay, chayyim*), and *nephesh* of animals. Indeed, as noted already (page 169), none of these terms are specifically human. Evidently the Adam must go beyond this in order to fulfil 'Let us make humankind'.

The sleeping Adam is divided. Seeing the woman for the first time, he declares the difference and the tie between them (2:23). Thus is fulfilled 'Male and female he created them' (1:27). This is not said of beasts, but only of humankind, and therefore is about sexual difference in its specifically human character. The Adam, having slept, says 'This at last is bone of my bones and flesh of my flesh' (2:23). The awakening of the human being to sexual difference and its power of attraction is the *third awakening*.

The forbidden fruit arouses to a new vision. 'And she ate, and she gave also to her husband with her, and he ate. And the eyes of both of them were opened, and they knew that they were naked' (3:6,7). In eating of the tree of the knowledge of good and evil, they come to understand these two, to make value judgments. At the standpoint at which this becomes possible they see themselves in a new way. The awakening to self-awareness is the *fourth awakening*.

This self-awareness does not long subsist alone, for there is an awareness of God, of a new kind, to follow as a consequence of eating the forbidden fruit. This new awareness of God is challenging, and summons not simply to be aware of oneself, but also to take stock of oneself, to answer for oneself. 'And the Lord God called to the Adam and said to him "Where are you?" ' The awakening to the knowledge that one is responsible, this is the *fifth awakening*.

Cain also awakens. At first he denies what he has done. When the Lord leads him to hear his brother's voice cry out from the ground, he realises the weight of his deed and the weight of its consequence. 'And Cain said to the Lord "My iniquity is too great to forgive" ' (4:13). The awakening to the realisation that one has committed a sin is the *sixth awakening*.

'And Noah awoke from his wine, and he knew what his youngest son had done to him' (9:24). It had gone well for Noah. To him it was vouchsafed that the ground would be no longer cursed and he, man of the ground, planted the vine. He enjoyed the fruit of the vine and drank. At peace with the earth, at peace with his Creator, midwife to the ground's new blessing, was he not right to be contented, to enjoy the consequence of all this, and to allow the sleep which came from his enjoyment? Nevertheless, although Noah was in a family and had saved alive humanity and beasts, we have had no mention of any personal relationship between Noah and another human being. He awakes to the knowledge of a personal relationship, a personal relationship gone wrong. What the Noah of our story has lacked, now comes to him as tragedy. The awakening to the depths, even bitter depths, of relations with others is the *seventh awakening*.

In the making of the Adam, the dust into which the Lord God breathes is the result of the wakening of matter, the first awakening. The breath of life by which there is not just dust, but a living soul, is that animal life which comes at the second awakening. The other five awakenings then befall Adam, Eve, Cain, and Noah, all of whom are in each of us. Thus is humankind created, more than matter, more than beast, but with both, each human being by awakenings becoming another creation, into which is drawn all creation.

***

If we look at the seven awakenings in the natural history of human life, we need not suppose that their order in the story and their order in life is always exactly the same, nor need we suppose that they do not overlap in time. Nevertheless they depend on each other in such a way that they have a logical sequence. Let us consider them in turn.

The matter which arises at the first awakening is the dust into which the Lord God breathes the breath of life. This matter is potent with new things arising by division and distinction (1: 4,7,9) and with life of the vegetative sort (1:11). Thus are we conceived and thus we begin life.

Next, matter awakens to animal life. In our human story this is at the Lord God's breathing into the dust. In ourselves this is not a sudden event. It is partly fulfilled in us when we have been born. Nevertheless animal life is blessed, to be fruitful and increase. This we cannot do in our infancy. This fulfilment awaits our sexuality, which has the specially human quality that is implied when the story says only of humankind that the Lord God created them male and female. Not only are the awakenings in our lives not necessarily sudden events (although a moment during an awakening may be seen retrospectively as critical), but they also may overlap each other.

The third awakening, which is to sexual difference, does not, in the story, allow any separation of physical sexuality from love. The Adam awakes, now a man face to face with a woman although the sexes are not previously distinct, and immediately expresses acceptance of the woman as a person. 'This at last is bone of my bones and flesh of my flesh' (2:23). The man echoes the longing, suffered by the Adam, during the naming of the beasts, we may understand, for the 'help matched with him' (2:18) which was impossible to the sexually undifferentiated human being. The transformation of the Adam into woman and man implies physical sexual difference, but the man's reaction on awakening is of sexual love. The sexual act itself is not mentioned until 'the Adam knew Eve his wife, and she conceived, and bore Cain' (4:1). The word 'know' (*yada'*) is often used in the Hebrew scriptures for sexual intercourse, but this should not obscure its meaning. The word *yada'* is not merely knowing a fact or knowing by acquaintance. It is having an awareness with one's whole being. The total loving acceptance of 'bone of my bone' goes on to the consummated love of 'knew Eve his wife'. The sequence is this: first there is physical difference, then there is sexual love, and next there is sexual intercourse. The position of sexual love between the difference and the act makes love integral with sexuality. From the point of view of this story, even though one has recognized sexual difference and has had sexual congress, one is still not through them alone fully awakened to sexual difference. Sexual love is an essential feature of the awakening.

The fourth awakening necessary to the fulfilment of our being created is to self-awareness. This is not simply an awareness of oneself as distinct from what is not oneself. It arises from eating of the tree of the knowledge of good and evil. That is to say, one can have a meaning for the terms better and worse, and can make value judgments which are of oneself or of what is distinguished from oneself. Also, beings like oneself, since they can be evaluated, are perceived among what is other, and so may themselves be felt as perceivers of oneself. Thus arises the possibility of shame. Therefore, to call the fourth awakening one of self-awareness is to give it a handle by naming its central feature, but it is not to say fully what this awakening is.

When therefore there is self-awareness, the possibility of value judgments, and the ability to judge one's own actions, there can be shame on being seen. This would, however, be a chaotic guide to action, since one is visible from no constant point of view. The viewpoint of oneself that can be a standard, a point of reference, comes with the summons of the call 'Where are you?' The call has meaning at two levels. Its undivided source sets it apart from other sources of questioning, while the question itself is a call to responsibility, that is, answerability for what one does. Thus the fifth awakening is the birth of a further self-awareness, knowing that one is responsible for what one does.

Cain denies what he has done. The voice which said 'Where are you?' to Cain's father has asked Cain where his murdered brother is. The same voice meets Cain's denial by forcing him to face the deed. Cain now comes to the realisation of his having sinned, and it is more than he can bear. The self-awareness which has awareness of responsibility now awakens further, to the consciousness of having sinned. (Cain's murder of Abel is the first act which the story calls 'sin' and, within the Creation story, is the only instance.) Thus this, the sixth awakening is to knowledge that a deed for which one is responsible may be a sin. That the notion of sin is not arbitrary, but has something to do with the way the world is created, is shown by the part played by the blood's crying out, and by the realisation of danger from people's natural reaction to a murderer.

This is not all there is to awareness, for there is awakening to others as agents capable of responsibility, with deeds that can be evaluated and which may be sins. This awareness comes, in the story, at the point at which one is aware that one is the object of another's deed. When Noah awoke he knew what had been done to him, and who did it. This is the seventh awakening, which is to deeds viewed not simply from the doer's point of view, but in their social setting. The vengeful Lamech is concerned with the effects on himself of another's deeds, but Noah's awakening is not simply to the effect of Ham's action on himself. Noah puts the offence against himself into the context of the family, relating it not only to himself but also to Japhet and Shem. Noah's awakening is to social relationships.

Thus are we are each created. First, the primary creation is awakened to matter and energy. Through the creation of animal life, matter, as dust, becomes a living being. The third creation, of humanity, is now fulfilled through increasing awareness,—awareness of sexual difference and sexual love, of values and oneself as perceived, of responsibility, of having sinned, and of social relations.

***

Nevertheless the creation of humanity needs something else for its fulfilment. 'And God said "Let us make humankind in our image, according to our likeness, and they shall have dominion over the fish of the sea, and over the flying things of the heavens, and over cattle, and over all the earth, and over every creeping thing that creeps upon the earth". And God created humankind in his image, in the image of God he created it, male and female he created them. And God blessed them, and God said to them "Be fruitful and increase and fill the earth and subdue it, and have dominion..."' (1:26-28). At the third awakening humanity is male and female, and this difference is integral with the manner in which each has dominion over the non-human creation (pages 65-69). To be fruitful and increase is already in the second awakening, since it is a blessing on animal life (1:22) as well as human. What remains is to be in God's image. This does not come with any of the seven awakenings taken one at a time, but is inherent in all of them taken together. Since God is the source of humankind, according to the story, and since closeness to the source makes possible the truest imaging, the fulfilment of the divine image in the human being is a progress through the awakenings, in reverse order, finding in each, on the way back, an enlargement of it.

In this progress to one's source, the journey begins at what the seventh awakening shows, social relationships. Knowing oneself, there appears the oneness of being single and being social, so that the individual and society are polarities, not oppositions. Knowing others, the truth appears that they are not loved except with loving oneself, and that without loving them there can be no self love, only selfishness. The love for others gives meaning to the family, the society, the nation, in such a way that this love entails respect for the love that another may have for a different family, a different society, a different nation, and the differences make the harmony. Seeing within and beyond, God is known in oneself because known in the other, and known in the other because known in oneself. *And on the journey this is the step made possible by the awakening to social relationships.*

The journey takes in also what the sixth awakening shows, the sin that a deed may be. Knowing oneself, one's dark side is met, not to be rejected, but to be integrated with the rest. Knowing others, one's dark side is no longer projected on to them, and they may be known as doers of bad deeds but not as bad people. So, facing the evil that one does, one can repent and turn in another direction and, facing the evil done by another, one accepts, hoping to meet in its new direction the other's turning face. Seeing within and beyond, there looms the mystery of the polarity of our own good and evil, and the mystery of the One who 'makes peace and creates evil' (Isaiah 45:7). *And on the journey this is the step made possible the awakening to the sin that a deed may be.*

The journey takes in also what the fifth awakening shows, responsibility for deeds. Knowing oneself, blame is transcended so that one answers for one's deeds irrespective of moral responsibility, seeing the works of one's hands in broad perspective rather than from the cramped corner of a synthesised conscience. Knowing others, one knows mutual answerability, mutual indebtedness, and hence the humility that comes from consciousness of being a part of that which is beyond representation as the sum of its parts. Seeing within and beyond, there is always the Voice that asks 'Where are you?' so that the more one is summoned the more independent one becomes, since, in coming to terms with the Voice, one comes to terms with oneself. *And on the journey this is the step made possible by the awakening to responsibility for deeds.*

The journey takes in also what the fourth awakening shows, value judgments, the self-awareness that is in exercising them, and the awareness of being seen from outside oneself. Knowing oneself, one brings these fruits of awakening to the centre, to become inner-directed and not, to use Pirandello's phrase, 'as you desire me'. Knowing others, the constancy they may have is seen, and this, answering to the steadfastness of the inner-directed, increases trust. Seeing within and beyond, the God that is outside us and in the heights, and the God that is inside humanity and in the depths, are known to be One. *And on the journey this is the step made possible by the awakening to self-awareness.*

The journey takes in also what the third awakening shows, our sexuality, a human sexuality (1:27) not of beasts, which is therefore more than genital, although that also. Knowing oneself, the two sexes are found in each, as the two sides of a coin with one side uppermost, in the light, the other not openly manifest. Knowing others, the libido of sexuality is directed to them as a power in work and love, and is thus manifested as libido that is more than sexual. Seeing within and beyond, the union of the sexes in the perfected androgyne of the alchemists becomes apparent, and the universal meaning of sexuality enriches the awakening and stretches infinitely beyond it. *And on the journey this is the step made possible by the awakening to sexual difference.*

The journey takes in also what the second awakening shows, that we have animal life. Knowing oneself, the beast is seen as an essential, to be neither crushed nor allowed to exceed its place, integral with one's humanity. Knowing others, the appreciation of the beast in oneself makes evident, without sentimentality, the brotherhood between the human being and the beasts, and makes evident the differences between humanity and other animal life, differences which present an awesome mystery. Seeing within and beyond, one is led by the divine in the beast to God in the whole of creation. *And on the journey this is the step made possible by the awakening to animal life.*

The journey at last takes in what the first awakening shows, that we are dust, the very matter of the universe. Knowing oneself, the mystery unfolds, that the more I am at one with the created universe the more I am my peculiar self. Knowing the other, I stand in love and awe of all things, unable to do wanton damage without feeling the harm to myself. Seeing within and beyond, not only is the God in oneself and the God in nature known to be One, not only is the indwelling God and the God outside known to be one, but also there is one truth behind the personal God of some and the denial by others that there is a personal God, since this a truth which our words cannot encompass. *And on the journey this is the journeying at one still point.*

WE CAN WORK with the grain of the created order, thus in freedom expressing the Creator's image in us, or we can work without regard to the grain, and so be frustrated by the outcome. If we are to use the world around us, we have to heed Francis Bacon's* aphorism, 'Nature certainly is not overcome unless by being obeyed'. 'Nature', however, needs to be understood in its widest sense, not only as this or that phenomenon, but also as the workings of the universe taken as widely as we can take them. In the Creation story the opposition between working with the created order and working without regard to it, is integral with the opposition between respect for the name that cannot be spoken (Chapter 9, pages 31-38, especially pages 36*f*), on the one hand, and the worship of an idol, on the other (pages 201-204). Further to this, in Chapter 33 (pages 205-210) I have suggested that the two precepts *you are not to belittle the name that cannot be spoken,* and *you are not to serve an idol,* provide an axis for the other five of the seven precepts given or implied by the Creation story.

The seven precepts are such that they may be variously fulfilled in the laws of different peoples, but are nevertheless limited in the scope for variation which is compatible with each (pages 208-209). When the seven are set against actual laws and practices, therefore, they enable these laws and practices to be seen as working with or against the created order. In this chapter the seven precepts will be taken in turn, and some points of contact of each with to-day's laws and practices will be noted, so that, for this our own time, there may be indicated the challenge and the hope.

***

To respect the unspeakable name and to refrain from worshipping idols, are complementary. The Creator who is to be respected is one, and is that by which all things are one. An idol is a part and an end in itself, so that it draws its worshipper on a path irrelevant to the rest of reality, and therefore towards contradictions, frustration, and destruction. For the human being, made in God's image, the choice is between being oneself, and being stunted into a closed-off fraction of what one can be.

The theologians distinguish God as indwelling (immanent) in us and in the rest of creation, and God as over and beyond (transcendent). These two are all one, and the difference is a polarity in our awareness. In the story the Creator is not the created, but the breath of life which is in the Adam is of the very Creator (2:6). Those who speak of no personal God but seek the reality within themselves, as is the Budhhist emphasis, and those who find God when they lift their eyes to the hills, and in history, are not opposed to each other. The unity has many aspects.

The word 'God' can be used to name an idol, even if the namer deny that this is being done. God speaks the creative word and is infinite, and is taken only partially if one restricts the openness by which one may receive divine promptings. This openness is not some kind of woolly open-mindedness, but is the state in which one finds oneself when free of idols. 'God' is the name of an idol when what the word represents is an incompleteness surrounded by other idols, which confine it. The other idols may include, for instance, a book given authority, or a particular social order, or our own horror of growing up and of freedom. Between the idols, what is then left to be called 'God' is some respectable or unchallenging residue, detached from the wholeness of our living, and unthreatening to the other idols. Thus there is 'religion' as a department of life, distinguishable from other departments. So it is that we find Lucretius* to have written truly that religion could prompt such evil deeds. When God, dwelling in us, turns one of us against the idol called 'God' the person so affected, not recognizing the enlightening power as divine and taking the enlightenment only negatively, may become an atheist. Since this atheism is primarily the rejection of an idol called 'God', the atheist may be much nearer to the worshipper of the Creator than are many whose 'religion' belittles the unspoken name with constricting God-talk.

One of the commonest idols is the state. The idol's prophets and priests may try to legitimise their god by identifying it with the nation, which corresponds to something in human nature. This nation is not that of the Creation story, an element of the God-appointed variety of humankind, but an end in itself. As a god, the state takes on the function of defining right and wrong but, since idols are dead and therefore cannot define anything, this is a trick played by a self-seeking priesthood, who set the morality to suit themselves. The state idol is unstable unless it has something to lean on, and often it leans on the images of other states. If the state is the supposed definer of virtue, which it embodies, other states (sometimes with their associated nations) come to be seen to embody vice. Thus state priesthoods may speak of other states as 'the empire of evil' or 'the great Satan'. This facilitates the projection on to others of aspects of ourselves which we do not recognize. In this way we are reinforced in appreciating only a part of ourselves. So we become like the idol we worship, less than entire, and preventing ourselves from serving God, who, as Isaiah (45:7) reports, makes peace and creates evil. Thus we take the part for the whole, and good itself may also become an idol.

Wealth is also sometimes an idol, one for which all else may be forsaken. Flaubert* saw it in Nineteenth-Century France.

231

Then property rose in esteem to the level of religion, and became confused
with God. Attacks on it were seen as sacrilege, almost cannibalism.

Jesus of Nazareth warned that you cannot serve God and riches (Matthew
6:24, Luke 16:9-13, 'mammon' in these texts being simply post-biblical Hebrew
for 'wealth', 'accumulation'). Yet did he not also, at the same time, recommend
making use of the mammon of the unrighteous? Yes indeed, for using it is not
necessarily the same as serving it. As an idol, not only is wealth not itself
divine, but it has no voice towards God.

They worship idols that can neither harm nor help, and say 'These will inter-
cede for us with Allah'. (Al-Qurān* 10.)

Directed towards an idol, whatever the idol, the worshipper is narrowed by an
idolater's notion of what has absolute value, is diminished to be limited according to the limitations of the idol. In the words of Psalm 115:4-8,

Their idols are silver and gold,
the work of human hands.
Mouths they have and do not speak:
eyes they have and do not see.
Ears they have and do not hear:
noses they have and do not smell.
Their hands—and they do not handle:
their feet—and they do not walk;
no noise they make with their throats.
Like them will be their makers,
all who trust in them.

The failure of the idol of wealth is illustrated by faith in the growth of the gross
national product, to which everything, it is fashionable to assume, must be
directed. The pursuit of this growth gives false expectations and betrays, in
that, contrary to its proclaimed nature, it reduces the wealth of many, and it is
inherently false, since gross national product does not in fact measure useful
wealth (Mishan*). Those among economists and politicians who are the
prophets of this particular form of the idol of wealth, maintain the illusion, to
the benefit of its priests and those who use and support them. All are called on
to bow to this great god, which is dead to the touch for any who dare lift a finger
against it. Thus are people encouraged to diminish themselves, instead of
using wealth and its increase in creation, with God; the material of which an
idol is made can have other uses.

The worship of many gods is not necessarily idolatry. If there are supposed
gods, each with power and with nothing superior, then they are idols. If one of
the gods is superior to the others and to all things, and has nothing superior to
itself, then the worship of that highest god need not be idolatry. It is to be noted
that the word 'god' is sometimes used for one of an order of beings subject to

another power. Nevertheless, although talk of 'gods' in the plural, or the use of revered images, need not in fact be part of idolatry, either practice may increase the danger of idol worship. Therefore those who reject the worship of idols, while not confusing polytheism or the revering of images with idolatry itself, may, like Moslems and Jews for example, rigorously shun both. D.H. Lawrence* puts it this way:

> But surely the Jehovah of Genesis, and Numbers, Samuel, Psalms, Isaiah, Ezekiel, surely he is all the gods in turn, Dionysic, Apollo-like, strange like Ra, and grim like Baal or Bel. You can't make an idol to Jehovah because he has the qualities of all the ancient gods in turn, Ouranos or Kronos or Saturn, even the old Osiris, or the mystery gods of the first Sumerians. He is One because he is all of them, not because he is different from any of them. He does not sit absolute and apart, while all the other gods topple, mere fallen idols. He is himself all the gods and all the idols, savage and fertile, and even he is all the unknown gods that are yet to come.

When Lawrence writes 'He is One because he is all of them', we are near the heart of the matter (but Lawrence's examples might well have included some goddesses). Nevertheless it is not true to say that the Lord has all the qualities of the gods 'in turn', for these qualities are together in the Lord, not one after the other. Also, the splitting-off of an idol means that, in some respects at least, it lacks life and, as a possible god, denies itself. Therefore the actually indivisible Unity from which it is notionally broken off, the living Unity, is more than the sum of all possible gods and idols, and is of a different kind from them, for life is integral.

***

Since humankind is here, now, and always (pages 26-27) created in the image of God (1:26,27), reverence for the unspeakable name implies reverence for humanity. The divine is one and infinite; in the image of the divine we do not know what we may become. When human possibilities are reduced, the indwelling Creator is received only restrictedly and, certain aspects being taken as the whole, an idol can be made out of humanity. To attempt to subordinate humanity to one of its aspects, or to certain of them, is to attempt to transform it from being in the likeness of the Creator into being in the likeness of an idol. This happens when some aim or tendency, pleasure or social conformity for example, is allotted supremacy. The idol limits us. In idolising myself I am diminished as worshipper and as idol. The only total humanism is divine humanism, whatever it is called.

When a human being is used as a means to an end, without being an end, the infinite possibilities of the divine image are denied, so that an attempt is made to recreate the person in the image of an idol, and the manipulator or user is a servant of the idol, not of the Creator. To deny the absolute value of humanity is to belittle the name of God, in the image of which humanity is made. It is to treat that image as though it were of a mere idol.

Unemployment, under certain circumstances, provides an example of treating people as objects to be manipulated for an end made more important than they are. One set of such circumstances is the following threefold combination. First, it is implicitly (i.e. socially and economically) and explicitly taught to people that being employed is necessary to their fulfilment as human beings. Secondly, it is made inevitable that many of these people will be unemployed. Finally, the unemployment is a matter of deliberate policy. Those causing unemployment may, of course, find it expedient to deny that it results from their policies. Thus, in Britain in the 1980s and 1990s, the government attributed unemployment to conditions outside the country, to the failure of the unemployed to look for jobs, or to their pricing themselves out of work. However, the then British Secretary of State for Energy, Cecil Parkinson*, let slip the admission that depriving people of the opportunity to do paid, socially useful, work was an essential and deliberate element of policy. If the further aim was some kind of general economic benefit, as the policy-makers claimed, it is to the point to note that unemployment was accompanied by loss of industrial output, a decline in wealth-making investment, failure to export enough to pay for imports, and inability to use new technology. Thus does an idol repay trust in it.

The difference between a person as of absolute value, and as a tool, provides a differentiating criterion among the possible purposes of education. Respect for a person requires that education provides the understanding necessary for making a living and for contributing to the society in which the living is made, these amongst other things. However, to be taught to survive and fit in, without any further purpose, limits the possibilities of divinity in humanity, and devalues the one taught by attempting to make that one primarily an instrument in the hand of a future user. When education has in view the wholeness of people, however unremarkable its expression, then the manifestation of the divine within them can be an opening to that broad view in which their own part in society can be better understood by them and fulfilled, but in which also society and each person's part in it can be seen more critically, even when simplicity leaves understanding inarticulate.

Thus it is that the education which best serves the stability of society is also that which can prove subversive. Those who want education to serve social ends, as it must if it is to serve the divinity in those taught, have no choice but to live with the paradox and the uncertainty. The idolatrous confinement of pupils to what rulers see as useful is confinement to a space no bigger than the rulers' field of vision, outside which their brittle schemes crumble, ruler and teacher and pupil alike betrayed by trust in idols, whether the idol be wealth for its own sake, power for its own sake, or the narrowed thing that one may try to substitute for the divine image in oneself when avoiding the terrible thing it is to fall into the hand of the living God.

In friendship, in ease of acquaintance, in candour, in the honest handshake, there is the opportunity to find each other's worth and to glimpse into the depth of the divine image in others and in oneself. It is therefore in the nature of idolatry that it may be opposed to trust and a sense of community. The operators of the idolatrous state need to turn people from the God already present to an attempted ordering of existence around the idols. For this purpose society is denied and enmity cultivated. The enmity is not that of combatants who respect each other although enemies, but is the hostility expressed in a general and continuing antagonistic posture. There are various ways in which the priests of idols can stir up hostility. They may try to lead a quest for social unreliability in people or put forward the notion that the state has an 'enemy within'. Defence policy can come to be based not on defence, but on the existence of permanent enemies, whether outside or inside the state. Such a policy is unadapting and, being emotionally rigid and logically indefensible, becomes increasingly hypocritical, requiring people to submit to more and more of the evils which the 'enemies' are held to be ready to impose. Candour, trust, and a sense of mutuality can be eroded by fostering antagonism to outgroups, who are often, conveniently, those thought not to be conformable to official idolatry. Thus at one time or another violent emotion is called for against 'hippies', dissenting students, immigrants, social security 'scroungers', or protesters in woolly hats. Idolatry then, in the long run, can truncate humanity by denying sociality and, since the latter is necessary for civil existence, generate the very conditions that make repression seem reasonable, so giving a presentable basis for antagonism as a tool of policy and a feature of its aims. So it is that idolatry can reinforce itself, by generating the conditions for the hostility on which it depends for blocking our understanding of what it is to be human and our sense of God's image, in which we are made. However antagonisms tend to cause social instability, especially because new outgroups are for ever being distinguished, while personal instability arises from opposition to our own nature. The natural history of idolatry, therefore, can pass through self-reinforcement to self-destruction.

There is a story that summarises some of the main features of idolatry, features already noted. In the Apocrypha attached to the Bible there is the tale of Bel, an idol worshipped in Babylon. Every day this image was provided with twelve bushels of fine flour, forty sheep, and fifty gallons of wine. Since these could be seen to have been consumed, Bel was evidently a living being. Daniel challenged the seventy priests of Bel to let it be seen whether the food and drink would be consumed if the door were sealed by the king. Before the door was sealed, Daniel spread ashes over the floor. The priests of Bel came as usual by their hidden entrance under the table, and feasted with their families. When the door was opened the king showed Daniel that the provisions must have been eaten and drunk, but Daniel showed the king the footprints of men, women, and children on the floor, so that the king realised the falsity of Bel's priests.

This tale declares truths about all idolatry, whether of a work by human craftsmanship, or of power, or of profit, or of any other idol. None of those named are necessarily idols, but any of them is if it is treated as an end in itself. To try to make an idol convincing as an end, with absolute value, there is commonly between idol and people a priesthood, as Bel had. The priesthood, together with those in league with the priests or using them, have a material interest in idolatry, as had the priests of Bel and their families. Since the idol, as a god, is a fake, the priesthood needs to limit opportunity for examining it and for examining the process of faking.

It is natural therefore that the idolatrous powerful should limit access to information and corrupt or massage it. Those who honour the Creator, and the image of the Creator in human beings, need, on the other hand, all knowledge that can help working according to the order of the Creation. This means a readiness for the unforeseen, since we cannot comprehend the whole, and therefore honouring the Creator requires an openness to knowledge. Because an idol is given absolute value, but is at the same time dead and in itself powerless, its priesthood arrogates to itself the real power. Such power in the hands of those who respect neither the Creator nor humanity has no stable limit in the minds of the idol's priesthood and their allies. Thus it is that the priests of idols can tend to a kind of madness, which has then to be made to appear as a qualification for office. Because an idol is a fake, those worshipping it or pretending that they worship it will, like the priests of Bel, stand to lose by exploration. They are threatened not only by Daniel's deed, but by the state of mind which made the deed possible. (This connects with what has been said about education.) Idolatry is, in the end, incompatible with the free exploration natural to humanity, whether this is independent research, or skills and arts, or the creativity of human hands and minds in general. The idol needs to have these limited, the partial serving the partial, not the inexhaustible serving the One. Understanding and creation are blocked, scope is given to the crowd's self-increasing roar rather than to the counterpoint of the various voices in it, and there is a muzak of vision, sound, and print, to swamp the inner being, with its indefinitely varied working, and to prevent the contentment through which can be heard the divine voice that awaits our listening, and is single, although aptly different for each. Thus idolatry is threatened by the arts. As for the art in ritual images and their ceremonies, not all such images are idols, and the art in the image can transcend even an intended idol. Even when human creativity does not negate idolatry, it always offers a threat.

For the idol, since it is a fake, protective lies are needed, lies which are called truth, in the manner of Orwell's* 'Newspeak'. For example, in the worship of the accumulation of money, abolition or gross reduction of competition by businesses big enough to lose temporarily while crushing smaller rivals may be called 'the release of market forces to give the benefit of competition'. Again, the centralisation of power by the priesthood may be called 'getting the government off our backs'. Idolatry corrupts language, that gem in mankind's crown of dominion.

Idolatry prepares for oppression by its effect on the oppressor and oppressed alike. The oppressor, by serving an idol, can see the oppressed as instrumental, not as in the image of God. The oppressed, for their part, can be confined in their knowledge of themselves and so be hindered in realising their dignity, a dignity which makes them ungovernable, even if unviolently, when it is asserted against rulers who deny the divinity in us. To be ungovernable for this reason is surely to have a masterly grasp of essentials.

The idol, whether a graven image, or profit, or pleasure, or power, or any other, eventually shows its self-contradictory nature. The god Bel decays on its plinth, the pursuit of profit brings diminishing returns, pleasure pursued for its own sake cloys, and power comes to lose control of the forces which it uses. The narrowness of idolatry prevents the worshipper from putting the deterioration into its wider context, the infinite relatedness of created things, one in their Creator. Therefore the failure of the idol is seen by its devotees as a universal rot and, as the idol fails, its priesthood runs out of ideas. Increasingly, expedients are preferred to policies. Since ultimate failure is something to which its priests cannot admit, the idol obviously needs bigger sacrifices. This or that idol is given its millions of Tasmanians, Jews, Cambodians, Amazonians. Eventually the devotees of idols, devoid of all creative purpose, cast their gaze over all humankind and, by knowledge and craft narrowed in vision not to transcend the idols, prepare the means for killing by the thousand million, whether the enemy by missiles or the world's poor by finance (George*).

***

In respect for the unspeakable name, in the rejection of idols, there is challenge and hope. To be in the image of God is a challenge to awake and, in a very particular sense, to pull ourselves together. It offers the hope of living with a sense of the meaning of life, a sense of the value of oneself, a becoming into one's unbounded possibilities by which each of us differs from all others and finds the human nature common to us all. Our differences necessarily have social consequences. These will now be considered.

Because of our divine variety, which we cannot wholly encompass by our understanding, toleration does not arise from indifference, but is active, born of respect for the divine in all. We cannot counter the belittling of the divine name by spurning the divine image, nor must we confuse that name with our susceptibilities, lest we make a human idol or make an idol of religion. Nevertheless, susceptibilities are of beings made in God's image, and therefore require our respect and serious consideration. Toleration of people does not imply toleration of all possible deeds, of course, and toleration of words may therefore be limited when they summon to certain actions. As Chief Justice Holmes of the United States pointed out, the right to free speech does not include the right to shout 'Fire!' in a crowded theatre; the dangers of the shout would mean that it was contrary at least to the precept forbidding bloodshed.

Strangely perhaps at first sight, toleration overrides any attempt to suppress words belittling the unspeakable name. This is because words cannot certainly be identified as doing this. What, because of its formal characteristics, attracts the label 'blasphemous' may be an attack on religion as an idol, and help to open up, perhaps unintendedly, the possibility of honouring God in truth. Conversely, what, in a formal sense, is speech honouring the unspeakable name, may be God-talk on behalf of an idol misnamed 'God'. If I have to tolerate what offends me, so be it. Injury beyond offence to feelings is another matter, a matter for others of the seven precepts of the righteous of humankind. The prohibition of belittling the name is, as already noted, generally inseparable from the prohibition of idolatry. When, however, the former prohibition is taken alone, its social force is to require conditions for the name to be honoured. As a direct prohibition of words it is applicable to the individual. Since, for reasons given, words may not be certainly identifiable as blasphemous, and since enforcing a law must refer to actual words used, the precept of not belittling the name can have a corresponding publically applicable law only in the special instance in which a society has a single way of speaking of the divine. Such a unity of mode of expression may not exist even in a single community of worship.

None of us knows fully how the divine in oneself may become manifest. We make ourselves (page 27) but can do this only because socially related to others. (Even the hermit is not solitary from birth.) Therefore a social structure, however deliberately shaped or, on the other hand, however spontaneous, is necessary for the fruition of divinity within us. This, however, can generate paradox, since social, economic, and political structures can limit the development of all people or many, while perhaps cloaking from consciousness the limitation which it imposes. The smaller the social unit, the more scope there is for mutual respect, and the more likely is an individual to be effective through influencing its behaviour, and therefore the more able to make membership of the unit an instrument of personal growth through doing. The larger the unit, on the other hand, the greater the opportunities for deceptions and self-deceptions that make action ineffective, and the greater the difficulty in finding a connection between personal action and its effect. Some human needs require the coordination of the work of large numbers, but this does not negate the different virtue of small-scale organisation. Therefore, if we are to be as open as possible to the consequences of being made in God's image, no decision should be taken at a level of social, political, or economic organisation higher than the nature of the decision requires. The need to be free to participate in, and influence as much as possible, those decisions which manifest or allow or limit the potential of one's being, is an argument for democracy, although not for its institutional forms when they disguise something quite other. Also, it is an argument for decentralisation, since size tends to deny humanity and imply human relations which diminish opportunity for mutual respect and recognition of the image of God in each other.

Humanity being itself, and therefore social, commonly needs, even while increasingly manifesting the image of God, to be served by economic behaviour, which may in turn need to be served by monetary behaviour. When, however, this is reversed, and finance determines economics, with people subordinated to the economics thus determined, irrespective of human becoming, then money is no longer a tool, but an idol, an idol to which human living is sacrificed. On the other hand, when priorities are those of the created order, and people are the purpose of economics, there is no shame, or awkwardness of bearing, when we care for each other. When human beings are seen as made in the image of God, and cannot therefore be placed below tools turned idols, such as money or power, they are subjects for persuasion that respects their dignity, not objects of mass advertising and manipulated information. To tell someone something new, or remind someone of something, though it be in the interest of the teller, may help the one being told, but when the aim is manipulation by the suppression of critical faculties, then people are objects, not subjects, and you may be sure that the purpose of the manipulation is the service of an idol. (To call both activities by the same name, whether 'advertising' or 'information', according to context, is an example of idolatry's corruption of language.)

The society which directs itself according to the created order opens up space for the manifestation of the image of God in which each of us is made. It is therefore a society of freedom and hope. For its members, what are called the arts are not a luxury, beyond necessity, nor is research and scholarship. Also, being of life and not just added to it, the arts are more than that which the papers usually review. They are in the work of one's hands done with pride, in amateur skills, and in popular arts, whether commercialised or not. In conventionally unimportant matters people can unassumingly or unwittingly touch upon the immensity of themselves as creators, as much as they may do in more deeply trying to shape their lives, in more widely using and working with the world, or in self-consciously expressing themselves.

Because none can encompass all the working of God in creation, or know all the possibilities of God's image in us, the society which is in accord with the created order, depending as it does on our partial understanding, has within it that openness to new realisation which is the seed of its own subversion. And why should it not if it neither is nor serves an idol, the end of which is, as already noted, inherent in its inability to fulfil promise and in its need for antagonism? Change due to adaptation or self-realisation need not cause bloodshed, violence, or robbery. When people are moved towards the fulfilment of God's image in themselves, violence can nevertheless be caused by the rigidity imposed by idolatrous rulers, afraid to risk the fragility of their idols and afraid of the uncertainty of events, an uncertainty which the idol's priesthood tries to ward off by brute force as their authority fails, and by louder and more querulous shouting as it becomes increasingly difficult to conceal that they are lying. Then, as already said (page 237), the panicking priests collapse from policies into expedients, and become ever less restrained in the enormity of the sacrifices that they will offer to their idol. Then the challenge becomes more urgent. The hope—in life's meaning, in one's own value, in the limitless adventure of freedom—remains nevertheless, and in remaining it does not deceive.

***

These two precepts, *you are not to belittle the name that cannot be spoken,* and *you are not to serve an idol,* are two of the seven precepts stated or implied by the Creation story, and therefore presented as applicable to all humankind. With these two, the other five of the precepts form a coherent system. (page 207) Each of the five offers, as do the first two, a challenge and a hope.

That *you are not to shed human blood* (pages 148-149, 207) is based, in the story (9:5,6, and see page 148), on the killer's responsibility for the life taken, on the reciprocal killings set in train by the bloodshed (9:6, and compare the story of Cain, 4:14), and on the creation of humankind in God's image, which is given as an explanation of the other bases of the prohibition of bloodshed. That is, bloodshed is an offence, according to the Creation story, because we are made in the image of God.

There are boundary regions of the field of the precept's effectiveness, in which peoples and communities observing the precept may nevertheless draw exact limits differently. One of these regions is where responsibility for bloodshed is unavoidable. For example, an attacker might be about to kill an intended victim when one finds oneself able to prevent the killing and save the intended victim's life, but only by killing the attacker. According to one legal code, one might be obliged to save the one attacked while, according to another, one might be absolutely forbidden to kill the attacker. Both legal systems, however, could be fulfilling the precept prohibiting bloodshed, but resolving in different ways the problem what to do when all possible courses lead to responsibility for bloodshed. (We are, of course, morally responsible for the foreseeable consequences of deliberate inaction, just as we are for those of deliberate action.)

A second boundary region is that in which life is risked in order to gain livelihood, or follow a vocation. Where a dangerous occupation is made more dangerous than its purpose requires, and where lives are lost on this account (as, for example, according to McCrae*, on North Sea oil rigs), there must surely be an infringement of the precept against bloodshed.

A third boundary region is that of health. Since being alive is more than a state of not being dead, it is arguable that causing ill-health takes away life. Whether one accepts this or not, there is another connection between health and prohibiting bloodshed: causes of ill-health can thereby be causes of loss of life. Therefore the authors of a health threat, and those who connive with them, can be, and often are, shedders of blood. Examples range from baby food, through unsafe factories, the suppression of information on health hazards, and the sale, in countries where knowledge lags behind purchase, of products too dangerous to be permitted at home, to policies designed to force into motor transport those who prefer less lethal modes of travel.

In causing death by statistically probable means, such as avoidable ill-health, one is concerned with moral certainty, certainty of a degree sufficient in everyday life to imply responsibility, for absolute certainty is not given in human affairs, and we would hold responsible for broken bones someone who greases steps, although we cannot prove logically that the owners of the bones would not have been injured on ungreased steps. A similar view is taken by judges and juries, as is seen when someone is hurt by a fall due to failure to mend a broken pavement. Therefore, although there is no infallible healer, to impede access to healing can also be bloodshed. If the needless endangering of life is due to the pursuit of profit, which thus has a value above that of humankind made in God's image, then profit is an idol.

Respect for the prohibition of bloodshed is one of the conditions for the hope that we may dwell in safety, unafraid, nourished by peace, and growing in our being. Awareness of the precept links us to the Creator and to humankind at a point from which we can develop our relations with both. Prohibition of bloodshed makes a space for respect for life.

In the Creation story the forbidding of human bloodshed is coupled with respect for the life of the beast, which is presented as a member of one society with us (9:5, which makes a beast responsible if it sheds human blood, page 147). Further, since it is eating blood which is explicitly prohibited, attention is drawn to respect for the beast when making use of it. Since the reason given for not eating blood is that blood is the life of the beast, the prohibition implies a general precept, *you are to respect the life of the beast* (and see pages 143-147, 207). In the telling, the mention of the beast's blood leads into the beast's answerability for human blood, and then to human responsibility for bloodshed and the basis of this responsibility in the creation of humankind in God's image. When we turn back to this creation in God's image (1:26-28) we find it coupled with dominion over the non-human creation. Thus the story presents not an isolated prohibition, but a complex of interdependent statements concerning not eating the beast's blood, not shedding human blood, the creation of humankind, and the relation of this last to the non-human creation. The key link is, of course, that the reason given for prohibiting human bloodshed rests upon the creation of humankind in God's image, since this links the prohibitions with the work of the sixth day. Since not eating the blood of the beast is coupled with not shedding human blood, the reader is presented with a restriction on eating blood, 'its life', coupled with giving humankind dominion not only over the beasts but 'over all the earth' (1:26) which is to be 'subdued'. The reason for not eating blood is therefore not simply respect for animal life, which the blood is (9:4), but rests upon the sixth day's work, with its granting of dominion over the earth. It implies respect for the non-human creation generally.

Like all living things, we necessarily change the earth on which we live. Because we have dominion over the earth, we decide how we change it. The practical choice is whether we work with it as a continually renewing source of life, or whether we leave our children and our grandchildren an earth less and less able to support them, and more and more constricting of their possibilities even if they survive. It is evident that devastation of the earth arises for the most part from the worship the idols of power and profit. Even when the suffering poor can truthfully be told that they are the spoilers of their own land, and that they saw through the bough on which they sit, the conditions which have driven them up the tree and on to the bough will often have been contrived by an idol's priesthood.

The other way, that of hope, is still open to us, to maintain, to restore, to improve, and to enjoy the fruits of the good earth continuingly. Only we need to turn from idols and refuse either to serve them or to follow their priests. Then we become co-creators. Then the words 'The earth is the Lord's and the fulness thereof' (Psalm 29:1) are not just a theological proposition, but are a way of expressing the contentment and wonder of humankind at the earth and its Creator spirit.

***

Respect for human beings requires that there are means of exercising justice between them. The precept that *you are to have judgments among you* has meaning at four levels, as already noted (pages 120-121, 207). First, the law itself must be consistent with respect for the name that is not to be belittled, and therefore for the divine image in which we are made. Correspondingly, the law may not force people to whorship an idol. These requirements do not arise from the precept of judgments but underlie it.

Secondly, the law has to be made known as widely as possible and, conversely, it may not be deliberately concealed, as happens if, for example, it is deliberately made difficult for people to know what their legal rights are.

If the law is well-founded and made known, then, at a third level, it must be impartial. That is to say, it must have arisen from uncorrupted lawmaking and must be impartially administered. Concerning corrupt lawmaking, it is to the point that Members of Parliament in the United Kingdom are, many of them, paid by interested outsiders for specific items of legislation or of influence on law-making (Raphael*). Similarly, the impartial administration of justice cannot be taken for granted, even where it is commonly so taken. We may recollect that, when the British government in 1984 brought an action against a civil servant, Clive Ponting, and the interest of the state had by law to be considered, the judge ruled that the interest of the government, a party to the action, was the same as the interest of the state, so that one only of the interested parties had the right to define the law to suit itself. As it happened, the jury disagreed with the judge who, however, remained in office to represent the impartiality of the law.

If the law is well-founded, made known, and impartial and uncorrupt in its making and administration, there is yet a fourth level of meaning of the precept of judgments. Respect for the divine image implies that access to justice may not be denied (through pricing or communal affiliation, for example)orby-passed. By-passing may be not only in administration, but may be wilfully arranged by legislators when their laws are designed to be hard to enforce against some, such as public officials or the police when these act outside the law, perhaps with violence to the unthreatening under conditions which impede or prevent redress for the victims. If it is conceded legally that someone may cause another to be the victim of, for example, violence, robbery, or murder, all prohibited by the seven precepts, then the law is not in accord with the precept of judgments. This is because of partiality and because of what is permitted.

The challenge of the precept of judgments can be very great for the individual. To refuse obedience to an unrighteous law, or to refuse co-operation with an unrighteous priesthood in its pursuit of injustice, may require great courage. Nevertheless there is also hope, since our ways of trying to be just can express our respect for each other and our desire to live together in quietude and at ease.

The precept enjoining us to have judgments among us is one of two related precepts referring directly to social relations in a context wider than the family. The other is that *you are neither to rob nor to do violence* (see pages 125-126 on why violence and robbery are two aspects of one thing, also page 207). Robbery can arise from idolatry. If the highest good is wealth, or power served by wealth, it is an idol which is worshipped by the pursuit of monetary profit and of possessions as the ultimately good activity. All things are subjected to the idol by having a price put upon them. Putting a price upon them makes them alienable goods.

It works like this. Those with wealth at their disposal may by their enterprises rob others of quiet, of health, or of some other benefit, or of their lives. Those against whom violence is done can remedy the matter perhaps by spending money on alleviation, buying back some or even all of what was already theirs, as if in response to a highwayman demanding 'Your money or your life!' I myself have been present at an exercise on the cost of a development destroying people's livelihoods and amenities, and at this exercise the non-financial losses were, in principle, valued at what people would be prepared to pay to avert the loss. In other projects, even the life one already has is given a price, as when the expected fatal accidents on a projected road were costed at the average value of a life insurance, a few thousand pounds. Were it a million pounds, the idolatry would be the same, although perhaps less profitable to the idol's priests and their backers. Also, how much one is prepared to pay depends in part on how much one has, so that the same good is made to have a lower price when it is the possession of the poor than when it belongs to the rich. (Incidentally, this is different from an open market, where a rich seller and a poor may sometimes get the same price for the same commodity, because that is what buyers will pay.)

Of course, whenever human activity by one person will change the circumstances of another, this other may suffer loss or hurt. There is, however, a difference between saying 'The idol rules and I serve it: out of my way!', and saying 'We are, all and equally, made in God's image: let us see therefore whether we can act to our mutual advantage or, at least, without unacceptable harm to either'. That it may not be possible to arrive at an ideal solution, is not a reason to set out, in the first place, to seize by violence what is another's.

Those who serve idols are threatened by reality. Therefore they try to prevent people discovering themselves and understanding the world. This also entails violence and robbery. In the service of the idol substitutes for thought and feeling are made to abound. There is continual violence against the human mind with robbery of human faculties.

The challenge is to delegitimise the robbery and violence that is legal, and to maintain the law against them when illegal. The hope is of dwelling at peace with each other. In this connection we may note that robbery and violence by one individual against another, and contrary to law, can be carried out, in various common circumstances, with little risk of detection. The principal reason why there is not more crime against the person and against personal possessions is that people do not want to commit it. Many people would find it repugnant to be violent or to rob, and most would find it repugnant to do so person to person, with no process between. The beginnings of the future are alive and well, and awaiting development.

***

The precept that *there are nakednesses that you may not uncover* indicates a requirement for rules about permitted and impermissable sexual relationships (pages 163, 208). These rules differ among the earth's peoples, but they need three features if they are to satisfy conditions implied by the Creation story. The first of these is that the rules must assume mutual respect, including respect for each other's mental and material needs. Secondly, this respect is to be related to some wider order of things, some view of the Creator and the created, whether the creator is known as personal or not. Third is provision for the needs of such offspring as a union may produce. ('Be fruitful and increase', 1:28.) Opposed to the precept are rules which do not have the three features. Also opposed to it is the notion that no rules are necessary because there is no certain principle on which they can rest.

Whatever the exact norms of a people for the fulfilment of the precept of nakedness, it will, in general, have exclusions based on family relationship (breach of these being incest) and those based on existing marital relationships (breach of these being adultery). More positively, the norms of a people whose rules have the three features mentioned will include some form of marriage. The structure of marriage, if fully in harmony with the created order, will impede neither the human development exemplified by Noah (Chapter 29, pages 164-171) nor the awakenings noted in Chapter 36 (pages 223-229).

When the divine Unity is replaced by fragments, so that our being is broken up and our desires isolated, sexual pleasure can become an idol. It is then not a consequence of serving or pursuing that from which it has been isolated, but is an end in itself, denying other aspects of our being and, indeed, of our sexuality. The worship of money is also destructive of completeness when, for example, it leads to the attempt to increase sales by disseminating a picture of human sexuality which is one-sided, uncreative, and likely to be only transiently satisfying, if at all.

The challenge is in the sickness of meaning and in joyless sexual activity, in the confusedness of children and parents, and in a diminishing of love's inspiration of art. The hope is in the discovery of each other, in singleness of pleasure, in the joy given by children and by their growth as creators, and in the civilising influence of the choreography of social relations between the sexes.

***

Through the awakenings in the Creation story, something is said of the development of the individual, and through the story's stated or implicit precepts of right action something is said of the behaviour of a society aiming at harmony with the created order. The individual and social aspects of the matter are, however, inseparable.

A society can provide conditions more conducive, or less, for personal awakening. This is because, in the society not worshipping idols, the fulfilment of the precepts of right action are possible and these, in their turn, permit and cultivate the respect within which love for one another can most readily arise. Human love is an aspect of the image of the Creator who adopts (page 12) what has been created. When we, being in the image of God, imitate God by our loving, we fulfil our being, and so make possible our awakenings. With our awakenings we feel the need for a society yet more in accord with the created order, and try to bring it about. Thus the conditions for loving are further advanced, and the happy spiral continues.

It can be that, in our awakening, and in furthering our awakening, right action may be performed in awareness of its being a channel from the totality of things and that totality's godly mystery, whether or not the awareness can be expressed in words. When this is so there can be no distinction between the letter of the law and its spirit, and no line drawn between formal ritual and everyday living. Then, as by the spreading light of the dawning day, more and more things become charged with felt divinity, and we become holy.

CHAPTER 38: *THE MEANING OF LIFE*

IN THE CREATION story the characters behave as free agents. They choose what to do, and are held responsible for what they have done. The purpose of a person's life is for that person to choose. We can live according to the created order or contrary to it. Like a wood carver or sculptor, we can work with the grain of the material, being then free to be creative in an indefinitely large number of ways, and so fulfil ourselves, each differently from all others. Alternatively, we can work without attention to the grain of the material, liable at every minute to shatter it, always to be frustrated in the long run.

Nevertheless, this is not quite an open choice. We are ourselves part of the created order and, if we do not work in accord with that order, do not become fully ourselves. There is also another reason why the choice is not symmetrical. Our completeness, integral with the order of creation, includes even our desires to oppose that order. Good does not thrust away evil but includes it, and what could be evil in isolation contributes to wholeness when we increasingly fulfil the image of God, who makes peace and creates evil (Isaiah 45:7, discussed on page 15).

Life according to the created order has inner and outer aspects. It is in me, in my development towards perfection (see Chapter 29, pages 164-171). It also points outside me, providing direction, purpose, meaning. Through living with the order of created things I live according to my nature, while also giving that nature meaning. If I do not live according to my nature, I am unable to pursue a purpose beyond myself, to find meaning. Conversely, if I do not seek meaning, do not pursue a purpose beyond myself, then I am not living in accord with my nature, in accord with the Creator in whose image I am, for this nature includes having purpose, having meaning. Thus life in accord with the created order might be described as having two aspects, but they cannot be separated. This talk of the double aspect of life is misleading if taken to mean that there are two distinct sets of activity. Rather, in considering one's life, one sets out from a single question that can be asked in two ways: what am I?—where am I going?

Since we are made in the image of what is infinite, we are infinitely variable when compared with each other. Therefore, among all who direct themselves towards living in accord with the created order, no two people do it in exactly the same way. If they are true to their nature, they differ according to differences in their natures. Because of our various natures we start from different

246

places, and therefore have different journeys towards a common goal. We can still face towards the one tree of life (pages 71-72) and so, through our purposes, come to find a common meaning.

The purpose of life, then, is not part of our inner drives, activating us whether we like it or not. (Yet the need for a purpose is indwelling.) It is the meaning that life has when, as Frankl* puts it, we transcend ourselves. So we relate ourselves to the wholeness of the world, to the unity of its Creator, and to the Creator's variously manifested but indivisible image in which we are made, and which patterns our becoming.

Now, reader, we have ended the journey together from the place of invitation, where this book began. My wish is that you have no cause for regret for the time spent. If there is such regret, perhaps you will better understand your good reasons for it. After all, what matters is less whether we agree, than whether our agreements and disagreements are fruitful. Good-bye and fare well.

Authors and Works Cited

The *italicised* numbers are of pages where references to an author or work occur in this book. If more than one passage of a work is referred to, the location of each passage in the cited work is given after the page number in this book.

ALBRIGHT, WILLIAM FOXWELL, *The archaeology of Palestine*, Harmondsworth (Penguin), repr. 1951; chap. 6. (*181*)

AL-QURĀN , *The Koran*, transl. and ed. N.J. Dawood, Harmondsworth (Penguin), 1974, repr. 1979. (*Preliminary quotations*. Sura 85. *232* - Sura 10)

ALTER, ROBERT, *The art of biblical narrative*, New York (Basic Books), 1981. (*5*)

ALTER, ROBERT, *The art of biblical poetry*, New York (Basic Books), 1985. (*5*)

APOLLODORUS, *The Library*, with intro. and transl. by Sir James George Frazer, London (Heinemann: Loeb Classics), 1921; 2 voll.; 1:2:3, 1:7:1. (*176*)

> Flourished in Athens about 140 B.C.E.. The *Library* is a treatise on the gods and the heroic age. It is a rich source book for Greek myths and legends.

AUGUSTINE OF HIPPO, ST., *The Confessions of St. Augustine* (many editions and usually in print), Bk. 1, chap. 1. (*36, 170*)

> North African Church Father, 354-430. The original, Latin form of the quoted sentence is:
>
> Fecisti nos ad te et inquietum est cor nostrum donec requiescat in te.

BACON, FRANCIS, *Bacon's Novum Organum*, ed. T. Fowler, 2nd edn., Oxford (Clarendon), 1889; Bk. 1, aphorism 3. (*230*)

> The Novum Organum was published first in 1620, in the author's lifetime.
> The original, Latin form of the quoted sentence is:
> Natura enim non nisi parendo vincitur.

BACON,FRANCIS, 'On beauty', in *Essays, moral, economical and political* (many editions and usually in print). (*153*)

> First published in 1597.

BEALBY, JOHN T., 'Georgia (History)' in *Encyclopaedia Britannica,* 11th edn., London and New York, 1910; vol. 11, p.758. (*178*)

BENSON, LEWIS, *Catholic Quakerism*, Gloucester (pubd. by the author), 1966. (*164)*

BERLIN, ADÈLE, *Poetics and interpretation of biblical narrative,* Sheffield (Almond. Press), 1983. (*5*)

BERLITZ, CHARLES, *The lost ship of Noah: in search of the ark at Ararat,* London (W.H. Allen), 1987. (*217*)

BIBLIA HEBRAICA STUTTGARTENSIA, Stuttgart (Deutsche Bibelstiftung), 1977. (*14*)

An edition of the Massoretic text of the Hebrew scriptures (see page 4) with notes on variant readings, textual difficulties etc., using a range of manuscripts and early translations and editions. A cited note is to be found in it at the verse under discussion.

BLAKE, WILLIAM, 'The marriage of Heaven and Hell', in *Poetry and prose of William Blake,* London (Nonesuch Press), 1946. (*34* - p.181. *106* - p.189. *203* - p.187)

BRANDON, S.G.F., *Creation legends of the ancient Near East,* London (Hodder & Stoughton), 1963; pp. 141-144. (*158*)

BROCKE, MICHAEL, 'The "imitation of God" in Judaism', in A. Falaturi, J.J. Petuchowski, and W. Strolz, *Three ways to the one God,* Tunbridge Wells (Burns & Oates), 1987; pp. 55-75. (*28*)

BUNAM OF PZHYSHA, in *Forms of prayer for Jewish worship,* ed. Assembly of Rabbis of the Reform Synagogues of Great Britain, London (Reform Synagogues of Great Britain), 1977; vol. 1, p. 378. (*Preliminary quotations*) Chassidic rabbi, 1765-1827.

BURNS, DAN E., 'Dream form in Genesis 2.4b-3.24: asleep in the Garden', *Journal for the study of the Old Testament* **37**, 3-14, 1987. (*56*)

CASSUTO, UMBERTO, *A commentary on the Book of Genesis,* transl. I. Abrams, Jerusalem (Magnes Press), 1961, repr. 1978; 2 voll. (*90* - I, 248. *98* - I, 252-262. *127* - II, 66-67. *140* - II, 43-45. *151* - II, 30-33. *176* - II, 172-225. *181* - II, 205-206)

CHILDE, V. GORDON, *Man makes himself,* revd. edn., London (Watts: Thinkers' Library), 1941. (*27*)

COOTE,ROBERT B. and K.W. WHITELAM, *The emergence of Israel in historical perspective,* Sheffield (Almond Press), 1987. (*89*)

DAVIES, DAVID, *Centenarians of the Andes,* London (Barrie & Jenkins), 1975. (*98*)

DONNE, JOHN, 'The Sunne Rising', in *John Donne, complete poetry and selected prose,* London (Nonesuch), 1946; p.6. (*155*)

EDINGER, EDWARD F., *The Bible and the psyche: individuation symbolism in the Old Testament,* Toronto (Inter City Books), 1986; pp. 116-118. (*111*)

FLAUBERT GUSTAVE, *L'éducation sentimentale: histoire d'un jeune homme,* Paris (Garnier), 1984; pt. 3, chap. 1, p. 299. (*231*)

Recollections and experiences, first published in 1869, in the author's lifetime. The original form of the quotation is:

Alors la propriété monta dans les respects au niveau de la Réligion et se confondit avec Dieu. Les attaques qu'on lui portait parurent du sacrilège, presque de l'anthropophagie.

FOKKELMAN, J.P., 'Genesis', in R. Alter and F. Kermode, *The literary guide to the Bible,* London (Collins), 1987; p. 41. (*47*)

FORD, JULIAN, *The story of Paradise*, Richmond, Surrey (H. & B. publications), 1981. (*2, 217*)

FRANKL, VIKTOR E., *Men's search for meaning: an introduction to logotherapy*, revd. edn., Boston (Beacon Press), 1962. (*247*)

FRANKL, VIKTOR E., *The will to meaning: foundations and applications of logotherapy*, New York (New American Library), 1970. (*247*)

GEORGE, SUSAN, *A fate worse than debt*, London (Penguin), 1988. (*237)*

GERHARDSSON, BIRGER, *Memory and manuscript: oral tradition and written transmission in rabbinic Judaism and early Christianity*, transl. E.J. Sharpe, Uppsala (Gleerup), 1961. (*4*)

GINZBERG, LOUIS, *The legends of the Jews* transl. H. Szold, Philadelphia (Jewish Publication Society of America), 1937, repr. 1968; 7 voll. (*15* - I, 162; V, 17-18 n.50; V, 27 n.74.; V, 182-3 n.39. *19* - I, 8-9; V, 8-9 n.19. *23* (on the tannin) - V, 41 n.117; V, 45. *23* (on Rahab) - I, 18; I, 156; III, 25; V, 26 n.73; VI, 8 n.42. 86 - I, 108; V, 145 n.42. 95 (4th para.) - I, 125-140. 95 (last para.) - I, 146; V, 167-8 n. 5.)

GOWAN, DONALD E., *Eschatology in the Old Testament*, Philadelphia (Fortress Press), 1986; chap. 4 especially. (*34*)

GRAVES, ROBERT, *The Greek myths*, Harmondsworth (Penguin), 1955; 2 voll.; vol. 1, p. 34. (*176*)

HALIFAX, JOAN, *Shaman: the wounded healer*, London (Thames & Hudson), 1982; pp. 21-22. (*71*)

HERODOTUS, *The Histories*, with transl. by A.D. Godley, London (Heinemann: Loeb Classics), 1981; 4 voll.. (*177* - 3:94:2. *178* - 1:163:1. *184* - 2:73:3.)

　　Born at Halicarnassus, in Asia Minor, in or about 484 B.C.E..

HERTZ, J.H., ed., *The Pentateuch and Haftorahs*, 2nd edn., London (Soncino Press), 1981; pp. 193-194. (*217*)

HICK, JOHN, *Evil and the God of love*, 2nd edn. reissued, London (Macmillan), 1985; p.287. (*61*)

HITTI, P.K., *History of the Arabs*, London (Macmillan), 1937; chap. 4. (*186*)

HORA, JOSEF, *Kniha domova*, Praha (Borovy), 1947; p. 35. (*220*)

　　The original Czech of the quoted couplet, which opens a poem titled by the first line, is:

　　I smutno mi i veselo je.

　　Co bylo mé už není moje.

JABÈS, EDMOND, 'The key' (transl.), in G.H. Hartman and S. Budick, edd., *Midrash and literature*, New Haven (Yale U.P.), 1986. (*Preliminary quotations*)

　　Jewish poet. Born 1912 in Egypt. Lived in Paris. Died 1991.

JOSEPHUS, FLAVIUS, 'Antiquities of the Jews', in *Josephus*, ed. and with transl. H. St.J. Thackray *et al.*, London (Heinemann: Loeb Classics),

1926-1965; 9 voll.; 1:6:1. (*177*)

> Born 37 or 38 C.E.. Participated in the Jewish war of attempted liberation,
> against the Romans under Vespasian and Titus.

JUNG, C.G., *Collected Works,* ed. Gerhard Adler *et al., London (Routledge & Kegan Paul), 1960; 22 voll.;* vol. *12,* para. 420. (*111*)

LAWRENCE, D.H. *Apocalypse,* London (Granada), 1981. (*Preliminary quotations, 220* - pp. 2-3. *233* - p. 119)

LIVY (TITUS LIVIUS), *History,* 1:8:6. (*87*)

> Roman historian, 59 B.C.E.-17 C.E..

LUCRETIUS (TITUS LUCRETIUS CARUS), *De rerum natura* ('On the nature of things'), ed. and with transl. by Cyril Bailey, Oxford (Clarendon), repr. 1972; 3 voll.; Bk. 1, line 101, p. 180.   (*231*)

> Latin poet and philosopher, c.98-55 B.C.E.. The original form of the quoted
> line is:
>
> Tantum religio potuit suadere malorum.

MABINOGION, THE, intro. and transl. G. Jones and T. Jones, London (Dent: Everyman), 1949, repr. 1970; p. 152. (*4*)

McCRAE, CALLUM, 'Government "fiddling" on oil rig toll', *Observer,* 15.1.89. (*240*)

MIDRASH RABBAH, ed. H. Freeman and M. Simon, transl. by various hands, London (Soncino Press), 1939; 10 voll.. (*11* - Genesis Rabbah I,5. *34* - Genesis Rabbah IX,7. *61* (both refs.) - Genesis Rabbah XIX,3. *71* - Numbers Rabbah IV,8. *83* - Genesis Rabbah XXII,1.)

> Hebrew commentary on the Pentateuch and other scriptural books. These
> are from the 6th-12th Centuries C.E., but incorporate older material, espe-
> cially from the 1st Century B.C.E.-3rd Century C.E..

MISHAN, EZRA, *Economic myths and the mythology of economics,* Brighton (Wheatsheaf), 1986. (*232*)

NAVEH, JOSEPH, *Early history of the alphabet,* Jerusalem (Magnes Press) and Leiden (Brill), 1982; p. 44. (*179*)

NICHOLAS OF CUSA, *Nicolai Cusae Cardinalis opera,* Parisiis, 1514; offset repr. Frankfurt-am-Main (Minerva), 1962; 2 voll.; 'De docta ignorantia', Bk. 2, chap. 4, fol. XVa. (*15*)

> Born 1401 at Kues, on the Mosel; Cardinal; Archbishop of Brixen
> (Bressanone); died 1464.

ORWELL, GEORGE, *Nineteen eighty-four,* London (Secker & Warburg) 1949. (*236)*

OTTO, RUDOLF, *The idea of the holy,* transl. J. W. Harvey, Oxford U.P., 1923. (*26* - *passim. 129* - p.77)

OVID (PUBLIUS OVIDIUS NASO), *Metamorphoses* (many editions in the original and in English translation, usually in print); Bk. 1, line 131. (*58*)

> Roman poet 43 B.C.E-17C.E.
>
> The original Latin of the quoted phrase is:
>
> Amor sceleratus habendi.

PARKINSON, CECIL, cited by William Keegan, in 'How Parkinson blew the gaffe', *Observer*, 21.2.88. (*234*)

PINDAR, *The Odes of Pindar, including the principal fragments,* intro. and with transl. by J. Sandys, London (Heinemann: Loeb Classics), 1937, repr. 1968; fragment on p. 602. (*19*)

Born in Thebes, in or about 522 B.C.E..

PLATO,*Republic* (many editions in the original and in English translation); Bk. 4, section 427. (*209*)

Athens, 427-347 B.C.E..

PLINY THE ELDER, *Historia naturalis,* 6:30:118. (*185*)

North Italian by birth but Roman by education. Materials for the *Natural History* had been collected by 23 C.E. but publication began only in 77. Two years later Pliny was killed by Vesuvius at Pompeii while he was trying to get a better view of the eruption.

POPE, ALEXANDER, 'Epilogue to the Satires, Dialogue I', in *The poems of Alexander Pope,* London (Methuen), repr. 1984; p. 693, lines 135-136. (*62*)

Ralph Allen, in the quoted couplet, is the original of Squire Allworthy in Fielding's *Tom Jones.*

PTOLEMY (CLAUDIUS PTOLEMAEUS), *Geographia,* 6:1:2. (*184*)

A Hellenised Egyptian of the 2nd Century C.E.. His mathematical, astronomical, and geographical works remained standard texts for over 1300 years.

RADAK, *The commentaries of Rabbi David Kimche on the Pentateuch,* ed. M. Kamelhaar, Jerusalem (Mossad Harav Kook), 3rd imp., 5742 (i.e. 1981-2); p. 14. (Hebrew) (*21*)

Of Narbonne, 1160-1235. The name 'Radak' is an acronym, following Hebrew custom, of Rabbi David Kimche.

RAPHAEL, ADAM, 'A £10m trade in influence', *Observer,* 9.4.89. (*242*)

RASHI, *Pentateuch with Rashi's commentary,* ed. and with transl. by M. Rosenbaum and A.M. Silberman, London (Shapiro Vallentine), 1946; 2 voll.. (Each cited passage will be found at the verse of scripture on which it comments.) (*11, 14, 20, 57, 61, 105, 140*)

'Rashi' is the acronym of Rabbi Solomon ben Isaac of Troyes, 1040-1105, who not only wrote on scripture but also composed, on Talmud Bavli*, a commentary printed in every edition.

SAWYER, JOHN F.A., 'The meaning of *barzel* in the biblical expressions "chariots of iron, yoke of iron", etc.', in J.F.A. Sawyer and D.J.A. Clines, 'Midian, Moab, and Edom', *Journal for the study of the Old Testament,* suppl. 24, 1983. (*88*)

SEDER OLAM RABBAH, *Chronologia Hebraeorum maior* etc., interprete Gilb. Genebrardo, Parisiis (apud Martinum Iuvenem), 1578; chap. 5. (A Latin translation of the Hebrew.) (*206*)

A chronology of the world from the Creation to the 1st Century C.E.. Probably written in the 2nd Century. The title means Elder 'Order of the

World', to distinguish it from a later work, *Seder Olam Zuta,* the Younger 'Order of the World'.

STERNBERG, MEIR, *The poetics of biblical narrative: ideological literature and the drama of reading,* Bloomington (U. Indiana Press), 1985. (*5, 160*)

STEWART, R.J., *The mystic life of Merlin,* London (Routledge & Kegan Paul: Arkna), 1986; pp. 8-9. (*171*)

STUTTGART BIBLE, see BIBLIA HEBRAICA STUTTGARTENSIS

TALMUD BAVLI (many printed editions,—the folio number being the same for all,—Warsaw 1887 being used by the author; one complete translation, as given here), *The Babylonian Talmud,* ed. I. Epstein, various translators, London (Soncino Press), repr. 1961; 18 voll.. (*34* - Sukkot 52a. *57* - Sanhedrin 58a.   *62* - Pesachim 54a, Nedarim 39b. *145* - Sanhedrin 56a. *160* - Sanhedrin 70a. *184* - Gittin 46b-47a. *206* - Sanhedrin 56a,b.)

> The Babylonian Talmud, i.e. the Talmud of the Jews of Mesopotamia, consists of *Mishnah* and *Gemara.* The *Mishnah,* completed 200 C.E., is a collection of teachings, mostly of the three centuries preceding its completion. The *Gemara* is commentary on Mishnah, and includes material down to the end of editing, in the 5th Century.

TALMUD YERUSHALMI, Jerusalem (Shiloh), 5729 (i.e. 1968-9); Nedarim 9:1. (*61*)

> The Jerusalem Talmud, i.e. the Talmud of the Jews of the Land of Israel, has a *Gemara* different from that of the Babylonian, but commenting on a common *Mishnah.* The Jerusalem Talmud was edited about a century earlier than the Babylonian, and is much smaller than the latter.

TAO TE CHING, with transl. by G.-F. Feng and J. English, London (Wildwood House), repr. 1982. (*Preliminary quotations* - Stanza 52. *36* - Stanza 1)

> By tradition (but not necessarily by modern scholars) attributed to Lao-Tse, the founder of Taoism, of which the *Tao Te Ching,* the 'Classic of the Way', is the most important writing.

TAYLOR, GABRIELE, *Pride, shame and guilt,* Oxford U.P. 1985; p. 84. (*62*)

THOMPSON, FRANCIS, 'The hound of Heaven', in *The works of Francis Thompson—Poems,* London (Burns, Oates & Washbourne), 1925; 3 voll.; vol. 1, pp. 107-113. (*63*)

TOSEFTA, ed. M.S. Zuckermandl, Jerusalem (Sifrei Wahrmann.), 5735 (1974-5); tractate *Avodah Zarah.* (Hebrew) (*206* - chap. 8, pp. 473, line 12 - 474, line 3. *209* - chap. 2, p. 462, line 29)

> The *Tosefta* is a collection of rabbinic material of the period of the *Mishnah,* on which see the note on Talmud Bavli*.

TRIBLE, PHYLLIS, *God and the rhetoric of sexuality,* Philadelphia (Fortress Press), 1978. (*5*)

WARLOW, PETER, *The reversing earth,* London (Dent), 1982. (*217*)

WARNER, SYLVIA TOWNSEND, 'The rival', in *The Albatross Book of Living Verse,* London (Collins), n.d.; pp. 599-600. (*67*)

WENHAM, GORDON, 'The coherence of the Flood narrative', *Vetus Testamentum* **23** (3), 336-348, 1978. (*151*)

WESTERMAN, CLAUS, *Genesis 1-11,* transl. J.J. Scullion, London (S.P.C.K.) and Minneapolis (Augsburg Publishing House), 1984. (*8* - pp. 88-89. *47* - p. 78. *113*- p. 410. *176* - pp. 504-528. *213* - pp. 563-565)

ZOHAR, THE, transl. H. Sperling and M. Simon, London (Soncino Press), 1934, repr. 1970; 5 voll.; vol, 1, p. 75 (i.e. Bereshit 18a) and p. 144 (i.e. Bereshit 46a). (*14)*

> This translation from the original Aramaic is incomplete.
>
> The Zohar has the form of a commentary on the Pentateuch. It is of 13th-Century origin, although it claims greater antiquity for itself, and may indeed incorporate much older material. It lies within the Cabbalistic tradition and has proved to be the most reprinted, quoted, and loved mystical work among Jews, despite being almost impossibly difficult for a reader with no prior familiarity with Cabbalistic discourse and no teacher.

Index of Scriptural References and Citations

HEBREW SCRIPTURES

(Bracketed numbers refer to English translations where these differ from the Hebrew in verse numbering)

Genesis

1: 1 - 2: 3,   6, 7, 205
  1 - 5,   11
  3,   63
  4, 7, 9,   225
  6, 7,   208
  6 - 8,   14
  8,   16
  9, 10   16
  11 - 13,   17
  11,   225
  14 - 19,   18
  16,   168
  17,   153
  18, 19,   168
  20 - 23,   22
  21,   223
  22,   57, 153, 227
  26, 29,   169
  24 - 25,   25
  26 - 28,   227, 241
  26, 27,   148, 207, 233
  26,   26, 63, 95, 203, 223, 241
  27,   27, 51, 57, 64, 154, 223, 224, 228
  28 - 30,   29
  28,   57, 125, 153, 244
  29, 30,   70, 143, 153, 168
  31,   30, 125

2: 1 - 3,   31
  4 - 3: 24,   40, 205
  4,   47, 94
  5,   49
  6,   50, 231
  7,   32, 66, 71, 169, 224
  8,   54, 70

  9,   60, 71
  10 - 15,   52
  10 - 14,   50
  10,   54
  11,   52, 179, 187
  15,   55, 67, 70
  16, 17,   60
  16,   206
  17 - 20,   66
  17,   61, 66
  18,   225
  19 - 25,   55
  19,   67, 68
  20,   56, 68
  21,   56
  22,   56, 67
  23,   56, 224, 225
  24, 25,   25
  24,   57, 167
  25,   57, 60, 62, 159

3: 1 - 7a,   59
  1 -5,   60
  3,   60
  5,   60
  6, 7,   224
  6,   60
  7b - 13,   59, 62
  8,   63, 95
  11,   63
  12,   63, 167
  14, 16,   65
  14, 15,   167
  16,   68
  17 - 19,   167
  17,   67, 168
  19,   71, 113
  20,   67
  21 - 4: 1,   70
  21,   67, 70
  22 - 24,   71

  22,   61

4 : 1 - 16,   205
  1 - 17,   73
  1,   60, 67, 70, 106, 225
  13, 14,   84
  13,   204, 224
  14,   204, 240
  15,   38
  17 - 26,   85
  17,   87
  18,   87
  22,   105
  23, 24,   89, 118
  23,   189
  25,   67, 94, 106, 107
  26,   90, 162

5: 1 - 32,   91, 212
  1, 2,   128
  3,   94, 106
  5,   61
  15,   67
  22,   95
  24,   95
  28,   158, 159
  29,   95, 105, 168
  32,   114, 158, 212, 213

6: 1 - 7,   119
  1 - 8,   107, 114, 158
  2,   119, 207
  4,   201
  5, 7,   119
  5 - 7,   206
  5,   125
  8,   114, 162
  9 - 7: 5,   122
  9,   95, 127, 164
  11 - 13,   206

GENERAL INDEX

Words within the translated passages are not indexed unless appearing and being discussed elsewhere. Names appearing alphabetically in the index of authors and works are not indexed here.

« , precept against 149, 206, 208-9, 240
« , warning against 26, 147
b'nei elim 109
Bo tree 71
bone 68
boneh 87
brass 88
breath 51, 169
bricks 198, 201
b'rit 149
Britain in the 1980s and 1990s 234
bronze 88
brother 213
Buddha 71

C

cabin 127
Cadiz 178
Cain 38, 86, 89, 104-5, 107, 111, 118, 120, 128, 148-9, 155, 162, 166, 205, 214
« , comparison with parents 75
Cain's family 85
« , wife 87
Calah 180
Callirhoe 183
Calneh 180
Calno 180
Canaan, Canaanites 3, 158, 161-2, 176, 178-181, 183, 186, 188-9, 192, 194, 200
Caphtor, Caphtorim 180-1, 188
Cappadocia 177
Carthage, Carthaginian empire 3, 192
Casluhim 180-1
castration 160
Catalonia, Catalan 196
Caucasus 178, 185
Chaboras 186
chalon 136
chamas 125-6
chance 35
chanakh 87, 104
Chanokh 87, 104
chapters, biblical 5

Charan 212
charash 67
charity 209
chat'at 80
Chaulctaei 186
chawilah 187
Chawwah 67
chay, chayah, chayyim 24-5, 51, 67, 169, 223-4
cherubim 71, 169
chiasma 115-6, 148
choice 34, 246
chol 184
chosen people 146, 195
chowl 187
Christian, Christians 164, 195, 202, 215, 220
« tradition 209
chronology of the Flood (see 'Flood calendar')
Church, Christian 195-6
Cimmerians 177
city 87
cloud 50
coastal nations 178, 192
co-creator 27, 86, 95, 111
co-creatrix (see Eve)
cold and heat, of the year 139
comfort 168
concentric parallelism 151, 198
consciousness, stream of 155
Cornovii 184
corporations 204
Cos, Coan 71
couple 57
courtesy 36
covenant 125, 149
create, meaning of word 23, 29, 223
created order 246
Creation story 1, 151, 171, 195, 201, 207, 210, 214-5, 217
« « , four stages 208
« « , sources 2
Creation, The (oratorio) 22
creativity, human 27, 236
creeping things 23
Crete 180, 194
Cross, Christian 71

crowd, its counterpoint 236
« , its roar 236
cubit 124
cubitum 124
curse 163
curse on the ground 66, 139, 153. 158-9, 167-8. 205
« « snake 65, 68, 167, 205
Cush 53-4, 179, 188-9, 192, 201
Cushan 54
cybernetic adjustment of the universe 62
cycles of the story of the seven days 9
« « Garden story 39, 45-6, 72
Cyprus 178, 180
Cyrenaica 180

D

dalet 178
dam 148
Damascus 186
Daniel 235-6
Danube 177
Dardanians 178
darkness 12, 13
darshan 202
date-palm 186-7
daughter 213
daughters of humankind 109, 112, 117, 119
David 96, 101, 183
day 13, 19-21, 48, 94
« and night 12, 19, 139
« , 1st of the Creation 11, 20, 223
« , 2nd of the Creation 14
« , 3rd of the Creation 16
« , 4th of the Creation 12, 13, 18, 20-1, 139, 154, 217
« , 5th of the Creation 22, 153, 223
« , 6th of the Creation 25, 39, 65, 148, 153-4, 241
« , 7th of the Creation 31

262